MANUAL

OF

BIBLICAL INTERPRETATION.

BY

JOSEPH MUENSCHER, D.D.

GAMBIER, O.
PRINTED FOR THE AUTHOR.
MDCCCLXV.

PREFACE.

A work of convenient size on the Principles of Biblical Interpretation adapted to the wants of ministers and theological students, and at the same time of a cast sufficiently popular to be acceptable to intelligent laymen, has long been regarded as a desideratum. It has been the aim of the writer in the preparation of the following unpretending manual to supply this want. That the subject of which it treats is one of great importance, no intelligent reader of the Bible will be disposed to deny; and yet for the want, perhaps, of a book on the science easily accessible, and neither too concise and technical on the one hand, nor too copious and diffuse on the other, it has not received the attention either from ministers or from the readers of the Bible generally, to which it is justly entitled. That the present work may be instrumental of promoting a more general appreciation of the science, and of directing the minds of Biblical students to a more attentive study of the Principles which lie at the basis of all sound and rational interpretation of the Sacred Volume, is the earnest prayer of

THE AUTHOR.

MT. VERNON, O., May 2, 1865.

PRINCIPLES OF INTERPRETATION.

CHAPTER I.

INTRODUCTORY REMARKS.

The blessed God has been pleased to communicate to man a revelation of himself, of his providential arrangements and designs of grace and mercy towards our race, of his relation to us and our duty to him, to ourselves, and to the human family. This revelation was not made at one time in all its entireness, and through a single individual, but in sundry parts or portions, through different persons and at various times, extending through a period of four thousand years. Embodied in permanent records originally written in languages which have long since ceased to be spoken, this revealed religion, together with its history during the long period just named, has been handed down to the present day, and still claims to be the rule of our faith, the ground of our hope, and the guide of our life. The sacred oracles have been placed in our hands with the solemn and oft repeated injunction that they be made the subject of earnest and prayerful study by all men without exception who have the ability and opportunity; and that we "so read, mark, learn, and inwardly digest them," as to become wise unto salvation through faith in Christ Jesus. For this end they have been translated into the different languages of men, and widely circulated over the face of the earth. In the contents of these sacred records all men are equally interested, and the same responsibility rests upon all in respect to the use they make of them. But that which is the duty of all Christians in this regard, is especially and pre-eminently incumbent on the Ministers of Religion, because it is their particular vocation to apply themselves closely and diligently to the study of the Scriptures, and to acquire an extensive and critical knowledge of them, so as to be able to explain them to the people committed to their charge, and so to exhibit the truths they contain to the minds of their hearers as that their understandings may become enlightened, their affections moved, and their wills rightly directed and controlled. They are the authorized public teachers of revealed religion, by whom the Church is to be thoroughly instructed in the principles of that religion, and grounded in the faith once delivered to the Saints, and they are expected to be qualified to divide rightly the word of God, and to bring forth from the treasury of that word new things as well as old. It becomes, therefore, a question of profound interest and importance to every private Christian, and especially to every minister of the Gospel, and to all those who are looking forward to the sacred office, in what manner and spirit, and by the aid of what helps and guides, shall I apply myself to the study of the Divine Word, so as most successfully to acquire a proper understanding of its meaning, and, if need be, so as rightly to explain and unfold that meaning to others.

That the sacred scriptures should not be interpreted according to the whims and caprice, the fancy or the prejudices of each individual, but according to some fixed principles, and in the use of appropriate helps and guides, must be quite obvious to all, and is so generally admitted as hardly to require an extended argument. But what principles shall be adopted, and what guides followed, and what weight shall be given to each respectively, are points of very grave importance, in regard to which Christian men and Christian ministers are by no means agreed. Hence the almost innumerable and contradictory interpretations which have been given to the Scriptures; and hence the multiplicity of sects and denominations into which the Christian Church is divided. That entire unanimity of opinion in regard to the meaning of every part of the Bible will ever be reached by any process now known to man, is more than, as the human mind is now constituted, we are warranted to expect. A miracle greater by far than has yet been performed, would be required to accomplish such a result. At the same time, it cannot be questioned, that a great approximation may be made towards it by a better appreciation and a more diligent study of sound and well-defined principles, and by a more careful, independent and discriminating use of such aids as we possess for the correct understanding and interpretation of the Bible. In the following work an attempt is made to exhibit and illustrate the principles and laws of Biblical interpretation, and to show the grounds on which they rest, in a form adapted to the comprehension not only of scholars and clergymen, who may be supposed to be somewhat familiar with the subject, but also of that large class of intelligent laymen, who are honorably and usefully employed in imparting biblical instruction to the rising generation in our Sunday Schools and Bible Classes.

CHAPTER II.

THE IMPORTANCE OF BIBLICAL INTERPRETATION.

The only verbal revelation which God has made to the human race, is contained in the Bible. No other writings than the canonical books of the Old and New Testament are regarded by the Protestant Church throughout Christendom as of divine authority. No others are, in the truest and highest sense of the term, *inspired.* The Bible, and the Bible alone, divested of all apocryphal additions, and as distinguished from all oral and apostolical tradition, is the only infallible and sufficient rule of faith and practice, and is possessed of paramount and final authority. This is one of the fundamental principles of Protestantism,—one of the two main pillars which support the superstructure. Other books may contain truth of the greatest value, and be worthy of all commendation. But however excellent, they are merely human; they have not God for their author; they cannot command our implicit belief, homage and obedience. This exalted position is accorded to the Bible alone. What say the Scriptures? Here is the appeal, and this appeal is final in regard to all questions in which the vital interests of the soul are concerned. "Holy Scripture," in the language of the Thirty-nine articles of the Protestant Episcopal Church, "containeth all things necessary to salvation, so that whatsoever is not read therein, nor may be proved thereby, is not required of any man, that it should be believed as an article of faith, or be thought requisite or necessary to salvation." The Confessions of all Protestant Churches are in harmony with this declaration.

Now, the Bible being the record of a Revelation, is necessarily written in human language. Intended for the use and instruction of mankind, it could not have been otherwise. If it had been clothed in signs and symbols which were unintelligible to us, it would not have been a revelation,—it could not have been understood. It might as well not have been communicated. The language then, in which the Bible is written is human, marked with all the imperfection which characterizes human language, and subject to all the laws which govern it. The thoughts, the ideas and sentiments conveyed to our mind through this medium, are divine; but all else is of the earth earthly. The languages in which the sacred scriptures were originally written, are foreign to us, and became long since, as to all practical purposes, dead. Hence, if the Scriptures are to be understood in the original, these languages must be thoroughly and critically studied in the use of all the appropriate helps which we can command. If they are to be read and understood by the masses of mankind, who have not the opportnnity of becoming acquainted with the original, they must be translated into the living vernacular languages of the earth.

The Scriptures, we believe, were written to be read and understood by all men, and not exclusively by any particular class. Every man has an equal and common interest in them. They contain the doctrines and principles by which he is to govern his belief. They contain the law by which he is to regulate his life. But, although the Scriptures may be faithfully translated into the vernacular language, so that all who are able to read may have access to them, yet many circumstances may and do operate to prevent them from being fully understood by the majority of those who read them. The want of competent learning, the want of sufficient leisure, the imperfections which unavoidably adhere to human language as an instrument of thought, an imperfect knowledge of the laws of intrepretation, or an incapacity to apply them rightly; the changes which are constantly taking place in the usages of language, the difference in the forms of expression and modes of thinking, in the manners and customs of different countries, and nations, and ages of the world; the great antiquity of the scriptures; the extent and variety of the sacred volume, the different periods in which, and persons by whom it was written, and to whom it was immediately addressed, together with the loftiness and mysteriousness of the subjects presented, are among the circumstances which render it exceedingly difficult for the uneducated to obtain, by personal study merely, an accurate knowledge of every point revealed in the Scriptures. Hence an order of living teachers, thoroughly instructed themselves in the Bible, and competent to aid and instruct others, is required. Our blessed Saviour accordingly ordained twelve apostolic men for this purpose, and empowered them to commission others for the same work, so that there might be to the end of time duly authorized and qualified living teachers in the church of Christ

To defend, explain, illustrate and apply the sacred Scriptures, is the chief part, the highest function of the Christian ministry. The ministers of the Gospel are, by virtue of their office, emphatically and pre-eminently *teachers*—expounders of God's word. By the requisitions of their master, and by their ordination vows, they are bound to feed the flock committed to their care. There are, doubtless, other duties appertaining to their office of great importance, which they may not neglect; but their main business is to explain, illustrate and enforce the truths whieh are contained in the Bible. The Bible is the Protestant minister's text book—the *open* Bible, which others may read as well as he, and by which they may judge of the correctness of his statements and views. From this fountain of truth he must be constantly bringing forth things new and old, for the edification of the Church, the refutation of error, the conviction of the individual conscience, and the establishment of the truth. For the accomplishment of this object, he must be conversant with the sacred scriptures, with their evidences, history, doctrines and precepts. He must be acquainted with them not merely in a translation, but acquire a competent knowledge of the languages in which they were written, and be able by an examination of the original text, to draw his expositions from that. In all matters of controversy the appeal must be made to this original text. This alone is final and conclusive. The foundation, therefore, of a theological and ministerial education must be laid in the critical, grammatical, and exegetical study of the Holy Scriptures. Exegetical theology must be the groundwork of a thorough ministerial education in every age; but it is especially important in the age in which we now live. That education should, doubtless, be such as will enable the ambassador for Christ to cope with living men, and living ideas, and to employ most successfully those weapons which the present mode in which the Christian warfare is conducted, demands. That theological training which might have been of great service and quite sufficient in the mediæval ages, would be entirely inadequate and answer no valuable purpose now. It must be adapted to the demands of the present age, and to the present advanced state of biblical and theological science.

A thorough and critical knowledge of the Holy Scriptures is particularly necessary for the ministry of the Church at the present day, because the Bible is the battle-ground of skepticism and infidelity. The chief assaults from this quarter are now directed against the Bible itself. Many scientific men of skeptical views and proclivities, are laboring hard to prove that the facts of natural science and the statements of Scripture are contradictory. Rationalism, also, which is but another name for the most subtle form of infidelity within the bosom of the Church itself, is wholly occupied with attacks on the Bible, and the position it occupies and the facilities it enjoys for mischief. render it a far more formidable and dangerous enemy than open and avowed infidelity. On the ground of philosophical criticism, it aims to overthrow the canonicity, the integrity, the credibility, and the inspiration of Scripture; and while it professes great respect for the morality of the Bible, and claims to be its true friend and advocate, and has really done some service in elucidating its contents, the legitimate and inevitable effect of its labors is to impair, if not entirely to destroy, all confidence in that blessed volume as containing a supernatural revelation.

Nor is Rationalism any longer a distant enemy confined to the country which gave it birth. It is rapidly making its way over the Christian world. Its deadly poison is working extensively in England, both in the Established Church and among the Dissenters; nor has our own country entirely escaped its polluting touch and destructive influence. Now one indispensible means of checking the progress of this foe to piety is the thorough training of candidates for the ministry in the critical study of the Bible. It is impossible for any minister to contend successfully with this great evil who is not thoroughly versed in exegetical theology; who does not understand the languages of the Bible, and who is not familliar with the principles of Biblical criticism and interpretation.

The Bible is, moreover, the battle-ground of the numerous sects and parties into which Protestant Christendom is divided. These acknowledge no other standard than the Bible. They recognize this and no other authority as final and conclusive. They plant themselves on the Word of God interpreted in accordance with the laws of language and of rational exegesis. No minister, therefore, can be properly prepared to defend and maintain the distinctive doctrines and peculiarities of his own church, or to appreciate the arguments by which others support their peculiar views, who does not understand the right method of explaining the Word of God.

The field of research in exegetical theology, is both attractive and boundless; the mine to be explored is inexhaustable. This interesting department of study, from its very nature, is progressive. All other branches of knowledge,—philology, history, chronology, antiquities, geology, astronomy, geography, etc.—are constantly pouring their treasures into its lap, and shedding light on the pages of the Bible. The minister, therefore, who diligently applies himself to the cultivation of this field, and acquires a taste for it, cannot fail to find it a constant source of delight, and to derive from it a perpetual incentive to increased diligence. He will gather from it the best materials of thought for the pulpit and become eminently fitted for that expository preaching which consists in the faithful presentation of the Word of God in all its truthfulness and fullness.

CHAPTER III.

THE THREE GREAT LIGHTS.

Three great lights have been furnished us to be our guides in the study and interpretation of the Word of God, to which it is of the utmost importance that we should take heed, if we would avoid the numerous mistakes and errors into which so many have fallen. These are the light of *reason*, the light of *authority*, and the light of the *Holy Spirit*. Of these the first named is of primary and paramount importance, because it is a gift bestowed upon all mankind, and conferred for the very purpose, among others, of enabling us to hold intelligent communication with our fellow beings, and impart reciprocally to one another, by means of oral and written language, a knowledge of our individual thoughts and feelings, desires and purposes, views and opinions. Human language is the product of human reason. And as the faculty of reason is the *parent* of language, so it is likewise the proper *interpreter* of it. The light of *authority* is not an original, distinct, and independent light, like that of reason, but like that of the moon, it is a borrowed light, and derives all its illuminating power from the other two—reason and the Holy Spirit, and its aid is valuable and reliable only so far as it is a true reflection from these. The light of the *Holy Spirit* is an inward, hidden light, not outward and manifest to observation, and not distinguishable from the ordinary operations of the intellectual powers or the natural conscience by him who enjoys it. Hence it is liable to be mistaken and misapprehended. No one of these guides is to be followed exclusively, and to the neglect or rejection of the other two. Errors without number have sprung from a disregard of this simple, but most important rule. An exclusive reliance on reason is the fruitful source of rationalism and skepticism. A like exclusive reliance on human authority, whether it be that of an individual, or of the Church, tends to degrade the human intellect, to destroy all self-reliance, to weaken our sense of personal responsibility, and becomes the foster-parent of blind credulity, bigotry, intolerance, and persecution. An entire dependance on the supposed inward light or illumination of the Holy Spirit, in disregard of reason and authority, is the prolific source of mysticism, fanaticism, and latitudinarianism. But where the aid of all these is sought in proportion to their intrinsic and relative importance, there we may expect to find a safe, sound, reliable interpreter of the Word of God.

1. *The light of reason.* By this is meant the exercise of our natural faculties in connexion with the use of such means and instrumentalities as are afforded us by literature and science for the investigation of truth. This is necessary to the attainment of any branch of knowledge, and to the understanding of any production of *human* genius and learning. And it is not less necessary for gaining a knowledge of *revealed* truth; for the Deity, in condescending to employ human language as the vehicle of communication with his rational creatures, manifestly intended that it should be understood, and that the meaning of the communication should be

ascertanied by the same means and in the same manner as the import of all other oral or written communications is determined. Otherwise it could not be comprehended, and the professed revelation would be no revelation at all.

The exercise of our intellectual faculties in the investigation and discovery of revealed truth, implies of course the right of *private*, i. e. of *individual judgment;* for to employ our reason in the Study of Scripture, would be of no avail, unless we are at liberty to embrace the *deductions* to which our reason may lead us. Deny this right, and the injunction of our blessed Lord to "search the Scriptures," would be but a solemn mockery. This topic will form the subject of the next chapter.

It is of the utmost importance that we should entertain correct views as to the *proper province of reason* in the investigation of revealed truth. It is not the province of reason to determine before hand what the Bible, as a revelation from God, *ought* to contain, but to ascertain what it *does* contain; not to decide in advance what the Scriptures *ought* to mean, but to determine in the use of all legitimate and appropriate means, what they *do* mean. Neither is it her province to sit in judgment on the truths revealed in the Bible, and to admit or reject them according as they may or may not coincide with our pre-conceived opinions, or as they may or may not be comprehensible by us. She is not competent to such a task. It would be transcending her powers. It would be an abuse, a perversion, a usurpation of reason. And to this abuse and usurpation may be traced a vast multitude of the most dangerous errors and false doctrines which have prevailed and do still infest the Church. The rationalism and neology prevalent at the present day in some portions of the Christian world are attributable to this cause. Unitarianism and Universalism are also measurably chargeable with this abuse.

Reason is competent, however, to investigate the evidence both external and internal for the truth of Revealed religion. She is competent to ascertain by the application of sound critical laws the genuine text of Scripture. She is competent to determine amid the various interpretations of which a passage of Scripture is supposed to be capable, which is probably the true meaning.

And this she is to do not arbitrarily and capriciously or under the influence of an unrestrained imagination, or of prejudice, but by the application of the established laws of language and the acknowledged principles and canons of interpretation; for these principles and canons are merely the deductions of reason, approved by the common sense of mankind. Here for the most part her task ceases, and Faith steps in with her mighty power to appropriate the living truths which Reason has thus developed in the word of God, and to accomplish in the individual soul the great moral work for which the Revelation was given.

CHAPTER IV.

TRADITION.—RIGHT OF PRIVATE JUDGMENT.

We have said that one of the two main pillars on which the superstructure of Protestantism rests is *the sufficiency of Holy Scripture* for all the purposes of the divine life in the soul of man, and its exclusive divine authority as the Rule of faith and the Law of life. The Romish Church, on the contrary, maintains, as appears from the acts of the Council of Trent, that "the truth is contained *in the written books*, and in the *unwritten traditions*, which, having been received by the Apostles, either from the mouth of Christ himself, or from the dictates of the Holy Spirit, were handed down even to us," and that Church "receives and venerates with equal *feeling of piety and reverence* all the books of the Old and New Testament, since one God was the author of them both, and *also the tradition*, relating as well to *faith* as to *morals*, as having, either from the mouth of Christ himself, or from the dictation of the Holy Ghost, been preserved by continuous succession in the Catholic Church."* Against this claim

* A few words may be necessary in order to explain what is here meant by *tradition*. It properly denotes that information which Christ and his inspired servants communicated to men, which is not embodied in the Canonical Scriptures, but which, it is alleged, was handed down by other means. The New Testament is not a large book, and must be supposed to contain but a small part of what our Saviour and his Apostles said and taught. Several of the Apostles, indeed, committed nothing to writing, at least nothing

of coordinate authority for a vague, uncertain tradition with the written word of God, the Reformers protested, and this constitutes one of the fundamental points of difference between the two great Communions into which the Western Church is divided. "In the books of the

---

that we possess or of which we have any knowledge. Tradition, therefore, in the strict sense here intended, is the entire body of those apostolical instructions and facts which have been transmitted otherwise than by writing, otherwise than by the New Testament, in the state in which it has reached us. As the Jewish Rabbies maintained that in addition to the *written law* of Moses, there was also an *unwritten traditional law*, which had been handed down *orally* from the times of the Hebrew lawgiver, by which the written law contained in the Canonical Books was to be interpreted; so the same thing is alleged in regard to many of the sayings and doings of Christ and his Apostles. This tradition is termed *Oral*, from having been transmitted at first by word of mouth from one to another, but at length committed to writing, or said to have been so, by the Fathers, or Councils. "The rule of faith in the Church of Rome," says Bishop J. H. Hopkins, "professes like our own, to be the Word of God, and of course, it includes the Holy Scriptures. But they maintain that besides the Scriptures, there was an *oral* delivery of divine truth to the Church which is equally obligatory on every believer; of which *unwritten* word, the Church is the sole depository, and in the safe preservation of which, as well as in her power of interpreting the written word, she cannot err, being absolutely infallible." "By the *unwritten* Word of God," says Dr. Wiseman, "we mean a body of doctrines, which in consequence of express declarations in the *written* word, we believe not to have been committed to writing, but delivered by Christ to his Apostles, and by the Apostles to their

New Testament alone," says a late English writer, "is to be found a trustworthy record of the life and conversation of Christ—of all [so far as we know] that he said and did—of his labors and sufferings, of his death and resurrection,—and of the efforts, happily the successful efforts of the apostles in diffusing far and wide the glad tidings of his Gospel. But having these, says the genuine Protestant, we have all that is needed. They are all-sufficient for the purpose of

---

successors. We believe that no *new doctrine* can be introduced into the Church, but that *every doctrine* which we hold has existed and been taught in it, ever since the time of the Apostles and was handed down by them to their successors, under the guarantee of which we receive doctrines from the Church, that is, Christ's promise to abide with it forever, to assist, direct and instruct it, and always teach in and through it. So that while giving our explicit credit, and trusting our judgment to it, we are believing and trusting to the *express teaching of Christ himself*." Strictly speaking then, the oral Tradition here intended, is a traditional revelation concerning doctrine, in matters of faith and morals, which is not to be found in Scripture, and which is equally certain, equally divine, and equally to be embraced, and reverenced with Scripture itself. In point of fact, however, the Word is commonly taken in a wider sense and made to include *ecclesiastical* tradition, i. e., Tradition concerning Church government, discipline, rites and ceremonies, and *hermeneutical* tradition, i. e., certain doctrines handed down from early times, and certain interpretations of Scripture, which are found in the writings of the fathers. And it is in this wide sense that, according to the Romanists and Anglo-Catholics, Scripture and Tradition taken together, are the joint rule of faith."

making us acquainted with the great truths of Christianity; with the mind and character of Christ; with the principles, the spirit and the genius of his religion. If we cannot learn from the New Testament all that is essential and necessary to make a man wise unto salvation; if from this source, we cannot derive an adequate knowledge of what Christ taught as most important to be believed, then there are no authentic documents to which we can have recourse, and in which such knowledge is to be found. If it exists anywhere, it exists in the writings of those who were his immediate followers and attendants. There, then, we shall seek it, and there we hope to find it." This is what the immortal Chillingworth meant when he said "The Bible, the Bible alone is the religion of Protestants." This is what is intended by the sufficiency of Scripture. "In contending for that sufficiency, it is not meant that Scripture alone should be read and studied, and that we throw aside every means,—that we should despise and reject every help, that might enable us more correctly to ascertain its meaning, and more fully to enter into its spirit. This would be a monstrous perversion, a most pernicious abuse of the maxim that "the Bible only is the religion of Protestants." All that is to be understood by it is, that no other work carries with it the same title to our regard and submission, and that when once its principles are clearly ascertained, they furnish the only authoritative rule for Christian faith and practice; that no other writings, of whatever age or country they may be, can be allowed to come into competition with them,—to qualify their statements or to supercede their authority; that on every question where they speak positively and explicitly, their decision is paramount and final; and that no opinion or practice, unsanctioned by them, is to be received as a necessary and essential part of the Christian scheme."

This view of the sufficiency of scripture is held universally by all who claim to be Protestant Christians. The only exception, if it may be called an exception, are a few English Tractarians, most of whom, however, have followed out their principles not only to their logical but their practical results, and apostatising from the Church, whose faith they had denied, have gone to Rome. It is unnecessary, therefore, to dwell longer upon this topic.

The second of the two main pillars on which the superstructure of Protestantism rests is *the right of private judgment in the interpretation of Scripture.* This right is denied by the Romish hierarchy, which claims either for its representatives assembled in council, or for its ecclesiastical head, the Bishop of Rome, or for both concurrently, an infallible judgment, and an exclusive authority to determine for the faithful the meaning of Scripture. The Protestant Church, however, utterly repudiates the idea that infallibility belongs to any individual man, or body of men—to the Pope or any ecclesiastical council whatever. This claim is regarded as a monstrous and arrogant assumption, wholly incapable of proof, and actually disproved by the contradictory decisions both of Popes and Councils. But while all Protestants agree in rejecting the Romish dogma of infallibility, and the coordinate authority of tradition, there are some who virtually deny the right of private judgment in the interpretation of Scripture itself by ascribing to the writings of the primitive fathers a judicial authority in determining its meaning. It must be evident to all that this is a vital point, which requires serious and attentive examination. For if men may not rightfully exercise their private or individual judgment in investigating the meaning of scripture itself, then it is entirely a work of supererogation, both useless and irreverent to invoke the aid of reason and prescribe laws and rules for the interpretation of the Bible. Then may the science of biblical hermeneutics be reduced to a very narrow compass, and the whole be comprised in this one simple law—"Follow your leader, right or wrong."

We are told by the advocates of Romish infallibility, that it is a very desirable thing, that there should be some authoritative umpire supernaturally qualified to distinguish with infallible certainty between truth and error; and that it is incredible that the Deity, in granting a revelation, should have left its meaning to be ascertained by so weak and erring a tribunal as private judgment. Admitting the desirableness of such an infallible umpire and arbiter in the interpretation of scripture, does this establish the fact that such a judge has been actually appointed by the Deity? If it can be shown that any one man, or that any body of men are gifted with infallibility,—that the judgment, in any case pronounced by him or them *must* be right, then, to be sure, there is no presumption in requiring me to yield unhesitatingly to his or their decisions. But that, since the time of Christ and his apostles, such a property has been lodged in any one individual or number of individuals, there is not an atom of evidence to prove. On the supposition of such an appointment by the Deity, is it not reasonable to expect that He would have told us explicitly and unmistakeably in his word, where that infallible judgment and judicial authority reside?—whether in the Pope exclusively, or in a general council exclusively, or in the Pope and Council conjointly? This is a question certainly of vast moment which the Church of Rome has never yet been able to settle.

It is indeed true, that human reason is fallible, and, consequently, that the decisions founded upon it may be, and in point of fact, often are erroneous. It is true, that sincere and intelligent Christians have been led in the exercise of their rational faculties to the most opposite conclusions, and have claimed with equal confidence and pertinacity, the authority of Scripture for their conflicting opinions and systems. It is true, that the right of private judgment may be abused, as may other inherent rights which men possess, and that its exercise involves great responsibility. But what warrant does all this afford for the conclusion that there must be some unquestionable umpire, from whose decisions in matters of religion there can be no appeal? Before such an idea can be seriously entertained, it must be shown that in granting a revelation the Deity *designed* to preclude the possibility of dispute and disagreement as to its meaning, and to secure beyond the possibility of failure perfect unanimity of opinion. But as diversity of opinion can be prevented only by taking away the liberty of individual judgment, it must be further shown, that He also designed to deprive men of this freedom, and to compel them to take their religious opinions upon trust, and with implicit submission to the decisions of some recognized arbiter and dictator. But most certainly it is impossible for us to determine what the Deity *intended* to do in this regard, except from what he has actually done. Entire unanimity, however, has never yet been attained even among those who recognize a self-constituted infallible interpreter and judge. We are therefore authorized to conclude, that it never was the *intention* of the Deity to prevent the incidental evils arising from a diversity of opinions by means of a human infallible guide.

The human understanding is so constituted that it cannot be *compelled* to the belief of anything by external force. Such force may make hypocrites, but cannot produce conviction. Hence all attempts to coerce men into the belief of certain dogmas have proved a failure. Wherever coercive measures have been resorted to, the result has invariably disappointed the expectations of its employers. The case of Galileo is here in point. Witness also Luther and the other Continental as well as English reformers and martyrs—the English Puritans—the Early Christians, of whom it was truly said, "the blood of the martyrs is the seed of the Church." The attempt to coerce men into a unity of belief, or even into a uniformity in respect to external ceremonials, so far from accomplishing the object sought after, has led to the principal divisions into sects and separate ecclesiastical organizations, which unhappily exist in the Church. And if entire unanimity of opinion in regard to material points of Christian doctrine, and even in regard to immaterial points of ceremonial and ritual observances never has been, and never can be effected by coercion, or by requiring implicit submission to an authoritative arbiter, whose right to control opinion is unacknowledged, how can we expect entire harmony and agreement in the interpretation of the whole volume of inspired truth by any such means? The idea is utterly preposterous, and even the infallible Bishop of Rome has never acted so absurdly as to attempt the accomplishment of such an impossibility; but allows in his paternal clemency the exercise of individual judgment and the use of our rational faculties in relation to such doctrines and passages of Scripture, as he has not authoritatively pronounced an infallible judgment upon.

Again: the fundamental verities of all religions rest necessarily and purely on the exercise of reason and consciousness. On no other ground can we believe even in the existence of a God, which must first be established before the idea of a Divine revelation can be seriously entertained. The free exercise of the reason and judgment in the intrepretation of Scripture, moreover, cannot be superceded without destroying human responsibility. For if there were an infallible preservative against error, a right belief could not be a matter of choice, just as if there were an irresistable safeguard against *vice*, obedience could not be a virtue. But in the divine government men are treated as free-agents and made responsible for their opinions as well as for their conduct. It is true that in the exercise of their freedom they may err, and thereby involve themselves in ruin : but liability to error is inseparable from a state of probation: and consequently an infallible guide in matters of faith and practice, would be incompatible with the exercise of a rational faith, and with a moral submission to the divine laws. Finally: the denial of the exercise of the right of private judgment in the concerns of religion is incompatible with the intellectual advancement of the human race. And accordingly it has ever been the settled policy of those who deny this right to shut out from the mass of mankind the sources of knowledge and to deprive them even of the Scriptures in the vernacular language except in peculiar cases and under stringent restrictions. This right is also fully recognized in the Scriptures themselves. Though our Saviour and his apostles were infallible, they never insist on their own infallibility as a reason for compelling men's faith. On the contrary, they uniformly address mankind as intelligent creatures, and invite them to examine and then judge of the truth of what they propound.

But it is said, all men are not competent to judge of the meaning of Scripture. On the one hand, there is so much of the Bible which is deep and mysterious, so much that is dark and intricate and hidden from common observation, as to render its interpretation extremely difficult even to the well-informed; and, on the other hand, many, from their education and the circumstances of their lives—from being altogether unaccustomed to think and reflect, are wholly disqualified for coming to a sound conclusion upon the various questions pertaining to religion. Hence it is proper, if not absolutely necessary that there should be some reliable guide—some fixed and certain standard by which the true doctrine and the true interpretation of Scripture should be distinguished from the false and erroneous.

In reply to this it may be observed that right, and ability properly to use the right, are very different things, and must not be confounded with one another. The one is not necessarily and in point of fact is not actually, the accompaniment of the other. A man may possess the right to do, what he is ill qualified for doing wisely and beneficially. "You may have the right to choose your physician, your lawyer, your engineer, and it is important that you should choose well; and yet, from the circumstances in which you are placed, you may not be very competent to make a good choice. In such a case we cannot say, it does not belong to you to determine the matter. That is left to another who will do this for you, and to his decisions you must unhesitatingly bow. We could not address to any one language like this; but we might reasonably and becomingly say to him; before you come to a decision upon a matter of such great importance, take care that you have qualified yourself to judge rightly. Avail yourself of the knowledge and experience of others. Learn from them the facts which will give you the means of coming to a sound and satisfactory conclusion. The power, the right of deciding is unquestionably yours. That we do not deny. You may choose whom you please. All we say is, see to it that you render yourself competent and qualified to choose well. Such advice, such recommendation as this would be reasonable and proper. And if this were all that is meant by questioning the right of private judgment on the subject of religion; if it were only intended to check presumption, to curb rashness, to prevent haste, to make men cautious and careful in their inquiries, willing to receive instruction and anxious to avail themselves of all the light which the labors and learning of others might throw upon the subject, there would be little or nothing to object to." (Madge.) No intelligent advocate for the right of private judgment ever claimed that men should willfully disregard all assistance from others, and proudly rely on their own superior discernment alone in the investigation of the Scriptures. And those who may have pursued this course in their inquiries, have been guilty of great rashness and presumption. On the contrary they should avail themselves gladly of all the lights of former ages and all the lights of the present age within their reach. "No person," says Dr. J. Pye Smith, "is competent to ex-cogitate for himself a religion out of the Bible, or out of any other book, without the assistance of all those various means, which in the Bible, as in every other book, are indispensible to his reading, understanding, feeling, analysing and judging of its multifarious contents. Our appeal should be to the Bible, with *every note and comment* from every quarter; from all those legitimate and necessary helps which are supplied by grammatical, critical, historical, moral and spiritual considerations, and which regulate our interpretation of every other book." There is unquestionably a *duty* as well as a *right* involved in the exercise of this privilege of judging for ourselves. In contending for the right we must not overlook or forget the duty. The duty is to see that we are competent to judge respecting the questions that come before us; that we are duly qualified, both intellectually and morally, for forming an opinion on the matter under consideration. It would then be felt that there is a right and a wrong use of the faculties of the intellect as well as of the body; and that we are answerable, not indeed to man, but to God, for the principles we adopt. "The question," says Archbishop Whately, "when plainly stated, is not whether men should follow the guidance of inclination and fancy; nor, again whether they should reject all human teaching, and refuse all assistance in their inquiries after religious truth; but, supposing a man willing to avail himself of all helps within his reach and to divest himself of all prejudice, is he ultimately to decide according to the best of his own judgment, and embrace what appears to him to be truth? or, is he to forego the exercise of his own judgment, and receive implicitly what is decided for him by the authority of the Church, laboring to stifle any different conviction that may present itself to his mind." "We are, all of us," says Madge, "a good deal dependent upon one another; we are, all of us, obliged to take much upon trust. This is the case not only with men of little learning and little information, but with men well accomplished in both these respects. Take as an example the case of two or three men of different talents and attainments inquiring into the evidences of the Christian religion. The first, we will say, is a scholar and well read in all the branches of Christian literature. The second is one who, though not able to read the New Testament in the original or the works of the Greek and Latin fathers, has still leisure and opportunity for reading such translations as have been made of them, or such writings as contain the best and fullest information concerning them. The third is possessed of plain good sense, but has little or no time for reading works of any considerable extent, and derives therefore most of his knowledge on the subject from those who are able to give him, in a small compass, the result of their reading. Now each of these gets hold of the same facts, though in different ways; and, possessing these facts, the one may be as competent to draw from them the just inference as the other. The first will say that, from his own personal examination, he knows that the books of the New Testament existed in their present form at a very early period of the Christian era, as is testified by the large quotations made from them in the works of the first Christian fathers, and which have come under his observation. The second will say that he also has ascertained the same fact, not indeed from a perusal of the ancient authors themselves, but from the account given of them in the works of Lardner, Less, Paley and others in whose representations he places the most entire confidence. Then comes the third, and he tells us that he has learnt this fact, neither from the Fathers themselves, nor from the writings of those by whom the Fathers are largely quoted, but from the verbal testimony or assurance of those who *did* thus obtain their knowledge, and on the truth and integrity of whose statements he firmly relies. Now, in these cases, it might perhaps be said, that the last person, the poor unlettered man, is altogether disqualified for drawing any argument in favor of the authenticity of the New Testament from the fact in question, because he has not been able to obtain a knowledge of it by means of his own personal examination of the authorities on which he depends. To this I answer that, availing himself as he may of the labors and learning of others for the desired information, he then becomes (unless there are other disqualifications to hinder him) quite as competent to reason from the fact thus made known to him, as the other two that have been mentioned, though without their aid and apart from their testimony no such competency would be possessed by him. It is certainly true that on the subject of religion,—on matters connected with the interpretation of the New Testament,—there is much concerning which many persons, from their situation and circumstances, from their state and condition intellectually and morally considered, are not very well qualified to form a correct judgment. If they think about them at all, their thoughts will probably be very crude and ill-digested; and hence perhaps we shall be told that they, more especially, stand in need of guidance and direction. Undoubtedly they do; but instead of saying to them, you have no right to look into these matters, you have no right to inquire and to judge of such things, you must look up to us, and take our opinions as the rule and measure of your own, the wiser course would be to say, The great essential points of Christian belief, all that it is most necessary and important for you to know, are so clearly and explicitly and emphatically taught in the Scripture of the New Testament, that all may understand them from the least to the greatest. 'Secret things belong unto the Lord, but those which are revealed belong unto us and to our children.' Upon these let your thoughts be chiefly exercised; they will instruct you in the one thing needful; they will make you wise unto salvation; and if you are desirous of extending your inquiries beyond these,—if you are anxious to become acquainted not only with the leading principles, the object, the purpose, the spirit of Christianity, but with the letter of the New Testament, with the exact meaning of all its various contents, argumentative as well as didactic, controversial as well as historical, obscure as well as plain,—remember that, for this purpose, certain qualifications are absolutely necessary, and that without these you will only trouble and perplex yourselves in vain."*

CHAPTER V.

PATRISTICAL AUTHORITY IN INTERPRETATION.

It is the doctrine of the Romanists that the Church, (by which they mean of course the Church of Rome, or rather the Hierarchy of that Church,) is the infallible judge and interpreter of Holy Scripture, on the ground that she is the

* Lectures on Puseyism.

only authority which represents Christ upon earth, and that ever possessing his mind and supernaturally guided by his Spirit, she cannot possibly err in her doctrinal decisions. This, as we have seen, is utterly denied by the Reformed Church. Some Protestant divines, however, distinguished for their learning and piety, who have no faith in the paramount or co-ordinate authority of oral tradition, and repudiate the papal claim to infallibility, do, notwithstanding, virtually deny or greatly circumscribe the right of private judgment in the interpretation of the Bible, by according to the early Church fathers an authority incompatible with the exercise of that right. They shift the ground of authoritative interpretation from the Church in all ages or the Pope its spiritual head and representative, to the primitive Church as represented by the fathers and early councils. Thus we are told that "the Scriptures are the Rule of Faith according to the primitive catholic interpretation, with *the right of private judgment to decide what that interpretation was.*" The Scriptures are represented as the *law*, and the early fathers as the *judges* and *interpreters* of that law, whose concurrent decisions we are implicitly to follow. "As judges and interpreters of the written word of God, they (*i. e.* the ancient fathers) have our absolute confidence. whenever they are unanimous. But where they are not unanimous, we are compelled to do as they did; compare their discordant sentiments with Scripture, and adopt that sense, which seems most conformable to the language of inspiration." Again: "there is a part of the English law, although it is not expressed in the [thirty-nine] articles [of the Church of England], and has no formal recognition in the system of the American [Episcopal] Church, which I consider important to a perfect understanding of our doctrine concerning the Rule of Faith ; and this is the provision that the Scriptures should be expounded according to the sense of the ancient fathers."

If this is the doctrine of the English Church it is extraordinary that it should have found no place in the Articles of that Church, many of which relate to points of far less consequence than this. Besides, why did not the Anglican Reformers append to their admirable translation of the Scriptures a catena of patristical interpretation, as the Romanists have done, so that the clergy as well as the unlearned reader might be enabled in every instance to put the authoritative interpretation upon them, and not by furnishing them with the naked text, leave them to exercise presumptuously their own private judgment in regard to cases already adjudicated? Or, why did they not at least cause the writings of the fathers to be translated into the English language and circulated among the people, in order that they might have the true key with which to unlock the treasures of the Bible? Even Mr. Newman saw clearly the propriety of this course, and he and his co-adjutors among the Oxford Tractarians undertook to supply this defect. Remarking on the tenacity with which Christians of the present age maintain the notion, that they are inadequate judges of tradition, he follows it up by saying, "It does seem a reason for putting before them, if possible, the principal works of the Fathers, translated as Scripture is, that they may have by them, what, whether used or not, will at least act as a check upon the growth of an undue dependence on the word of individual teachers, and will be something to consult, if they have reason to doubt the catholic character of any tenet to which they are invited to accede." It would seem, then, according to the views here presented, that although we may *read* the Scriptures, we may not *interpret* them in the exercise of our rational faculties, as we do any other book; but must first go to the early church fathers and ascertain what interpretation they put upon the sacred volume. That interpretation, as far as it goes, we are implicitly to receive and adopt as conclusive, whether it accords with reason and common sense or not. It is true, that, where the fathers are not unanimous, we are allowed *to do as they did.* And what did they do? They studied the Scriptures for themselves. And why may we not do the same thing, as well in regard to points on which they have expressed an opinion, as in reference to those upon which they are silent? The very fact that they have advanced discordant opinions conclusively proves that they were not infallible, and not always reliable. Truly this studying of the Scriptures through the writings of the fathers, instead of going directly to the fountain head, is a most recondite and circuitous, as well as unsatisfactory way of coming at their meaning.

But who are the primitive or ancient fathers, whose authority is decisive as to the meaning of Scripture? Does the term embrace the writers of the first two centuries only or of the first three? Or does it comprehend also those of the fourth, fifth and sixth centuries? Are Irenæus and Tertullian the latest writers who are entitled to this enviable distinction? Or are we to include Augustine and Jerome in the number? This is a point of very considerable importance, and yet it is one by no means settled among the advocates of patristical authority. By some much is said about Nicene Christianity, the Nicene Church and the Nicene Creed. These have been lauded to the skies as perfect, comprehending all Divine truth, and presenting nothing but apostolic truth. With such, doubtless, the authority of the Nicene or ante-Nicene fathers, as interpreters of Scripture, is decisive and unquestionable. Suppose, then, we restrict the term to these, who are the men, we may ask, that must be recognized as authoritative interpreters of the Word of God? In addition to the *soi disant* apostolic fathers, who are not of much account in reference to the matter under consideration, there are Justin Martyr, Clement of Alexandria, Irenæus, Tertullian, Cyprian and Origen. Now on what ground are the interpretations of these men to be implicitly followed by us? It must be either on the ground of their possessing superior literary qualifications for such a work, or on the ground of their proximity to the apostolic age, or on both.

What then were the personal qualifications and literary attainments of these men? No one claims that they were generally eminent biblical scholars. The works of most of them which have come down to our times are apologetic rather than exegetical. Where they belong to the latter class of writings, they are open to most weighty objection on account of the erroneous principles of interpretation which pervade them. Some of them carried the allegorical and mystical system to a most unwarrantable, extravagant and even ridiculous extent. At the head of Biblical interpreters during this period stands Origen. Possessed of great genius, extensive erudition, amazing industry and vast powers of memory, he holds the most conspicuous place among the Christian writers of the ante-Nicene age. But he pushed the allegorical mode of interpretation to a far greater and more dangerous extent than any of his predecessors. To the Scriptures he ascribed a three-fold sense, viz.: the literal or grammatical, the moral, and the spiritual or mystical. To the first of these he attached very little value; but regarded the hidden or mystical sense as the only one worthy of regard. None but the most wild and visionary of the present day would regard him as a safe and judicious expositor of the sacred volume. Swedenborgians might adopt him as a guide, but not any one who places common sense above fancies and dreams.

But it is alleged that the ante-Nicene fathers possessed the advantages of having lived very near the age of the Saviour and his apostles, and on this account alone are entitled to implicit confidence. To their writings the legal maxim is applied, *Contemporaneous interpretation is the best interpretation.* This principle is doubtless a sound one in reference to Biblical as well as secular writings. But the rule is not applicable to any great extent to the writers in question. They did not live near enough to the times and scenes of the apostolic ministry to impart to their interpretations the character of genuine and uncorrupted apostolic tradition.

The rule applies in their case only to general doctrines and facts, and not to particular interpretations of Scripture, and therefore cannot supercede a personal examination and an independent judgment of Scripture for ourselves. Testimony may be early and yet not contemporaneous. We should hardly affirm of two individuals who lived one or two hundred years apart that they were contemporay and that the latter was fully competent to tell us what interpretation the former put upon this or that passage of Scripture in the absence of all documentary evidence to that effect. The fact that a Christian father of the third century has put a certain construction upon a passage of Scripture would certainly be very inadequate testimony to prove that the Apostles of the first century put the same construction upon it. The Constitution of the United States has been in existence scarcely three-fourths of a century; and yet, notwithstanding all the light thrown upon that instrument from the well-known private opinions of its framers, the statesmen of our age have already begun to dispute about its meaning. But few of the ante-Nicene fathers lived soon after the death of the Apostles, and their writings are of no special value as interpretations of Scripture. Clement of Rome, Ignatius and Polycarp are all. Still the testimony of the others is comparatively early, and would be entitled to our respect on this ground provided *other things were equal.* But other things are not equal. They did not possess other requisite qualifications. Several of those who lived at a much later period, (e. g. Chrysostom, Augustine and Jerome,) are entitled from their superior learning and sounder judgment to much greater respect and deference, than are any of those who previously flourished and wrote.

Are the ante-Nicene fathers then, it may be asked, of no value? Most certainly they are of value; but this is not the question under consideration. They are of some value as interpreters of Scripture; but of much greater importance as credible witnesses of facts which came under their observation. A man may be perfectly competent to testify to a fact, and at the same time very incompetent to expound an ancient document. The testimony of the primitive fathers is highly important, no doubt, in reference to the canon of Scripture, the polity, rites and ceremonies of the Church, and her received and traditional doctrines. The following examples will illustrate our meaning. I take up the New Testament, and by a careful and critical examination of its contents, I come to the conclusion that the Divinity of Christ is most clearly taught therein. I find divine names bestowed upon him, divine attributes ascribed to him, divine works attributed to him and divine honors paid to him. I am compelled therefore to believe that such is the doctrine of that inspired book. But this doctrine by some is denied on the ground that such is not the teaching of this book. Now to satisfy myself more fully that I have read and interpreted the passages bearing on this point rightly, I turn to the history of the early church and its doctrines as these are developed in the writings of the fathers of the first three centuries and other authentic documents, and I find that, with few exceptions, the doctrine of Christ's divinity was held as a fundamental truth by the whole church, and that the few who denied it were regarded as heretical. This corroborative testimony from the universal belief of the early church affords the most satisfactory confirmation of the correctness of my interpretation.

Again: I read the historical account of the institution of the Lord's Supper in the Gospels, and also the command of the Saviour to his apostles to baptize all nations, and am led by a sound grammatical exegesis to the conclusion that these ordinances were designed by the Saviour to be perpetuated in his Church to the end of time. I then turn to the inspired records of the Apostolic Church as contained in the Acts of the Apostles and their Epistles, and am confirmed in the opinion that I have interpreted the words of Christ correctly. But a sect has sprung up which denies that such was the intention of the Saviour. I, then, in order to render assurance doubly sure, recur to the uninspired but authentic writings of the early fathers and their testimony and above all their practice puts the fact beyond a peradventure, for it is a sound principle universally admitted that *the early usage under a law is the best interpretation of that law.*

One more: I find our Saviour, on one occasion, washing his disciples' feet in order to inculcate in the most impressive manner the Christian duty of humility and condescension. But I am not sure whether this ceremony was intended by our Saviour to be continued in his Church, and was so understood by his disciples or not. Some maintain that it was so intended. To satisfy myself on this point I examine the remains of Christian antiquity and find that the early Christians practiced no such rite. The inference to my mind is irresistable, that our Saviour was not understood by his disciples to impose the perpetual obligation of such observance on his Church. Thus we see that the writings of the early fathers are of great value *historically*, and furnish much information and light to the student. In this point of view, no doubt, more deference was paid to them by the Church of England at the Reformation, than by the Continental Reformers. But *hermeneutically* they have no special claim to our regard or attention.

Our remarks thus far have been confined to the ante-Nicene fathers. Suppose now we extend our views somewhat beyond the ante-Nicene fathers, and take in those of the 4th, 5th and 6th centuries, we still fail to find what is claimed,—an authoritative exposition of Scripture, which in any sense supercedes the right and duty of exercising our own deliberate judgment in the investigation of the sacred volume. In regard to literary appliances and qualifications for the work of scriptural interpretation they were for the most part in far less favorable circumstances than are the Biblical interpreters of the present day. With only one exception (Jerome) they were entirely unacquainted even with the language in which the Old Testament was written, and were consequently obliged to rely on imperfect and in many instances inaccurate translations of it. They had never studied the principles of interpretation, and adopted such as are now universally admitted to have been unsound and derogatory to the Scriptures themselves. Their expositions are frequently so childish and absurd that we may well wonder how sober-minded men could have entertained them, and still more that the authors of them should be held up not only as the best, but as authoritative and nearly if not quite infallible guides and lights in the investigation of Scripture truth.

The doctrine that the Scriptures are to be understood according to the interpretation of the Christian fathers must proceed on the assumption that the Scriptures on the one hand, are so written as to be unintelligible in themselves, and on the other, that the writings of the fathers are clear and luminous. But such an assumption is without foundation. The Bible, notwithstanding its many difficulties, is a considerably more intelligible book than the works of the fathers; and the latter often stand much more in need of comment and elucidation than the former. The writings in question are frequently so obscure and unintelligible as to perplex and confound the most careful and discerning reader. "Let the Scriptures," says Milton, "be hard; are they more hard, more crabbed, more abstruse than the fathers? He that cannot understand the sober, plain and unaffected style of the Scriptures, will be ten times more puzzled with the knotty Africanisms, the pampered metaphors, the intricate and involved sentences of the fathers."

Again: The expository writings of the fathers of the first six centuries cover only a comparatively small portion of the Sacred Volume. On some parts of the New Testament they are somewhat copious and valuable, especially those of Chrysostom; but on the Old they are very meagre, and with the exception of Jerome, of little value. If we rely, therefore, upon them to enlighten us in regard to the true meaning of the Bible, we shall find ourselves in five cases out of six without a guide, and be compelled to pursue our way in the best manner we can in the exercise of our rational faculties.

The works of these writers also are so voluminous that but few could ever read them thoroughly, even if they were translated. It occupied Archbishop Usher 18 or 19 years of his life to read them through, although he read a portion of them every day. Besides, these expositors of the Word of God are far from being agreed in their interpretations. Many of their expositions are contradictory and irreconcilable to such an extent as to lead Chillingworth to remark, "there are fathers against fathers, and fathers against themselves: a consent of fathers of one age against a consent of fathers of another age." How, then, amid such conflicting opinions is the student to decide? Must he or must he not fall back on his own reason and judgment, however fallible they may be, to help him out of the labyrinth?

There is no evidence that the fathers either of the ante-Nicene or of the post-Nicene church claimed for their opinions any such authority and deference as are accorded to them by some. And if they had, there is abundant evidence that the validity of such a claim would not have been allowed by the Church. Their opinions in many instances, were rejected by the Church as heretical and unscriptural. Origen who was the ablest and most learned among the early writers was anathematised by the 2d council of Constantinople. Tertullian was grossly heretical during a portion of his life, and Lactanius was also charged with heresy.

Some writers more moderate than the rest, claim for the fathers not authority to *enunciate* doctrine, but simply to *test* it. To their interpretations of Scripture we must bring ours; and if we do not find ourselves in conflict with them we are at liberty to hold what we have excogitated. And where they have expressed no opinion we are at liberty to interpret for ourselves. But a test is of little value unless it be absolutely certain. A chemist's tests are unerring and therefore infallible If they were not, they would be discarded by science as useless. A test, moreover, must be complete in itself. It must not admit of appeal to other tests more complete or more certain, but must decide the point to which it is applied. Now to concede such a testing power or authority to the fathers is in reality to concede everything. To grant a *testing* power, is to grant a *judging* power, from which there can be no appeal. In all cases, therefore, in which they have given any decision, they are, according to this view, *judges*—supreme judges and consequently, infallible judges.

But it is alleged that we are bound to listen to the voice of the Church:—the fathers are the representatives of the Church in their different ages and the proper exponents of its teaching; consequently we are bound to yield implicit assent to their interpretations of Scripture. If the truth of the major premise in this syllogism be admitted, it does not follow that the minor is true; and if the minor be not proved, the conclusion falls to the ground. But we apprehend it would be difficult to establish the truth of the minor proposition. The Christian fathers whose writings have come down to our times, represent indeed the opinions of a certain number in their day, just as Dr. Pusey or Bishop McIlvaine represents those of a certain class in ours, or as Jeremy Taylor or Jonathan Edwards represented those of another class in a former age; and that is all. But to call Origen or Ambrose or Augustine the voice of the universal Church, is an assertion the truth of which cannot be substantiated. Doubtless the circle of their influence was great, but it was far from being universal. The vast tomes of the fathers embody, beyond dispute, much truth, much eloquence and much genius, and are therefore entitled to respect; but we are under no obligation to bow implicitly to their dogmatic or their exegetical theology.

If, indeed, it could be shown, that they lived for the most part so very near the apostolic age, as to render it improbable that they could have been unacquainted with the meaning which our Saviour and his apostles attached to their own language; if it could be shown that they possessed the requisite literary qualifications for explaining the scriptures in a satisfactory manner:—that they always expressed their own views with clearness and perspicuity, so as to render their meaning unmistakeable:–that their exegetical writings cover the whole or nearly the whole ground of Scripture:—that they are embraced within a reasonable compass, so as not to require years of laborious study to plod through them:—that the writers were generally agreed in the exposition of the sacred volume and of Christian doctrines:—that they claim for their opinions and expositions the authority accorded to them, and established that authority by proper evidence:—and finally, if it could be shown that their interpretations were generally regarded as of determinate authority in the age in which they lived, and fairly exhibited the dominant and prevailing views of the Church: —then there might be some ground, perhaps, for insisting that we should hold our own reason in abeyance, lay aside the study of philology, of hermeneutics, and of kindred sciences, and read the Bible only through the medium furnished by the fathers. But we apprehend the day is far distant when these things will be proved.

But it may be said that primitive interpretation of Scripture is to be gathered, not solely from the writings of the Fathers, but from the Creeds and Confessions and Decrees of the Councils, and especially the general or ecumenical Councils. Whatever doctrine or interpretation the primitive ages unanimously attest, whether by consent of the Fathers or by Councils, is to be implicitly received. It is in both these forms that the Church speaks, and from both we are to learn what the Scriptures teach. Let us pass then from the Fathers to the Councils. If we seek for the consentient testimony of the Church in the decrees of the Councils, we shall find ourselves in the same dilemma as before. For as there are Fathers against Fathers, so there are Councils against Councils. Suppose that we confine our view to General Councils, how does the matter stand? The Romanists reckon as many as eighteen General Councils. How many of these are we to regard as of authority in matters of interpretation and doctrine? Mr. Newman says that the termination of the era of purity cannot be fixed much earlier than the Council of Sardicia. A. D. 347. Suppose, then, we call the first four centuries "primitive antiquity" and the doctrines of that period "primitive purity." How many General Councils do we find in this period? Only two, viz. that of Nice, A. D. 325. and that of Constantinople A. D. 381. If we include the fifth century we get only four; and if we embrace the sixth and seventh centuries, we have in all, six General Councils. Will the decisions of any or all of these furnish us with an authoritative interpretation of Scripture? From the first two we get the Nicene Creed in its present form, and this is all which the Episcopal Church has received from them. The Apostles' Creed we also receive from primitive times, although it was never formally set forth by a General Council. And this Creed we venerate and love, not merely for its antiquity, but for its beautiful simplicity, its conformity to Scripture, and its remarkable freedom from all philosophysing and theorysing. But after all, upon how few points in the Christian system do these Creeds touch? They relate mostly to facts in the Gospel history which lie open and conspicuous on the face of the New Testament, and which, with the exception of the doctrine of the Trinity, as enunciated in the Nicene Creed, and the Descent of Christ into Hell in the Apostles' Creed, hardly admit of a diversity of opinion among those who acknowledge the supreme authority of Scripture. These councils, therefore, have done but comparatively little towards providing the student of the Bible with an infallible standard of interpretation. And on what ground does the Episcopal Church receive these Creeds? This is a question of the gravest importance and is vital to our present inquiry. "They ought thoroughly to be received and believed," says Article VIII, "*because* they may be proved by most certain warrants of Holy Scripture." The Scriptures then, according to the express teaching of this venerable Church, are the sole rule of faith, and the ancient Creeds are to be received not on the ground of any independent and special authority which in consequence of their antiquity they are supposed to possess to *command* our assent, but because, when brought to the test of Scripture, they are found to accord with its obvious teachings. The views of the Episcopal Church also in regard to the authority of councils are unmistakeably expressed in Art. XXI. "As they are an assembly of men whereof all are not governed by the Spirit and word of God, they may err, and sometimes have erred in things pertaining to God; wherefore things admitted by them as necessary to salvation, have neither *strength* nor *authority*, unless it may be declared that they are taken out of *Holy Scripture*."

In all that we have said with respect to the early fathers, it has been neither our purpose nor our wish to detract one iota from their value or diminish their influence as competent and credible witnesses of facts: and in this view their testimony is the more valuable the nearer it approaches the Apostolic age. For this purpose it is not necessary that they should be learned and able to explain in a satisfactory manner the many difficult passages of Scripture. All that is required is the opportunity of knowing and honesty in declaring what they know. The great advantage to be derived from the earlier Fathers is that they give us in their writings a faithful picture of the times in which they lived —that they make us acquainted with the external and internal state and condition of the primitive Church, its ecclesiastical polity, its rites and ceremonies, its moral discipline and influence:—that they tell us of the opinions and practices that prevailed in the early ages, and especially that they furnish us with the most abundant and satisfactory evidence of the existence of the books of the New Testament at such a period of the Christian era as to render it impossible for them, widely diffused as they were, to have been forged and palmed upon the world, in so short a time, as the genuine writings of apostles and apostolic men. All that we contend for is, that they were fallible men, who were not only liable to commit mistakes in their interpretation of Scripture, but who actually did commit many mistakes: that as interpreters they were clothed with no authority which obliges us to submit implicitly to their opinions: that the Bible is not the Rule of faith as interpreted by the Fathers, but that the Bible is the Rule of faith interpreted by all the lights we can bring to bear upon it.

CHAPTER VI.

RATIONALISM.

Thus far it has been our aim to advocate the claims of right Reason as a guide of paramount importance in the interpretation of Scripture, and to vindicate as a necessary consequence the right of private judgment, in opposition to the alleged judicial authority of the Bishop of Rome on the one hand, and of the early church fathers on the other. We have endeavored also to define briefly the legitimate province of Reason in reference to the interpretation of Scripture, and to show the necessity of restricting its exercise to its own proper domain. But while it is highly important to guard against an implicit reliance on the decisions of the Roman Pontiff, or on the opinions of the early expounders of sacred writ, it must not be overlooked that our greatest danger at the present day lies in the opposite direction, viz: in placing an exclusive reliance on human reason, and exalting it to the position of a supreme, exclusive and infallible arbiter, test, and judge of the truth or falsehood of the facts and doctrines of the Bible. This abuse, misapplication and perversion of human reason in dealing with the claims and statements of Divine Revelation, is usually designated by the term Rationalism. The system has its origin partly in the corruption of the human heart, which, while it cannot bring itself to an open rejection of the Gospel as a divine revelation, proudly rises in opposition to its humiliating and self-denying doctrines, and partly in a high. overweening and deceptive estimate of man's religious instincts and reasoning powers. The tendency to exalt and exaggerate the powers and capacities of the human mind, and to bring everything if possible down to the level and within the grasp of its comprehension is a very remarkable characteristic of the present age; and in no department of science has this tendency been more conspicuous than in that of theology.

Rationalism as a system differs from what is termed Naturalism in this respect. The latter recognizes nothing but the religion of nature, or pure Deism; it denies the possibility or at least the necessity and probability of a supernatural Revelation, and consequently denies that the Holy Scriptures are in any proper sense a Revelation from God. The former, however, acknowledges the doctrine of Scripture as a divine revelation, but brings that doctrine to the standard of human reason and conscience. The advocates of this system claim not only the moral *right*, but the full *capability* of each individual, not merely to ascertain by the application of sound and acknowledged principles of interpretation the meaning of the sacred writers, but to sit in judgment on the facts and doctrines of Scripture themselves, and either to reject them as untrue, or to put such a forced and unnatural construction upon the text as to make its teachings accord with their subjective feelings and philosophical speculations. Everything which the Bible contains must, according to this system, be brought down to the comprehension of human reason, and whatever is beyond the reach of the human faculties or offensive to the moral sensibilities of the individual is to be discarded. Rationalists proceed on the ground that whatever is not intelligible or comprehensible is incredible; that only what is of familiar and easy explanation, and involves no difficulties, is entitled to belief, and that all which is miraculous and mysterious in Scripture must be rejected. They either deny entirely the divine inspiration of the sacred writers, or else advocate such loose views of inspiration as practically amounts to a denial of it. By the application of a destructive criticism they get rid of entire books or large portions of books from the sacred canon. They generally take some system of philosophy to which as a touchstone they bring the evidences and doctrines of Revelation. Whatever passages of the Bible appear to be inconsistent with this standard, are discarded from their creed. This accounts for the varying aspects and numerous phases which Rationalism presents, according to the current of the prevailing Philosophy,—a circumstance which renders it extremely difficult to define it, or to describe fairly and accurately its prominent and distinctive features.

The system of interpretation followed by the Rationalists exhibits precisely the same treatment of the sacred books as of the Greek and Latin classics, in utter disregard of the divine and spiritual nature of the truths they contain, the unimpeached and unimpeachable character of the writers, their entire credibility and trustworthiness, and the divine guidance, superintendence and inspiration, under which they claim to have composed their writings. The principle which lies at the basis of their hermeneutics is *Interpret the Bible as you would any other book.* This principle, which is undoubtedly a sound one carried to a certain extent, and applied with proper limitations and qualifications, is grossly abused and perverted by this class of interpreters, and the Bible is treated by them as they would not treat any other book possessing the least claims to authenticity and credibility, much less to divine authority. "Possessed of no real reverence for the sacred documents, and destitute of humility in its approaches to the fountains of heavenly truth, Rationalism comes not to drink of the pure waters and be satisfied, but to disturb their placidity and to lessen the enjoyment of such as drink at the same hallowed source. It suffers little of a purely religious nature to stand in the Bible, and even that which it leaves untouched, is so affected by the breath of its scepticism, as to yield no salutary or solid nutriment to the hungry spirit. It levels the mountains of God into plains, and removes the ancient landmarks which ages have justly venerated. Nor does it spare the holiest discourses of Jesus, but reduces even these to barrenness by the withering blight of its presence."

It is not our purpose to attempt a refutation of this most fallacious, baseless, and pernicious system. This would require volumes instead of a few paragraphs, which is all the space we can give to it. We have endeavored simply to present an outline of its most prominent features, and to put our readers on their guard against a system which enthrones reason in the seat of supremacy, which strips Revelation of every thing peculiar to it, and hurls the divine fabric of revealed truth to the ground, leaving nothing for the faith or hope of a poor sinner to rest upon. From such an awful heresy, the offspring of the evil one—a lying vanity by which many who call themselves Christians, and some who occupy prominent positions have been unhappily deceived—the Church should be quickly and thoroughly purged, or we shall have no word of God left us.

CHAPTER VII:

THE LIGHT OF AUTHORITY.

One of the guides whose assistance should be invoked in the study of the Scriptures, is *the light of authority.* All men are influenced in a greater or less degree in the formation of their opinions on difficult and important subjects, by the views and sentiments of others, who are supposed from their superior talents, or education, their extensive learning, or favorable opportunities, to be better qualified than themselves for arriving at just conclusions. The field of knowledge is so vast, that it is impossible, within the short span of human life, for any man to investigate for himself every subject on which he is expected to have and to express an opinion. Hence, for a large part of what we profess to know, we are indebted to the testimony of others; and the authority of names is every.where confessedly great. This holds true in regard to every science and department of knowledge, and theology furnishes no exception to the remark. It is natural and highly proper that we should pay a suitable respect and deference to the opinions of those who may be possessed of superior qualifications and advantages to unfold the meaning of Scripture. The Bible is a collection of ancient records relating to a divine economy, composed by different authors, in different ages, and in different languages and styles, embracing a great variety of subjects, historical, prophetical, poetical and ethical. To investigate *de novo* every point of importance in respect to them, in disregard of the labors of other minds who have been employed in the same field of inquiry and research, is beyond the power of a single individual, however well qualified for the task. And the attempt to do this would only betray a profound ignorance of our own incompetency and consummate vanity and self-conceit. There is not one, therefore, who does not feel and at least practically acknowledge the necessity of resorting to foreign aid and relying more or less on authority in the interpretation of Scripture. Even the most learned and intelligent are not insensible to its influence, and the uneducated, who are disqualified for forming an independent opinion, depend almost entirely on authority. Its value on the one hand has undoubtedly been unduly magnified and exaggerated, and on the other, as unduly depreciated. With millions the authority of opinion has the force of law. It overrides every thing else, and is paramount to all other considerations. Thus Newman (on Romanism) remarks, "When the sense of Scripture, as interpreted by reason, is contrary to the sense given to it by catholic antiquity, we ought to abide with the latter." Others, on the contrary, have affected to despise authority, and to rely exclusively either upon their independent judgment or the inward light of the Spirit.

The term *authority* is not always used in precisely the same sense. We speak of the *authority of law*, and the *authority of testimony.* By authority in the former case, we mean *rightful power;* but in the latter, we employ the term as equivalent to *weight, influence.* The authority of law does not admit of degrees; it is perfect and complete in itself. But the authority of testimony does admit of various degrees, and is weaker or stronger according to the circumstances of the case and the nature of the testimony. The authority of law is obligatory and imperative within the sphere of its action. It is armed with power to command and to enforce obedience to its mandates by penal sanctions. Not so is it with the authority of testimony. That has no binding force, and it is in the power of each individual to admit or reject it, as his judgment may dictate. In determining the meaning of the Scriptures in the original languages, we depend chiefly upon testimony, and are governed by its authority, *i. e.*; we rely in most cases for the signification of particular words and their sense in combination, on approved lexicons and grammars, which embody in a convenient form and small compass the results of a laborious and extensive examination of the usage, which from the want of opportunity or facilities, we may not be able to investigate for ourselves. We ascertain, therefore, the *import* of a divine precept, through the medium of human authority, *i. e.*, of testimony; we *obey* the precept because it has the *authority of God.* It is to this human testimony and its authority, or that weight and influence we are accustomed to accord to it in the formation or confirmation of our opinions, that we refer in relation to the present subject. This testimony is of course fallible, and therefore liable to err, while the testimony of God is infallible, and is implicitly to be received.

Human testimony is of different kinds:— 1. There is the testimony of *tradition*, and hence we speak of the authority of tradition. The word *tradition*, (παράδοσις, traditio.) in its etymological and most extensive sense signifies any information, whether fact, doctrine, or precept, delivered from one person to another in any manner, whether orally or in writing. In this sense it is constantly employed by the early Church fathers in reference to the Gospels and Epistles of the New Testament—the first being called for the sake of distinction the *Evangelical* tradition; the second the *Apostolical* tradition. But in the strict and now more common and appropriate sense, the word signifies that which was originally delivered *orally*, and not embodied in the sacred volume, though it may finally have been reduced to writing in a subsequent age, to which it had been handed down by word of mouth.* This is a species of testimony, which, though elevated by the Jewish Rabbins and by the Church of Rome to the same position as the volume of inspired truth, is held in very light esteem by Protestants, because it corresponds to

* See Note, p 15–17.

what in courts of law is called *hearsay evidence*, which is universally regarded as of little intrinsic worth on account of the infirmity and treachery of the human memory, and the possibility of designed misrepresentation which cannot be detected from the want of direct and positive evidence.

2. There is next the *testimony of an eye or ear witness.* As the testimony of tradition is the weakest, so this is the strongest and most reliable of all testimony, so far as pertains to all matters cognizable by the senses. Because the early church fathers were competent witnesses of facts coming within their own personal observation and knowledge, although possessed of very limited information in reference to other things, we have no hesitation in relying on their testimony with regard to the received canon of Scripture, the change of the Sabbath, the mode and subjects of baptism, the different orders in the Christian ministry, the form of ecclesiastical government, the admission of females to church membership and communion, the doctrine of the Deity of Christ, of the Trinity, &c., and the authority of such testimony cannot be rejected without betraying great inconsistency and want of candor.

3. There is further the *testimony of opinion*, whether of one individual or of many collectively, and this irrespective of the grounds on which that opinion may be based. Of course this opinion is of greater weight where the grounds of belief are distinctly stated, but where this is not done the naked opinion of those whom we believe to be competent to form a correct opinion carries with it no little influence.

When we find, for example, that such men as Sir Isaac Newton, Locke, Pascal, Addison, Johnson, Bunsen, Daniel Webster, and a host of others possessed of the most vigorous and capacious intellects, of comprehensive and liberal views, and of profound and varied learning, were firm believers in the truth and divine authority of the Scriptures, though this fact does not directly *prove* the truth of these scriptures, it must and will have great weight with all dispassionate, unprejudiced and thoughtful men, in confirming their own previous convictions, and furnishes at the same time an irrefragable confutation of the assertion so often to be met with in the writings of infidels and sceptics, that none but men of shallow intellects and limited knowledge have placed confidence in the written word of God This remark applies also with equal truth and force to particular doctrines and expositions of Scripture.

The witness or testimony in question embraces: — 1. The teachings of the Universal Church, or of some particular branch of that church. 2. The teachings of individual members of the church. The first is contained in Church Creeds, Confessions of Faith, Articles of Religion, Catechisms, Liturgies, Homilies, and other symbolical writings. The visible Church was established to be "the *witness* and *keeper* of *Holy Writ*,"—not the exclusive witness or exclusive keeper, but especially charged with these responsible duties. Others may preserve and bear testimony to the Scriptures as well as she, but it is specially incumbent on her, because to her has been committed "the Oracles of Truth," and she cannot fail to do her duty in this regard without being wanting in her allegiance to Christ. But to be *a witness* of holy writ necessarily includes the office of teaching the doctrines and precepts which it inculcates and enjoins. Nor could she be "the pillar and ground of the truth," unless she were invested with the power and ability, not only to preserve, in her keeping, but to set forth, inculcate and maintain by her dogmatic and ethical teaching, Gospel truth. Revealed religion is a system of faith and practice, requiring instruction for its propagation in the world; and as the Apostles promulgated it by word of mouth as well as by their writings, so the Church was instituted to supply in some measure their place, by teaching the same to her members, no less than by placing in their hands the inspired volume. This privilege and duty she has aimed to discharge in her collective capacity by embodying the chief and most essential articles of the Christian faith in forms supposed to be best adapted to meet the wants of the people. The right to set forth in doctrinal, catechetical and liturgical formularies her sense of the general meaning of Scripture, has been almost universally accorded to the church catholic, and has been exercised by her from the earliest period of her establishment, as a duty which she owed to herself in order to preserve her unity, and to her members that they might under all circumstances have a summary of Christian faith, drawn up by the collective wisdom of the church, to which they may refer as a guide in the study of the sacred volume. It cannot be denied, that in the exercise of this right she has frequently erred, by setting forth dogmas which either find little support in the word of God, and which are by no means essential, or that are clearly at variance with the sacred record, and has enforced them with an intolerance utterly inconsistent with the spirit of the Gospel. But notwithstanding this, her right thus to embody the collective opinions of her members in creeds and confessions of faith, cannot well be questioned. And what may be done by the whole church, may be done by any portion or branch thereof The powers and privileges with which the church catholic is invested attach to any sound branch of the same. And there is not a single denomination of Christians claiming to be a part of the visible church, which has not either a written or a mental creed. But as the several individuals who compose the church or any branch of it are not infallible, so neither does infallibility attach to either of them collectively; and their symbolical books are to be received only so far as we are assured they may be proved by most certain warrants of Holy Scripture. At the same time, much deference and respect are due to formularies thus set forth under the sanction of ecclesiastical authority, and these are generally accorded to them. They are important helps in the investigation of Scripture.

But this method of propounding divine truth for the use of the members of the church is altogether inadequate for the purpose intended. Hence our Saviour instituted within the church a standing ministry, who should have ecclesiastical authority to explain the Scriptures to the people. Accordingly we find that those who are ordained to the sacred office are to be teachers (1 Cor. 12: 28, Eph. 4: 11); to give attendance to reading, to exhortation, to doctrine, (1 Tim. 4: 13); to labor in word and doctrine, (1 Tim. 5: 17); to rightly divide the word of truth, (2 Tim. 2: 14); to preach the word, to reprove, to rebuke and exhort, (2 Tim. 4: 2); to be mighty in the Scriptures, (Acts 18: 24); to be apt to teach, (1 Tim. 3: 2); to be an example to believers in word and in faith, (1 Tim. 4: 12)—all which plainly intimates that they should be possessed of the requisite qualifications to expound truly and faithfully the doctrines which they themselves have learned from the word of God, and to commend them to the belief and practice of mankind. Hence the Church is bound to furnish those who are preparing for the sacred office every facility in her power for acquiring a thorough and critical knowledge of the Scriptures, and to see that those whom she appoints to minister at her altars and to be the authorized expounders of the Word from her pulpits, are properly qualified rightly to divide the word of truth, that the laity who look to them for instruction, and who naturally and properly place great confidence in their teaching, may be rightly instructed in the way of life.

But in addition to the oral instruction of individual ministers, there are ample facilities for embodying their expositions of Scripture in a more systematic and permanent form by means of the press; and those who have left as a legacy to the church their views of its meaning in their writings, are entitled to our gratitude and respect. Of these writings, such as embody professed commentaries and exegetical treatises on the whole or separate portions of the Bible are of chief value to the student, and their use cannot be dispensed with without great loss to himself. The weight which we are to attach to the opinions of commentators must depend on various considerations: such as the age in which they lived, their literary attainments and qualifications, their exegetical tact, discrimination and judgment, and the state of their moral feelings. In reference to the last, it should be specially borne in mind that religion addresses itself not to the intellect alone, but also to the moral feelings of mankind, and that those feelings are deeply interested in the questions—What is Scripture? and What is its meaning? The heart will necessarily and unavoidably exert more or less influence over the judgment on all moral questions, and in all matters of Biblical criticism and interpretation involving important principles, or essential doctrines. Something more, therefore, than competent learning and exegetical tact is necessary to a right interpretation of Scripture. The moral feelings of the interpreter must be in unison with those of the sacred writer, else no sympathy will exist between them, and the meaning of the latter will be often missed, and misrepresented. Hence, before we adopt this or that commentator as a guide in our religious inquiries, we should endeavor to ascertain the character and inward life of him whom we consult—the state of his religious affections, and the influence which these may have had in giving a particular complexion and direction to his views of Christian doctrine. In many cases, it is true, adequate learning may be all that is requisite to give the true sense, and we should candidly and impartially examine and weigh the reasons which may be assigned in support of an interpretation, let it come from whatever quarter it may. Still no man can be qualified in the highest and best sense to be a reliable interpreter of the inspired writings, whose mind is not imbued with the spirit of Christ, and whose moral and religious feelings are not in unison with his.

CHAPTER VIII.

THE LIGHT OF THE HOLY SPIRIT.

There remains to be noticed one more guide, whose assistance should be invoked in the study and interpretation of the Word of God, viz., *the inward light of the Holy Spirit*, one part of whose office it is to guide the humble and sincere inquirer into the truth. The absolute necessity of the teaching of the Holy Spirit, in order to enlighten the mind in the knowledge of the Scriptures, is a fact as clearly asserted in the Word of God as any other doctrine of revelation. This divine aid is rendered necessary in consequence of the fall of man, by reason of which not only has his will become perverse and his affections estranged from God, but his understanding has become darkened, so that he cannot discern spiritual truths, in all their fulness, unction and power. "The natural man, (*i.e.* the unrenewed man,) receiveth not the things of the Spirit of God,"—the truths of his word—

"for they are foolishness to him; neither can he know them because they are spiritually discerned," *i. e.* they can only be fully understood by the assistance of the Holy Spirit of which he is destitute. The Spirit alone can fully interpret what was given by the Spirit. Accordingly the assistance of the Spirit for this purpose is repeatedly promised to all believers, who will seek for it in earnest prayer. But as the operations of the Holy Spirit on the understanding are not distinguishable from those of our own minds, the utmost caution is necessary, lest we impute to the Heavenly Teacher what is properly the offspring of human prejudice, superstition, fanaticism or ignorance. For while, on the one hand, the necessity of special aid from on high is denied, and even derided by Rationalistic interpreters, such aid has been relied on by others to the exclusion of everything else. This exclusive reliance on the *inward light*, as it is termed, has led its advocates to disparage human learning, to disregard the plainest principles of interpretation, and to undervalue the Bible itself as the highest source of religious knowledge, and the only standard of faith and practice. But while both these extremes, leading as they do to the most mischievous errors, are to be carefully avoided, there is a middle ground which every student of the Bible should occupy. The promised assistance of the Holy Spirit, it should be well considered, is not granted to believers in answer to prayer, for the purpose of communicating to them *new truths* not before revealed; for this would be equivalent to supernatural inspiration;—but simply for the purpose of enabling them rightly to understand those which have been already made known. The grace conferred is co-operating grace—grace not to supercede the exercise of our reason, the teachings of others, or the use of human learning and literary appliances, but to render them more effective. The promised illumination is only the ordinary assistance of the Holy Spirit extended to the understanding—an assistance which neither supercedes the use, nor overrules the decisions of our natural faculties. On the contrary, we are constantly exhorted to employ these faculties on the subject of revealed truth. While the Spirit assists and exalts, it leaves our reason free, and no more makes us infallible than the ordinary influences of the Spirit upon the heart render us impeccable. The teaching in question does not imply any peculiar difficulty in Scripture. Its necessity does not arise from the obscurity and intricacy of its language, or from the incomprehensibility of its doctrines, but simply from the natural blindness of the human mind with respect to spiritual things and its deep rooted aversion to the wisdom of God displayed in the plan of salvation. In truth, it is the things which are most clearly revealed, that are often most misunderstood. Hence some writers who have most grossly perverted the plainest language in relation to the distinguishing truths of the Gospel, have most successfully explained some of the most perplexing difficulties of diction and phraseology with regard to matters in which the great truths of the Gospel are not immediately concerned. Nor are we to suppose that the teaching of the Spirit communicates any meaning to Scripture which is not contained in the words themselves. He makes men wise *up to* what is written, and not beyond it. The Spirit of God teaches only what is contained in the Scriptures, and this always through the instrumentality of the Scriptures. "Open thou mine eyes," prays the Psalmist, "that I may see wondrous things in thy law;" but the wondrous things here spoken of, are not things which are not contained in the law, but things already there, which our natural blindness disqualifies us from seeing. Whatever is taught contrary to the Scripture, therefore, or in addition to them, or without their instrumentality, is to be ascribed to the Spirit of darkness, or to our own perverted understandings. Nor does it follow because true Christians are taught by the Spirit, that they are taught the true meaning of every passage of the Word of God. The correctness of the explanation must ultimately rest on the arguments by which they support it, and not on the alleged ground of divine assistance. The explanations of an inspired apostle are doubtless to be received implicitly, even though we may not able to see the legitimacy of the conclusion from the premises. But the explanations of every uninspired man must be received no farther than they are seen to be the necessary result of the word of inspiration. Nor because all true Christians are more or less taught by the Spirit, does it follow that they all must agree in their interpretations. This assistance is not granted in the same proportion and degree to all. Even good men are not able to divest themselves altogether of prejudice, and passion, or a regard to self-interest in their examination of Scripture. Prejudice is no doubt one of the greatest obstacles in the way of understanding and explaining the Word of God. While this will take out of Scripture the meaning which it manifestly contains, it will put into it a meaning which it was never intended by the writer to convey. Hence, while it was related of Grotius that he could find Christ nowhere in the Old Testament, it was said of Coccaous, that he found Christ everywhere. The doctrine of the teaching of the Holy Spirit, then, affords no warrant for implicit submission to the interpretation even of the best of men. At the same time, from what has been said, we clearly perceive the duty of prayer for divine guidance. Without this no sure progress or certain results can be expected in the knowledge of the Word of God. There is great truth and force in Luther's aphorism, when rightly understood, *Bene orasse est bene studuisse.* And yet even this is not, as to any particular passage, to be received as conclusive evidence that we have attained the true interpretation. We are warranted to believe that God will hear our sincere prayer; but the only evidence that he has done so is that we now have light when before we were in darkness: that we now perceive the meaning which before lay hid from us.

Intimately connected with the aid of the Spirit afforded to the *understanding* of the devout inquirer after truth, is his moral influence on the will and affections. As we look for a right disposition of heart in the commentator whom we consult as reliable authority, so the same disposition is equally important in ourselves, if we would rightly apprehend the meaning of the Scriptures. Literary qualifications are obviously necessary to the interpreter; indeed they cannot be dispensed with; but moral qualifications are no less indispensible. When Christ appeared on earth, the light of his teaching shone in the darkness—not in the midst of intellectual darkness, but of moral and spiritual darkness—among unholy and sinful hearts—and the darkness did not comprehend it. Unholy affections had surrounded the mental eye and prevented the apprehension and reception of divine truth. Such is the influence of the heart for good or for evil on our judgment, in regard to all moral questions, and of course in regard to the whole of Scripture verity, that it may be laid down as a fundamental principle, *that Scripture to be rightly understood must be contemplated from within and not from without.* The old maxim, *Pectus facit theologum,*—"the breast makes the theologian," will always remain true, and other things being equal or nearly equal, he will best understand and explain Scripture, who most loves Scripture. "God has determined," says Pascal, "that Divine things shall enter through the heart into the mind, and not through the mind into the heart. In divine things, therefore it is necessary to love them, in order to know them, and we enter into truth only through charity." "An inward interest in the doctrines of theology," says Hagenbach, "is needful for a Biblical interpreter. The study of the New Testament presupposes as an indispensible requisite a sentiment of piety, and religious experience. The Scripture will not be rightly and spiritually comprehended, unless the Spirit of God become himself the interpreter of his Word: the *angelus interpres,* to open us the true meaning." It was a favorite maxim with Augustine, "*Believe that you may know*,"—not first know in order to believe; for the understanding, while it is not the *way* to faith, is yet the *reward* of faith. "He who has not believed," says Anselm, "will not experience; and he who has not experienced cannot know." "The theologian," says Tholuck, "must himself believe the doctrines which he studies. Without this moral qualification it is impossible to obtain a true insight into theological truth." "If goodness," says Trench, "be so essential even to the orator, that one of old defined him as *Vir bonus*, dicendi paritus, and few I think will quarrel with that *bonus*, or count it superfluous in the definition, how much more essentially must it belong, and in its highest form of love towards God, and to all which truly witnesses of God, to the great theologian." The interpreter of Scripture must possess a heart in cordial sympathy with its writings, otherwise he cannot grasp their profound, spiritual import. He must have the mind of Christ in order to comprehend the word of Christ. He must earnestly desire to know the truth for the truth's sake. He must possess an humble, docile spirit. He must be willing to sit with meekness at the feet of inspiration and draw the pure water of life from the great fountain of revealed truth. "The meek will he guide in judgment; the meek will he teach his way." And not only are a confiding faith, a childlike docility, and an humble, prayerful frame of mind essential to the successful study of divine truth, but also an *obedient heart*. Some appear desirous to know the will of God, who yet are averse to obey it. They approve of it in theory, but not in practice.

But such will not succeed. There must be the willing mind and a sincere endeavor to exhibit in the daily tenor of life the great principles and precepts of God's Word. "If any man," says the Saviour, "will do his will, he shall know of the doctrine, whether it be of God." The Bible brings us into contact with holy men, who spake as they were moved by the Holy Ghost. To understand aright their language we must be holy ourselves. An analagous truth is universally admitted in relation to every other subject of inquiry. To understand the poet's creations we must be imbued in some measure with a poetic taste. To comprehend or relish the profound speculations of the mental philosopher requires a philosophic spirit. In like manner, what communion of soul can the unrenewed and selfish sinner have with the sacred writers? The possession of a loving heart, open to receive the teachings of heavenly wisdom, in connexion with a spirit of cheerful obedience to the divine precepts, is the great secret of the success of many interpreters who are not furnished with much human learning. On the other hand, the entire want of a spiritual taste and relish for divine and heavenly truths is sufficient to account for the failure of many a man who heaps together rich stores of erudition, which only serve to obscure the truth instead of elucidating it.

CHAPTER IX.

LANGUAGE—INTERPRETATION.

Before proceeding to exhibit in detail the principles and rules of Biblical Interpretation, it will facilitate our progress if we devote a few paragraphs to some general preliminary remarks on Language, with which Interpretation is concerned. Language is the expression of thought—the outward medium through which a communication is formed between mind and mind—the mode by which we convey to other minds a conception of the ideas, sentiments, and emotions, which exist in our own. There is no direct communication between the minds of men. One man cannot immediately perceive the thoughts and sentiments of another. If then we desire to make known to others the thoughts and feelings which lie within our breasts, we can do so only by resorting to some outward manifestation of them, *i. e.*, to signs and symbols cognizable by the senses. But the necessary intercourse of mankind in social life,—the progressive improvement and advancement of individuals and communities, and the intellectual and moral culture of the race, render a mutual communication and interchange of thought and opinion among the various members and orders of society unavoidable and indispensible. There is found in man, also, a primæval principle ever urging him to represent outwardly what moves him strongly within, independently of any idea of utility, or a conscious desire to obtain a certain end by this development. Hence means were devised and resorted to from the first to facilitate this mutual communication. The means employed for this purpose are denominated *the signs of ideas*, and the term *Language*, in its broadest sense, includes all these means. Language is not absolutely indispensible to the *existence* of thought, but only to its development and expression. Pure thought, like pure spirit, is certainly a conceivable thing, however rarely it may be found. It may exist in the mind as an idea in a dormant or latent state, just as a principle of action may lie dormant in the soul, till it is called out in the transactions of life; and just as heat exists in all bodies in a latent state. But that thought may possess an actual as well as an ideal existence, whether in the mind itself, or in its outward workings, it must be clothed in some form, and that form, whatever it may be, is called language. "Thinking," says Plato, "is the talking of the soul with itself." Thinking then, as an act, process, or operation of the mind, is distinguishable from a thought or idea existing *in* the mind, and this process cannot be carried on without the use of language, any more than can a communication of thought to others.

There are three modes of developing the thoughts which exist in the mind—three distinct varieties of signs of ideas. The first is the *material*, as in the plastic or fine arts. The second is the *phenominal*, as in outward actions, looks, gestures, pantomimic representations, &c. The third is the *verbal*, as in oral and written language. The signs employed in the first two are addressed to the eye, or the touch; those employed in the third are addressed either to the eye or the ear. Accordingly language, in its widest acceptation, is the expression, by visible, audible, or tangible signs, of the thoughts, feelings or state of one mind, in order to excite the conception of the same in another. Language is either natural, artificial, or mixed. It is *natural*, when the signs employed are spontaneously suggested to the mind, and are of such a nature that they may be easily and readily understood by any one without previous instruction, or any conventional agreement, or the introduction of arbitrary customs. Of this description are certain looks, cries, gestures, &c., indicative of some powerful emotion, of distress, joy, sorrow, fear or alarm. These signs are *universal* in their use, and limited to no particular nation or age of the world. Language is *artificial*, when it consists of signs which are not spontaneous, but arbitrary, and adopted by tacit convention or common consent as expressive of ideas. Such are words, hieroglyphics, some symbolical actions and emblems. It is *mixed* when it consists of signs partly natural and partly artificial. The language of the deaf and dumb is of this character, and is the most successful attempt to reduce inaudible signs and gestures to a scientific form. Arbitrary signs are of course partial and limited in their use, and understood only by those who agree to adopt them, there being no natural fitness in them to convey the ideas intended, but deriving their signification from previous agreement of the parties using them. Verbal language, whether oral or written, belongs entirely to this class, because there is nothing in the sound, with the exception perhaps of onomatopoetic words, and nothing in the forms of the letters or of the words calculated to suggest the ideas to our minds, which they are employed to convey. Spoken language is remote from thought and written or alphabetical language is equally remote from oral language, and there is no necessary connexion between the two. We express a thought by an arbitrary sound addressed to the ear, which has no natural connexion with it whatever; and this arbitrary sound is then represented to the eye by an arbitrary figure, which has no more natural connexion with the sound than the sound has with the thought. That both the words of speech and the characters of writing are in themselves entirely arbitrary, is manifest from the fact that a great variety of different sounds and different signs is used by different nations, with equal convenience, to express the same thing. Words, whether spoken or written, are the most perfect signs of ideas. As vocal organs were bestowed upon mankind for the purpose of intercommunion, the employment of articulate sounds is a natural process in itself, and hence universally prevails, though the particular sounds employed to convey ideas are arbitrary, and left to the choice of individuals or communities. As there never has been a time since the origin of the human race, when men did not possess the faculty of speech, so there never has been a time when oral language was not employed. At first man's wants and ideas were few, and he required but a few words to express them; but as his knowledge increased and his intellect expanded, additions were made to his stock of words, and those already in use received an accession of meaning. Alphabetical or written language was the invention of a later period, and did not most probably come into use, until about the time of Abraham. In the mean time, however, the longing desire to give a permanent form to thought, and to transmit information to distant persons and places and to future times, was gratified to some extent, by the invention of pictorial representations and hieroglyphics, such as were employed in Egypt, and in the East generally. These cumbersome and very inadequate signs of ideas were superceded by the introduction of phonetic characters. Words expressed in *sounds* are the *immediate* signs of thought: words expressed in writing, the *mediate*. We have remarked that the term *language* is applied to signs of any kind which are employed as the vehicle of thought. In like manner, the terms *to explain*, and *to interpret*, are not confined to words simply, but used in reference to symbols, emblems, human actions, and all the outward signs which men have adopted to give expression to their thoughts and emotions. In a more restricted sense, however, the term language is applied to verbal signs of thought, whether spoken or written and as in the Bible we have to deal chiefly with such signs, so the terms language and interpretation, when used without any additional expression, are to be understood in this work as employed exclusively in reference to words.

Words are articulate sounds, or the representatives of articulate sounds on or in some material, by certain adopted characters to which, single or combined, we attach certain ideas. The particular idea or action thus attached to any word, is called its *signification*, and the general idea, or assemblage of ideas, conveyed by several words grammatically connected together, is called the *sense* or meaning of the combined words or period. And it is the business of the interpreter, by the application of correct principles and rules, to discover and exhibit this true sense.

Interpretation is both a science and an art. As a science, it consists of axioms, principles and rules. according to which we ought to proceed in discovering the true meaning of an author. As an art, it is the practical and skillful application of those principles and rules to the explanation of particular passages. The former is technically denominated *Hermeneutics;* the latter, *Exegesis.* These stand to each other in the relation of theory and practice. Thus we speak of the *Exegesis* of a passage according to *Hermeneutical principles.* The theory by which the Sacred books are explained, as distinguished from Legal instruments or other writings, is called *Sacred* or *Biblical Hermeneutics*, which, when ranked as a part of Theology, is called *Exegetical Theology.*

As an art, Interpretation is co-eval with language itself, and men, following the light of their reason and common sense, discovered the true import of language long before Interpretation was reduced to a scientific form, just as they learned to speak and write their vernacular correctly without the aid of Dictionaries and Grammars. As a science, Interpretation is of comparatively modern date. The general principles of Hermeneutics are such as lie in the common mind, and those which every man who speaks or hears, unconsciously applies in the daily use of language. The basis on which they rest is reason and common sense, as applied to language; and any principles which can be shown to be at variance with these can never be admitted as rules in the science. The ability of good men, from education and careful observation, to explain Scripture correctly without having studied the theory of interpretation, by no means detracts from the utility or importance of the science. Rules of interpretation, themselves, it is true, can no more make a good interpreter, than rules of poetry can make a good poet. At the same time, they are highly serviceable in teaching us how to apply the requisite learning and natural talent and tact to the best advantage. Many Biblical expositors, of unquestioned piety and considerable learning and talent, have failed through the want of what is commonly called *judgment;* and it is to the culture of the judgment that the rules which appertain to this science are especially directed. Though the study of Interpretation may fail to render the Bible student a very good interpreter, it can hardly fail to prevent him from becoming a very bad one. It will not only assist him in forming an independent opinion himself, but enable him to judge with discrimination of the interpretations of others, and amid various and conflicting opinions, to adopt that which is best supported by reason; and this is by far its most extensive application.

CHAPTER X.

THE OBJECT OF INTERPRETATION—ITS NECESSITY AND DIFFICULTY.

The object of interpretation is to discover and exhibit the true sense of another's words—his real meaning, no more and no less. This of course implies that this sense is not obvious; for if it were, there would be no necessity for rules of interpretation—no room for the exercise of the art in question. But as words are employed expressly to convey ideas, how does it happen that, if properly used for this purpose, there can be any reasonable doubt as to the ideas designed to be conveyed? There are many circumstances which conduce to render a speaker or writer's meaning equivocal and capable of misconstruction. Some of these it may be proper briefly to notice.

In the first place, it should be borne in mind, that language is at the best but an imperfect vehicle of thought. Its nature and essence is not a direct communion of mind, but a communion by intermediate signs, and hence the total exclusion of every imaginable misapprehension is in many cases absolutely impossible. The words employed, taken by themselves, often express more or less than the speaker or writer intended, and consequently without further explanation and proper qualification are liable to be misconstrued. Nor would further explanations always remedy the difficulty, but rather increase it. For the explanations given might still be open to misconstruction and require further explanations to make them clear. And men have learned by experience that little is gained by attempting to speak or write with absolute clearness and endless specifications. We are, therefore, constrained in a multitude of instances, to leave a considerable part of our meaning to be found out by interpretation; and this circumstance must often necessarily cause greater or less uncertainty with regard to the exact meaning which our words were intended to convey. Mathematical precision is impossible except in mathematics themselves.

Again: Another circumstance which renders interpretation both necessary and difficult is the intrinsic ambiguity of language. By this is meant that a large portion of sentences considered in themselves, *i. e.* if regard be had merely to the words of which they are composed, are capable of expressing more than one meaning. Take the following passage of Scripture as an illustration of this remark. "Ye have an unction (anointing) from the Holy One, and know all things." I John 2:20. Now if we consider these words in themselves merely, admitting that they were addressed to Christians, it will be perceived that they are capable of several different interpretations. Thus the first clause may signify, "Through the favor of God you have become Christians or believers in Christ,"—anointing being a ceremony of consecration, and Christians being considered as consecrated and set apart from the rest of mankind as a peculiar people, devoted to the service of God. Or it may mean, "You have been truly sanctified in heart and life by the power of God,"—a figure borrowed from outward consecration, being used to denote inward holiness. Or, "you have been endued with miraculous powers—consecrated as inspired prophets and teachers in the Christian community." The term *Holy One* in this relation may denote either God the Father, God the Son, or God the Holy Ghost. The second clause "Ye know all things," literally expresses Omniscience, and if addressed to God would be understood in that sense. But besides this meaning, it may signify, "you are fully acquainted with all the objects of human knowledge." Or, "you know every truth connected with Christianity," or, "you have all the knowledge requisite to form your faith and direct your conduct." This ambiguity of language arises from a variety of causes, among which are the following:

1. Nearly every word in all languages is used in a variety of significations and with different shades of meaning. Now as we assign one or another of these meanings to different words in a sentence, we change the import of the whole sentence. Take the following example: "The child is learning his *letters*,"—"The merchant is writing his *letters*,"—Dr. Johnson was a man of *letters*." Now it is plain to every one, that the word *letters* is used in each of these sentences in a different sense, and no man of common sense would attach one and the same signification to it in the three instances specified. Many words too, have a different meaning in combination with other words, as in set phrases and idiomatic expressions, from what they have singly and separately. Now if words were all univocal, and invariably employed whether singly or in combination in the same sense, there would be little occasion for explanation, and the labor of the interpreter would be circumscribed within

very narrow limits. But, as it is, it is possible to understand all the separate words in a sentence and still not be certain of the writer's meaning. 2. In addition to the common and literal signification, words may be used in a multitude of figurative senses, and many sentences may be understood either figuratively or literally. 3. Many sentences not properly figurative, are yet not to be taken strictly and in the full extent of their meaning, but with some limitation. 4. In the Sacred Scriptures as in many other productions, much of the language employed is the language of emotion or strong feeling. The strict and literal import of this language may indeed express the meaning really intended, but such is rarely the case. A proper allowance must be made for the excited state of mind of the writer, and his words should not be interpreted with strict philosophical accuracy. 5. As language is conventional, its use varies in different ages and nations, according to the state of society, the prevailing customs and the temperament of the people. Some nations as well as individuals are in the habit of expressing themselves in common life far more strongly, figuratively and hyperbolically than others. Hence a sentence translated verbally from one language into another will often convey a wider meaning than was intended by him who uttered it. Our Saviour, for example, says of John the Baptist that he "came neither eating nor drinking," Matt. 11:18. This idiomatic expression, if uttered for the first time in our language, would appear exceedingly strange and paradoxical. But such was not its character as spoken by Christ. The words simply mean that John, leading an ascetic life, practiced the strictest self-denial, abstained from indulging in the use even of such food and drinks as were customary among the people, and contented himself with the poorest fare. He refrained from "eating bread and drinking wine," as Luke informs us in the fuller form of the same expression, (ch. 11 . 33) and lived upon "locusts and wild honey." Our Saviour, on another occasion said, that he who would be a follower of his "must hate father and mother." Luke 14: 26. Taken literally, the import of this declaration would be not only impious but impossible. But the Greek verb μισειν is frequently to be understood in a limited sense, and by this bold figure our Saviour simply meant that his followers must be willing and prepared to sacrifice their dearest earthly attachments in his cause, and allow no worldly ties to interfere with their allegiance to him, (compare Math. 6: 24 and 10: 37, where the meaning is more clearly expressed.)

Further: It will be recollected that the Bible is not the production of one man or one age, but composed of a number of separate and independent writings, penned by different persons, unknown to each other, living in different and remote ages, extending through a period of nearly 2000 years, and treating the subjects on which they write in a great variety of style, from the simplest prose to the most lofty poetry. And not only are we widely separated from the authors of the Bible by distance of time, in consequence of which we have to contend with the difficulties inseparable from written language in a greater degree than otherwise we should have to do; but we are separated from them, also, by distance of place and circumstance. Their laws, their manners, their customs, their modes of thinking, were entirely dissimilar to everything of the kind with which we are now conversant, and their allusions to existing circumstances among other people are sometimes so slight, and yet so intimately connected with an argument or illustration, as to require on the part of the readers a large measure of previous information and knowledge. Add to these considerations the fact that the Holy Scriptures were originally written in languages entirely different from our own, both of which have long ceased to be vernacular, and that as to one of them we have no contemporaneous literature to aid us in the interpretation of the Sacred books. The Scriptures, moreover, abound in references and allusions to supersensuous and spiritual objects and to events such as never occur in our times. All these and many other circumstances which might be mentioned, conspire to make it difficult to understand the Scriptures and render the labors of a skillful and intelligent interpreter necessary. But one of the chief causes of difficulty in the interpretation of the Bible and of diversity of opinion with regard to its meaning,—a cause which may be said to be peculiar to that book, —is the habit of perverse and pernicious interpretation, which has unhappily prevailed for ages, arising from the force of educational bias and sectarian prejudice, or from the unlimited indulgence of a misguided imagination, or from a desire to make the Bible mean all that it can by any possibility be supposed capable of meaning. Methods of interpretation have been adopted as erroneous as they are pernicious.

The Bible is constantly treated as if fancy or caprice and not reason and common sense were the proper organ to direct its meaning. Instead of following the inductive method, which is the only true and safe mode of discovering the meaning of the Word of God, as of every other book, men have resorted to the dogmatic method, the scholastic or philosophic, or the mystical and allegorical, by means of which they have succeeded in putting such a meaning into the Bible as supported their particular doctrinal or philosophical creed, or in giving free scope to the vagaries of a lawless imagination. Hence tomes upon tomes have been written professedly to elucidate the Scriptures, which serve only to perplex the student and lead him far away from the right path to truth. It is related in the Persian letters, that Rica, one of the correspondents introduced into them, having been to visit the library of a French convent, wrote thus to his friend in Persia concerning what had passed. "Father," said I to the Librarian, "what are these huge volumes which fill the whole side of the library?" "These," said he, "are the interpreters of the Scriptures." "There is a prodigious number of them," replied I, "the Scriptures must have been very dark formerly; and very clear at present. Do there remain still any doubts? Are there now any points contested?" "Are there!" answered he with surprise, "are there! There are almost as many as there are lines." "You astonish me," said I. "what then have all these authors been doing?" "These authors," returned he, "never searched the Scriptures for what ought to be believed, but for what they did themselves believe. They did not consider them as a book, wherein were contained the doctrines which they ought to receive, but as a work which might be made to authorize their own ideas. For this reason, they have corrupted all the meanings, and have put every passage to the torture, to make it speak their own sense. It is a country whereon people of all sects make invasions, and go for pillage; it is a field of battle, where, when hostile nations meet, they engage, attack and skirmish in a thousand different ways." Such are some of the difficulties, objective and subjective, which lie in the way of investigating the Scriptures and discovering their true sense. They furnish a wide scope to the labors of the Interpreter and impart to his work a dignity and importance, unsurpassed in the entire range of Christian Theology.

CHAPTER XI.

THE PECULIARITIES OF THE BIBLE.

From what has been said in the preceding pages we see the necessity of some rules and canons for the interpretation of the Bible. None will contend that the Sacred Scriptures are to be interpreted in an arbitrary manner, according to the caprice, the prejudices, the subjective feelings, or the wayward fancy of each individual. All who hold to the right of private judgment, admit the propriety and necessity of being governed in our investigation of the meaning of God's word by some acknowledged principles, and hence all allow the necessity of hermeneutics. The diversity of Biblical interpretation has arisen, not from the rejection of hermeneutical principles, but either from adopting false principles, or from a misapplication of right ones. The basis on which our science rests being right reason and common sense, not only should its canons be such as are obviously founded in reason, but they should be such as need only to to be clearly stated and understood, to be universally approved. Now the language of the Bible is the language of men—such language as they employ in communicating their ideas and sentiments to one another in the intercourse of life, and hence, if understood at all, its meaning must be ascertained by the same means and according to the same laws by which all other writings are understood. Accordingly it may be laid down as a general preliminary principle, that *the Bible should be interpreted as other books are interpreted.* The same laws which are considered legitimate and proper in regard to the explanation of other books, are applicable to the Bible. I say this is the *general* principle, but it is subject to certain limitations and modifications arising from the peculiarities of the Scriptures. The Bible, as we shall see, is a book in some respects *sui generis;* as such it has its distinctive peculiarities, and these peculiarities are of such a nature as to necessitate a somewhat different treatment from that which other books receive at our hand, and give rise to canons of interpretation which belong exclusively to Sacred Hermeneutics, and are not applicable to other books. And these limit and modify the general principle which has been stated.

1. One of these peculiarities is the fact that the Bible is the inspired record of a supernatural revelation. Not only are the truths revealed therein of divine origin, but the sacred writers were supernaturally assisted in the composition of their books. There is in the Bible a human element and a divine element. To the former belong the diction, the phraseology, the style, the selection and arrangement of topics and facts, and the mode of argumentation, of proof and illustration. To the latter belong the thoughts, sentiments and ideas, so far as these claim to have come from God. And with regard to the human element, the Bible differs from all other books in this important respect; that the sacred penmen were under the supernatural guidance and superintending care of the Holy Spirit, so far at least as to preserve them from all error or mistake in their statements of doctrine and of material facts, so that implicit reliance may be placed on the truth of what they have written. This is called the dynamic theory of inspiration, in distinction from the mechanical or organic theory. It is the theory which, since the Reformation, has been substantially adopted by nearly every respectable writer of the Church of England, and with few exceptions, by the orthodox continental writers on this subject. It is also believed to be at present the prevailing theory in the Romish Church. It has this advantage over the stricter theory of verbal inspiration, that it accords best with the facts as they lie on the face of the record, and obviates many difficulties created by the other,

which are sure to perplex the student in the investigation of the Word of God. The inspiration of the sacred writers rests mainly on the promises of Christ to his Apostles, and on the unequivocal testimony of the sacred writers themselves, whose veracity and credibility have been abundantly proved to be worthy of entire and implicit confidence. That the Bible was written under the special inspiration of the Holy Spirit, though not of the nature of a self-evident proposition, is nevertheless a proposition which has been fully proved by those who have written upon the subject, and is most firmly believed by all orthodox Christians. It is hence to be regarded as a foundation principle and axiom of our science.

Now the fact that the Bible is the inspired record of a supernatural revelation, obviously requires that we deal with it very differently in some respects from the way in which we deal with a purely human composition. "As the record of supernatural events we must accept them as beyond the reach of that historical criticism which we would warrantably apply to similar events recorded by a profane historian. Take the earlier pages of profane history—such for example, as the narrative of Livy of a prehistoric period of the Roman state, and we deal with the legends and prodigies which it records, as events not trustworthy, and with the historian as mistaken. The mythical theory of interpretation which reduces such histories to the level of unhistoric legends; or the naturalistic theory of interpretation which brings its supernatural events within the circle of common things, and the range of common criticism, may,

in such cases, each assert its claims to a hearing and be allowed. Not so with the Scriptures. These claim to be an inspired record of a supernatural religion. In such a case there must be superhuman events embraced in the narrative, which are not to be dealt with in the same way as events of a similar character recorded in any human history might be dealt with, and the authors of the narrative, because inspired men, must be judged of as infallibly true in what they assert."*

And this remark applies to doctrines as well as to events. In a book containing a divine element—a supernatural revelation—we are to expect a communication of truths of the greatest importance for us to know, which yet lie beyond our comprehension—which are too high and too vast for human reason to grasp, and which, therefore, we are to receive simply, yet implicitly, on faith, without attempting to explain the *modus* of the truths revealed, or without being capable of answering a thousand questions which may be proposed respecting them. Of this character are the doctrine of the Trinity—the Incarnation of Christ—his Atonement, and the regenerating influences of the Holy Spirit. There is in these and kindred truths very much that transcends human comprehension; but this furnishes no ground for rejecting the doctrines, or for attempting, as many have done, by a forced and unnatural construction, to explain away the obvious meaning of the passages which assert them.

2. Another peculiarity of the Bible is, that

---

* North British Review.

though composed of many treatises, historical, biographical, ethical, prophetical, poetical and epistolary, written by different authors and at different times, it is one organic whole, proceeding from the same divine pervading mind and having throughout a unity of plan, of object, and design. This circumstance also necessitates a modification of the common principles of interpretation in order to adjust them to this distinctive feature. "The unity of thought and consistency of opinion which in human compositions, are found within the limits of one author's writings, and which so greatly aid us in the interpretation of them, are in Scripture extended over the many authors' writings which it embraces from Genesis to Revelation, because all are the product, not of the same human person, but of the same superhuman inspiration. This fact evidently warrants and requires us to bring to our aid in the elucidation of the Bible, to a greater extent than to profane writings, the canon, that the one part of it must be interpreted by another, and that the doctrines and revelations of earlier and later times, the principles of past and present dispensations must be equally taken into account, as throwing harmonious light on its meaning."* We are not at liberty to infer real contradictions between the different writers of the Bible, but where there exist apparent discrepancies, we are to resort to every reasonable and legitimate mode of reconciliation, and if these fail us, we are to suspend our judgment and wait for further light.

3. This unity of plan, which under the control-

---

* North British Review.

ing influence of the Spirit of God, pervades the whole of the sacred volume, from Genesis to Revelation, gives rise to numerous prophecies, symbols and types, which bind the several parts together, and which being peculiar to this book, require special canons of interpretation, not at all applicable to other books.

4. "Another modification of the general principles of interpretation, when applied to the sacred volume, arises out of the consideration, that necessary and manifest consequences drawn from Scripture, are as really a part of Divine Revelation as Scripture itself. It is not so in the case of man and of human writings. The inferences drawn from human expressions of opinion, even though they be necessary and lawful inferences from such expressions, are not always to be taken as forming part of the opinions of the author. A man is not to be charged with the consequences of the opinions he avows, because he may not have foreseen or intended the consequences. But with God and divine revelation it is different. He both foresaw and intended all that he has revealed, whether in the shape of express statement or necessary implication. What is virtually contained in Scripture, because the lawful and unavoidable deduction from its statements, is as really part of the mind of God as these statements themselves. This demands a minuter and more anxious inquiry into the letter of Scripture, and a more thorough investigation into the dogmatic relations and import of each passage, than would be required in the case of other writings; and it warrants interpreters to educe a more extensive sense and a profounder

meaning from its statements, than could be safely elicited from human compositions."*

Such are some of the more prominent peculiarities of the Scriptures, which have a greater or less influence on the general principles of interpretation, and render a system of Biblical Hermeneutics, applicable especially to them, necessary. At the same time, these peculiarities affect rather the thoughts and facts of Scripture than the words in which they are clothed, and do not necessitate any other method of discovering the meaning of the language, than what is pursued in regard to the language of any other book.

CHAPTER XII.

BIBLICAL CRITICISM.

Before proceeding to investigate the *meaning* of Sacred Scriptures, the attention of the Biblical student should first be directed to the *text* itself, in order to ascertain whether it be pure or corrupt. By the *text* of Scripture is to be understood whatever the author has written or caused to be written, as an expression of his thoughts. We must know what an author has written before we undertake to explain its meaning. Hence Quinctillian justly remarks,

"Enarrationem præcedat emendata lectio."
"An emended reading precedes interpretation."

---

* North British Review.

Until the invention of the art of printing, the Holy Scriptures of the Old and New Testament, both in the original languages and in translations made from them into foreign languages, were handed down from age to age by means of manuscript copies. Of the autographs or original manuscripts of the New Testament no less than of the Old, it is universally admitted that none are now extant, though there is evidence that at least some of them for many years were carefully preserved among the ancient Christian churches. Their final loss is probably to be attributed in a great degree to the dreadful persecutions which raged against the Christians in the earlier ages, and to the efforts of their barbarous persecutors to destroy all their sacred books. All the manuscripts of the scriptures extant, therefore, are but copies of the original. Now anterior to any particular investigation of the facts in the case, a reasonable presumption exists that many various readings have crept into these numerous transcripts of the Scriptures during the lapse of so many centuries. This antecedent presumption is founded upon the very nature of the case, and upon the fact that all other ancient books have suffered from this cause. Such is the frailty of man, and his liability to error and mistake, that in transcribing any book it is impossible entirely to prevent mistakes. The utmost diligence and carefulness will not secure immaculate purity and uncorruptness to any text. Verbal mistakes will occur in spite of the greatest vigilance. And the only way to arrive at the true reading, where more than one exists, is to weigh carefully the evidence by which the various readings are respectively sustained, and the claims they severally present to a favorable reception, and to adopt that which on the whole seems best supported by appropriate evidence. As it is with the works of the ancient heathen and gentile writers, so is it with the Biblical writers, notwithstanding the extraordinary care exercised in their uncorrupted preservation. Nothing could prevent this but a perpetual miracle, of which there is not a shadow of evidence. There was indeed a time when not only the Jews, but learned men in the Christian Church, maintained the absolute inviolability of the Scriptures. The Buxtorfs and men of that class, gigantic scholars, in their particular line of study, did not hesitate from the force of prejudice to maintain that not only all the Hebrew letters were the same in all manuscripts the world over, but that even the vowel points and accents were and always had been identically the same from the time of Moses down to their day. And when Dr. Mills (1707) published his edition of the New Testament with various readings, Whitby, the celebrated commentator, sounded the tocsin of alarm, as though the volume of divine truth were in danger of being thrown overboard. Investigation has, however, dissipated the pleasant dream of the Buxtorfs and allayed the groundless fears of the Whitbys. In point of fact Providence is found to have left the words of Scripture to the same casualties as the writings of uninspired men. While at the same time the great doctrines and duties of revealed religion have, notwithstanding, been all sacredly guarded and effectually preserved. While the critical investigations, which have been made in modern times, have resulted in bringing to light a vast number of various readings, both of the Old and New Testament, a careful examination of these various readings shows that they are of such a nature as not to shake in the least our belief in a single doctrine or duty of Christianity; at the same time it imposes on the Biblical student the duty of giving sufficient attention to this subject to be able to sift the evidence adduced in support of different readings and to form an independent judgment as to the true reading of the original.

That department of Sacred Literature which has relation to the purity of the text is called Biblical Criticism. This expression is often used in a more extended sense, so as to embrace Biblical Interpretation also. But the difference between the two is capable of being made perfectly intelligible to the most ordinary capacity. The object of Biblical Criticism (*i. e.*, of lower, special, verbal criticism,) is the genuineness of the *text itself;* the object of Biblical Interpretation is the *sense* or *meaning* of the text. The one is conversant with the mere *letter* of Scripture; the other with its *import.* It is the province of the former to ascertain what an author has written, and of the latter to determine what he intends by it. Criticism, therefore, in the order of nature, precedes interpretation. The former is properly introductory to the latter, and serves as a basis for it. And the nearer one comes by the application of judicious critical laws to the very words of an author, the nearer he will be to a correct interpretation of them. The application of textual criticism to the treatment of the Bible is quite as necessary and useful as to that of any ancient writer whatever. Indeed it is more important and beneficial with regard to the former in proportion to the greater importance of its contents. Accordingly we find that Criticism has always been held in high estimation by all truly learned and scientific theologians; and those skilled in it have always been reckoned in the first class of divines. Such were Origen, Gregory Nazianzen, Basil, Chrysostom. Jerome, and others among the ancients. Augustine declared it as his opinion, that the talents of those who sought to understand the Scriptures, ought in the first place to be exercised upon the correction of the text.

The sources of Biblical Criticism are—Manuscripts, or written copies of the Scriptures, both ancient and modern—Ancient versions or translations into various languages—the writings and remains of those early ecclesiastical writers or Church fathers, who have quoted the Scriptures —Parallels, or repeated passages—and Critical conjecture. The last of these, however, has no place in the criticism of the New Testament. There is no need of it there. The materials for procuring a correct, unadulterated text, are abundant. Critical conjecture, therefore, is rendered superfluous by the very copious array of proper resources; and hence none of the critical editors of the New Testament sanction the adoption of conjectural emendations into the text. In reference to this portion of the Sacred volume, the authority of manuscripts, versions, and quotations by the fathers, is paramount; and in no case ought the words of the New Testament to be altered from mere conjecture. The internal probability in favor of a particular reading is only taken into account, when it is at the same time accompanied with at least an equal amount of external authority. But with regard to the Hebrew Scriptures the case is different; and here there are various reasons against the *total* exclusion of conjectural emendations. The instances of accidental error in the transcribing of Hebrew manuscripts are far more numerous than in the transcribing of the Greek manuscripts, notwithstanding the extraordinary care observed by the Jewish Scribes. The long period, also, which elapsed between the time when the books of the Old Testament, especially the Pentateuch, were composed, and the time when even the oldest Hebrew manuscripts now extant were written, may have occasioned in various places the genuine reading to be entirely lost. And the circumstance that all the Hebrew manuscripts now in existence belong to one edition, family or recension, viz., the Masoretic, renders the probability that in various places the genuine reading is contained in no known Hebrew manuscript still greater. The means, therefore, of correcting the text of the Old Testament from authority, are far less ample than in the New Testament, and consequently conjectural emendations may be allowable in the former, though not in the latter. Instances occur where the very exigency of the case (*exegentia loci*) requires the aid to be derived from conjecture. In some instances the received reading is such as we can not conceive it possible that the Sacred penman could have written; it bears on the face of it evident marks of corruption. In such cases, the amount of external evidence in favor of such a reading as this is comparatively of little importance. A single version may be conclusive. Nay, the exigency may be so strong, that a reading which will meet it in a satisfactory manner may have irresistible claims to be received into the text of a critical edition, though sanctioned by no existing manuscript or version. At the same time, this liberty should doubtless be taken with extreme prudence and caution, and should be exercised only in cases where all other means of reconciliation fail. Many conjectural emendations proposed by Bishops Lowth, Blaney, Horsley, Dr. Kennicutt and other distinguished Biblical scholars of the 18th Century, have since been shown to be entirely unnecessary and unjustifiable, in consequence of a more thorough method of studying the Hebrew language inaugurated by Gesenius and other German scholars.

The genuineness or spuriousness of an ancient book or passage is a question of fact to be determined on the ground of *external* and *internal* evidence. By the former is meant the testimony of competent *witnesses;* by the latter, the testimony arising from certain *tokens* or *indications* observable in the contents, language, style, and character of the book or passage in question, which show it to be in all probability the production of a certain author, or at least of a certain age. The following fundamental laws of evidence will show the relative importance of external or historical, and internal critical evidence.

1. The genuineness of a book, passage, or word, whether profane or sacred, inspired or uninspired, is to be established by evidence, either external or internal, or both. When these two species of evidence coincide in support of the

affirmative, then the conclusion is irresistible that it is genuine.

2. If either of these be wholly wanting, still the book, passage, or word, may be shown to be genuine by the other alone, provided it be clear and indisputable.

3. But if they disagree, and contradict each other, then the following laws apply:—1. If the *internal* evidence be clearly and unequivocally *against* the genuineness of the book, passage, or word, then no amount of external evidence can prove it genuine; *e. g.* if it contains anacronisms, or manifest allusions to persons and things which did not exist until after the time of the reputed author; or if the passage as it stands affords no intelligible meaning, or one wholly incongruous or unsuitable; or if it makes a prudent, consistent, and conscientious writer contradict himself. With regard to the last point, however, a profane writer may sometimes, in a long discourse or treatise, say something inconsistent with or contradictory to what he said before; but this cannot be admitted in regard to the sacred writers. Not only must they be consistent with themselves, but with one another. We may find apparent discrepancies in their writing, but can impute no real contradictions to them. 2. But if the *external* evidence be clearly and decidedly *against* the genuineness of a passage, then no amount of *internal* evidence can establish its genuineness. In such a case internal criticism is of small value in determining what an author might have said, or might not have said. A *spurious* passage may be surreptitiously introduced and fitted to the context as well as a *genuine* passage. It may be so dove-

tailed into the text as to render it nearly if not quite impossible to detect it. When the genuineness of a particular passage of a sacred writer is disputed, therefore, the proper questions to be asked are, Is the passage found in the manuscripts, especially the earlier and more ancient manuscripts? Is it contained in the ancient versions? Is it quoted by the early fathers, where from its relevancy and appropriateness, we should have expected it to be quoted or alluded to? Is its genuineness admitted in critical editions of the Scriptures? If the answer to these questions must be in the affirmative, then its genuineness is indisputable. But if, on the contrary, the passage is not found in the ancient manuscripts; if it is not contained in the ancient translations; if it is not quoted or alluded to by the fathers, when it would have been appropriate in them to quote or refer to it; if its genuineness is not recognized by the best and most reliable critics, then we may infer that it is spurious, no matter what may be said in its favor on the ground of internal evidence.

The necessity of examining the original authorities for the purpose of textual criticism, even if it were in the power of the student to do so, is now entirely obviated by the researches of learned divines who have embodied the results of their laborious investigations in critical editions of the Scriptures. Griesbach (1774–5) first applied these results to the correction of the text of the New Testament, and for this purpose classified his authorities into three recensions or families. These were subsequently reduced by Scholz to two. But the whole system of classification introduced by Griesbach, after suffering severely from repeated blows, has been compelled to give way before the new and popular theory of Lachman (1831–42), who professes mainly to exhibit the text as contained in the oriental manuscripts and versions, or as it was received in the East in the fourth century; but especially of Tischendorf (1541), who gives the text according to the authority of the more ancient witnesses. Of his work in its later editions, Alford remarks, "I cannot but regard it as the most valuable contribution which has been yet made to the revision of the text of the New Testament. And I believe that all future texts arranged on critical principles, will be found to approach very closely to his." These principles have been followed by Alford, whose work on the Greek Testament, both for critical and exegetical purposes, is undoubtedly the most convenient and valuable for theological students and ministers which has yet appeared. No application has yet been made of the critical materials collected from Hebrew manuscripts and other sources, by Kennicutt, De Rossi, and others, to the emendation of the text of the Old Testament. A critical edition of the Hebrew Scriptures, with a revised text, is therefore still a desideratum. The nearest approach to such a work will be found in a thin octavo volume from the pen of Dr. Samuel Davidson (1855), entitled "The Hebrew text of the Old Testament revised from critical sources," which in a convenient form exhibits, but without the text, all the important various readings, and the authorities for each.

CHAPTER XIII.

THE GRAMMATICO-HISTORICAL SENSE—USAGE OF WORDS.

In the study of the Bible as in that of any other book our aim should be to get at the true sense and meaning of the Sacred writers. Divine Revelation consists not in the words of Scripture, but in the thoughts, sentiments and facts, which are communicated to us through the medium of the words. This idea was clearly expressed long ago by Jerome when he said, "Let us not imagine that the Gospel consists in the words of Scripture, but in the sense."* The sense is the nut; the letter is the mere shell which encloses the nut. Hence the legal maxim,

Qui hærit in litera, hærit in cortice.
"He who sticks in the letter, sticks in the bark."

He who considers merely the letter of an instrument, goes but skin deep into its meaning. The sense of a word, phrase, or proposition, may in general be stated to be that meaning which appears to be the natural, obvious and customary meaning of the language, as ascertained from usage, irrespective of extrinsic considerations. This is called the *grammatical sense*. In a majority of instances this is the true and exact sense intended by the writer. But it is not always the case, not merely because the language employed may be ambiguous and fairly susceptible of different interprétations equally

* "Nec putemus in verbis scripturarum evangelium esse, sed in sensu." Comment. in Epist. ad Gal. cap. 1.

accordant with usage and grammar; but because an author may have unintentionally expressed himself improperly or loosely. He may have carelessly or ignorantly chosen a wrong word or words to express his meaning, or assigned a wrong position to them in the sentence; or he may have employed words in a different sense from the customary one—in a technical, provincial or foreign sense, or in one entirely new, in order to convey an idea peculiar to the system of religion or philosophy which he has embraced. It is frequently necessary, therefore, in order to arrive at the true sense, to take into consideration a variety of extrinsic circumstances. Some knowledge is requisite concerning the age and country in which the writer lived, his education, temperament, style of writing, his religion and various surroundings, and the prevalent opinions, usages and customs of the times. We must understand the design and scope of his writings, the logical connexion of his thoughts; in fine, it is necessary to attend to all those historical circumstances and considerations, and to those subjective influences which would be likely to affect or throw light upon his meaning. This is called the *historical sense.* The following example will illustrate the difference between the grammatical and the historical sense. The Greek word αἰών grammatically considered, simply denotes *time, age*, but if we consult the history of Jewish dogmas we find that the phrases αἰών οὗτος and ὁ αἰών ὁ μέλλων *this world or age* and *the world or age to come.* (Heb. 2:5, 6:5.) mean the time present, and the time subsequent to the advent of the Messiah; in other words the Jewish and Christian Dispensations. The first would be the interpretation according to general usage, the latter, according to the usage of a particular age and people—the one classical and grammatical, the other historical and Jewish. But though the grammatical sense is in itself distinct from the historical, there is no contradiction between them. In a majority of instances they are perfectly identical, and when we have ascertained the one, we have determined the other. And where there is a formal difference between them, they still uniformly coincide. For no historical interpretation can be admitted which violates or sets aside and contravenes the grammatical. The true sense is the only one in every case; and this is made out by the application of the laws of universal grammar, modified, if need be, by historical circumstances. As grammatical interpretation must lie at the basis of all sound exegesis, the attention of the student in the investigation of Scripture should be first directed to the customary signification of the words employed, whether singly or in combination. But if he stop here, he will in very many cases miss the real sense. Hence we find that many Commentators particularly among the Germans, have excelled as verbal critics and thrown much light on the diction and phraseology of Scripture, while at the same time, from disregarding the logical connexion, from over-looking important extrinsic considerations, or from want of the ability or disposition to enter into the spirit of the sacred writers and to sympathize with them in their religious feelings and sentiments, they have entirely failed to comprehend and exhibit the true spiritual and profound import of their writings. Grotius, for example, was a profound scholar and excellent verbal critic, but beyond this he did not go. Hence it has been justly said of him that "the *shell* he took off with wonderful dexterity; but the *nut* he seldom tasted, and still more seldom relished." The only true method of interpretation therefore, is the *grammatico-historical.* This compound term is used to indicate that both grammatical and historical considerations are employed in making out the sense. The basis on which this method of interpretation rests is the *use of the language* (*usus loquendi*) employed in the expression of ideas. It may be laid down as a fundamental principle of Interpretation, that *use is the only arbiter of the meaning of words.* In other terms the signification of words depends on the usage of those who employ it. "*Usus est jus et norma loquendi.*" Use founded on human institutions and customs has constituted the connexion between words and ideas. Words have not the particular meaning or meanings attached to them from nature or necessity, but only from human institutions and customs, by which a connexion has been conventionally formed between them and the ideas they are employed to convey. But though this connexion was in its commencement and institution arbitrary, yet being once established by custom, it has become necessary; and hence we are not at liberty to give what sense we please to a word either in writing or in interpreting. The fact that usage has attached any particular meaning to a word, like any other historical fact, is to be proved by adequate testimony. But once established, the meaning can no more be changed at pleasure or denied than any other fact whatever.

The usage of language is affected by many things; by the time in which the writer lived, the religion he professed, the sect or party to which he belonged, his peculiar style and mode of expressing himself, the habits of ordinary life and the political institutions of the country. For the sense in which words are used, either originates from or is modified by all these; and thus the same word may signify one thing in ordinary life, another in religion, a third in the schools of philosophers, and a fourth as used by a particular writer. The same word or expression may convey one idea when employed by a Heathen, another when used by a Jew, and still another when employed by a Christian. It may have a classic sense, and a Jewish sense, and a Christian sense. Thus the words *victim*, *sacrifice*, *law*, in the Old Testament are often employed in a sense which differs from that of the same words in the New Testament. The verb to *perceive* in common life means to *feel* or *experience;* in philosophy, *to form an idea in the mind;* and among the academic sect it meant *to know a thing with certainty*, in opposition to mere conjecture. So *purification*, *flesh*, *regeneration*, &c., differ in meaning as employed by a Heathen, a Jew, or a Christian. Usage, accordingly, may be divided into *general*, *particular*, and *peculiar*. General usage is that which is commonly employed by writers in the language; particular usage is that which is confined to a particular age or portion of the country where the language is spoken; and peculiar usage is that which is limited to an individual, and forms a distinctive feature of his style. As an example of the last, we have the use of ὁ λόγος, *the word*, by St. John, as designating the compound person of the Messiah, or God incarnate. We learn the usage in living languages from conversation and personal intercourse; in the dead languages, as the Hebrew and Greek, it is ascertained from various sources, such as the writer himself, contemporary writers, Scholiasts and Glossographers, ancient translations, made when the languages were still living, kindred dialects, &c. But it is not at all necessary for the critical student of the Bible to dig into all these deep mines. This labor is in a great degree saved by the use of good dictionaries, grammars and concordances. He has but to provide himself with such works as the Septuagint and Vulgate Translations, Robinson's Gesenius' Hebrew Lexicon, Conant's Rodiger's Gesenius' Hebrew Grammar, Robinson's Lexicon and Winer's Grammar of the New Testament and the Englishman's Hebrew and Greek Concordances, and he is thoroughly equipped for determining the usage both of the Old and New Testament writers. The mere English scholar will derive great assistance from the use of such works as Brown's Dictionary of the Bible, or some other similar work, and Cruden's Concordance.

CHAPTER XIV.

LAWS OF INTERPRTATION—MEANING OF WORDS.

Having shown in the preceding chapter that the *Grammatico-historical* sense (i. e. the grammatical sense modified when necessary by the

historical,) is the true sense ef Scripture, we are prepared to lay down the following:

CANON I.

The language of Scripture is to be interpreted according to its grammatical import; and the sense of any expression, proposition, or declaration is to be determined by the words employed.

It was the just remark of Melancthon that "Scripture cannot be understood theologically unless it is understood grammatically." In other words, no one can be a good theologian, who does not interpret Scripture according to its grammatical sense. The reason of this is obvious. Theology is nothing but the grammatical sense of Scripture classified and arranged in systematic order. Theology is not one thing and the meaning of Scripture another; but the sense of Scripture is the whole of theology. Luther also truly observed, that "the knowledge of the sense can be derived from nothing but the knowledge of the words." As soon, therefore, as we learn the meaning of the words of any passage of Scripture, singly and in combination, we possess the knowledge of the sense of that passage. Any system of theology is consequently sound just so far as it accords with and is based upon the grammatical or true sense of Scripture, and no farther. Hence there is a necessary and most intimate connexion between a *bonus textuarius* and a *bonus theologus*. Plain and obvious as this Canon of Interpretation is, it is constantly violated by those who bring their pre-conceived opinions to bear upon the Scriptures, and by forced and unnatural or frigid interpretation, make them speak in accordance with those opinions, and thus attempt to banish from the New Testament all its peculiar and distinctive doctrines, such as the Deity of Christ, the Atonement, etc. Not only is this violation chargeable upon the German Rationalists, who eliminate from the Bible every thing supernatural, and whose systems of theology are any thing but scriptural, but also upon many who claim to occupy a higher position. Such, they say, cannot be the meaning of this passage, and such cannot be the meaning of that passage, because it would not be in accordance with the truth. The doctrine enunciated by the words of Scripture interpreted according to their obvious and grammatical import is not true; therefore such cannot be their meaning. These men consequently put a forced and arbitrary sense, unauthorized by usage, on the words, so as to make them speak in accordance with the opinion they may have previously formed on the subject to which they relate, independently and irrespective of Scripture. Few books perhaps abound more with instances of this error than the Improved Version of the New Testament, published by the English Unitarians in 1808. For example, John 1: 2, *the word was in the beginning with God*, is thus rendered in the note; "Before he entered upon his ministry, he was fully instructed by intercourse with God in the nature and extent of his commission." And again at v. 14, *And the word was made* (or became) *flesh*, i. e. "a mere mortal man." Again, John 6: 62, *What then if ye shall see the Son of man going up where he was before*, i. e. says the note, "What would you then do, if I should still farther advance into the subject of my mission, and reveal truths which would be still more remote from your apprehension and more offensive to your prejudices." These examples furnish striking instances of the abuse of reason, and an utter disregard of all sound hermeneutical principles, in the interpretation of Scripture.

Other religionists adopt certain notions of God from their own fancies, and then make this character of him their standard of the meaning of Scripture. Fanatics in every age have also perverted the Scriptures in the same way. Our Canon requires us to derive our theological opinions from the words of Scripture faithfully and conscientiously interpreted, and not to bring our previously formed opinions to the Scriptures, and put upon them, under the influence of prejudice, a meaning not warranted by the words. And this we are to do irrespective of the truth or the erroneousness of those opinions: for a sentiment may be true in itself and conformable to scripture, and yet not contained in the particular passage under examination.

CANON II.

In all its communications the Bible has one meaning to convey, and no more; consequently no word can have more than one fixed meaning in each occurrence.

There are few words in any language, if we except the names of persons and things, or proper nouns, which have not more significations than one. Custom has, by degrees, attached various meanings to words, in order to facilitate the acquisition of language, by preventing the infinite multiplicity of terms. But, while words may have a variety of meanings, they can not have this variety at the same time, and in the same place. In every instance of its occurrence each word in a passage has but one meaning, and every passage has but one sense; and, consequently, there can be but one interpretation of it genuine and correct. The words employed may be used in a literal or in a figurative sense; in their primary or in a secondary meaning; but not in both at the same time. The whole passage may be interpreted as history or as allegory; but as it can not be both, so the interpretation can not be double.

All men, in the daily intercourse of life, and in their writings, attach but one meaning to the words they employ, unless they design to speak in enigmas, and are playing a game at riddles or double entendres. No prudent, fair-minded, and conscientious person in common life, who, whether he expresses his thoughts orally, or commits them to writing, intends that a diversity of meanings should be attached to what he says or writes, and hence his hearers or readers do not affix to it any other than the single sense which they suppose he intended to convey. Now, if such is the practice in all fair and upright intercommunication between man and man, can it be supposed that the Deity, in his communications with his creatures, would depart from this simple and truthful method? The Bible was written, under Divine guidance and inspiration, by men, in the language of men, and for the use of men: it is to be presumed, therefore, that it would be written in such a manner as to be intelligible to men,—as other books are written,—in accordance with the common laws and usage of language. But other books are not written with a double or threefold meaning. In them we expect to find one clear, definite, and intelligible meaning, and no more. The antecedent presumption that the Scriptures were written in the same way, is so strong and violent, that it can be overcome only by evidence so manifest and indisputable as to amount to a demonstration. The perspicuity of the Scriptures requires this unity and simplicity of sense, in order to render intelligible to man the plan and purpose of their great Author, which could never be comprehended if a multiplicity of senses were admitted. "There can be," says Ernesti, "no certainty at all in respect to the interpretation of any passage of Scripture, unless a kind of necessity compel us to affix a particular sense to a word, which sense *must be one.*" The words of Scripture, then, like the words employed in profane writings, have, and can have, but one determinate signification attached to them in each and every instance of their occurrence, if the Bible is what it purports to be—a revelation from God. A single sense must be chosen, and it is the proper business of the interpreter to discover what that is. In doing this, it may often be a matter of reasonable doubt which of two or more interpretations is the right one. But they can not all, nor any two of them, be right. If we approve of one, we must, if they really differ, reject the others. The breach of this canon is most derogatory to the Scriptures, and destructive of all distinct views of divine truth. But plain and essential as it is, in one form or another it is more frequently violated than any other principle in the whole science of Hermeneutics. The practice of attaching more than one meaning to each passage of Scripture may be traced back to a remote age. It sprung, indeed, from the schools of the Jewish Rabbies, and passed from them, in early times, into the Christian church. It was a Rabbinic maxim, that, "on every point of the Scriptures hang suspended mountains of sense." The Talmud says, "As a hammer separates into many particles, so each text of Scripture has many meanings." Again; "God so gave the Law to Moses, that a thing can be shewn to be clean and unclean in forty-nine different ways." The Rabbies even invented a science or art called Caballa, which, by changing, disjoining, or transposing letters, or by calculating their value as arithmetical signs, elicited worlds of profound mystery. According to this system, letters instead of being taken in their alphabetical force, so as, in their combination to represent words, which words are, in their turn, signs of ideas, indicate, by peculiarities in their own structure and position, a mystical sense aside from or explanatory of the sense expressed by the words to which they belong. From the Jews this method of interpretation, so far as respects a multiplicity of senses, passed into the Christian church, being suggested, probably, by the variety of interpretations given to ambiguous passages, more than one of which appeared probable, and were recommended by a sentiment of respect for their authors. Nor was it confined in early times to minds of an inferior order, or to men of little information; but it was adopted by such men as Origen, Augustine, and Jerome. These men, and others like them, held that, in addition to their grammatical and obvious sense, the Scriptures have an occult, mystical, or allegorical sense. Some of the ancients subdivided this occult or mystical sense into the allegorical, the tropological (or moral), and the anagogical; hence these well-known lines:

> "*Littera* gesta docet ; quid credas *Allegoria ;*
> *Moralis* quod agas ; quo tendas *Anagogia.*"

By the *allegorical* sense they meant the mystical sense, which has reference to the church upon earth; by the *tropological*, that which refers to moral conduct; and by the *anagogical*, that which refers to the church in its glorified state above. Somewhat after this fashion are the three different senses which Emanuel Swedenborg attached to every word of Scripture in every instance of its occurrence, viz., the *literal*, the *moral* or *spiritual*, and the *heavenly*. In the Roman Catholic Church the practice of giving various senses to the same passage of Scripture has prevailed to a very great extent. Thus, Pope Innocent III. (A. D. 1216), who excommunicated King John of England, and threatened even the Emperor of Constantinople, maintained that the two great lights spoken of in Gen. I., signified mystically the office of *Pope* and the office of *King*—the *greater* light meaning the *former* office, and the *lesser* light the *latter ;* so that as the light which rules the day is superior to the light which rules the night, the dignity of Pope is superior to the dignity of King. This is merely a specimen of the kind of interpretation which has been common in that church. But Protestants have not been behind the Catholics in their invention of a multitude of senses. The earlier Reformers were more free from extravagant fancies of this sort: but Cocceius, a celebrated Dutch divine of Leyden, (1669), advocated the principle that *all the possible meanings of a word in the Scriptures are to be united;* in other words, whatever a word *may* mean it *does* mean. A single noun could thus have twenty different significations in the same place, and refer to twenty different things. He held that the whole of the Old Testament was an anticipatory history of the Christian church, containing a full recital of every thing which should happen to the end of time. Even the Lord's Prayer, according to him, is a prophecy, and its six parts denote six great epochs in history. Every good man in the Old Testament is a type of Christ or his Apostles; and every bad man a type of the devil or the unbelieving Jews. By the learning and influence of Cocceius, a powerful party was raised up in the Protestant Church in favor of this groundless and absurd principle. They pressed each word of a text until every idea which, by mere possibility, it might contain, etymologically or otherwise, was forced out; for, by this operation, the *pregnant sense* of Scripture, as they termed it, and the holy emphasis of its expressions, which had heretofore been neglected, could alone be discovered and received in all its fullness. John Bunyan, whose beautiful and nearly faultless allegory of the Pilgrim's Progress, there are few to be found who have not read with delight, wrote a treatise, in which he undertook to show that not only the temple, with its solemn ritual and impressive service, was significant of future good things, but that even its minutest parts were in like manner significant. The vases, the censors, the trays, the snuffers, yea, the snuff itself of the lamps—all had an important spiritual meaning. We find much of a similar character in Witsius on the Covenants, and other works of a like-nature. Such schemes of interpretation, however edifying they may be to some people, are to be utterly rejected, for they destroy all certainty of interpretation. They take the ground from beneath our feet, and make the Scriptures a nose of wax, which a man may turn into whatever shape his fancy or imagination may suggest. Later and more sober writers, it is true, have disavowed these extreme views, but without abandoning the principle of a double sense. This is still held by a large number of commentators and divines, though with considerable diversity as to the extent of its application. It is generally confined to the Allegories and Parables of Scripture, to the Book of Psalms generally, and to those passages from the prophetical and other writings of the Old Testament, which are quoted or alluded to in the New Testament with reference to Christ and the Church.

The *Double sense* may be thus explained. If we ascribe to any passage of Scripture a literal, obvious, historical sense, and interpret it as conveying and intended to convey the meaning which the words naturally seem to convey, and yet at the same time ascribe to the same words another and dissimilar meaning as designedly referring to another person or event, or as relating to another subject, and intended to be conveyed by those same words, we then make out a double sense. Take the following examples: If the second Psalm is interpreted as a description of the coronation of David or of Solomon on the hill of Zion, and all that is there said be literally and historically applied to him; and if then we go on to find in the words of the same Psalm a secondary sense as prophetically descriptive of the Messiah, or of believers, we give them a double sense. Again: If we give to the language of the sixteenth Psalm a grammatical and historical interpretation as designedly applicable to David and descriptive of his feelings on the bed of sickness and of his faith that God would again restore him to health; and then regard the language as designedly and prophetically descriptive in another sense of the resurrection of Christ from the dead, we manifestly give to the language a double sense. Once more: If we interpret the forty-fifth Psalm as an epithalamium or nuptial song, composed on the occasion of Solomon's marriage with a foreign princess, and as referring primarily and historically to that event: and then proceed to show that a secondary, deeper and mystical sense, distinct from and independent of this, runs through the whole, by virtue of which the words are found to be designedly descriptive of the King Messiah and of his spiritual union with the Church, then we give to the Psalm a double sense.

Now the question arises, is such a system of interpretation admissible according to the acknowledged laws of language? To this question, as it seems to me, the answer must be in the negative. If the principle be admitted in regard to these and other Psalms of a like character, why not with regard to all the Psalms? And if applicable in regard to one part of Scripture, why not to every part? Who shall decide within what limits the principle shall be confined? And if we are at liberty to invent a secondary sense equally true and perhaps more important than the primary, why may we not invent a third sense and a fourth? But would not this destroy all certainty in the use of language? "When we receive a letter on an important subject from a friend," says Dr. J. Pye Smith, "we read it with a view to ascertain its meaning, to know the real sentiments and intention of the writer, and having obtained this we are satisfied. That which it is our duty in all cases to seek after is the true, genuine, intended sense of the word of God, the mind of the Spirit, and this must be ultimately and essentially *one.*"

It is true there are kinds of composition in which an apparent sense is presented, which every intelligent reader sees is only an envelope for another, and it is this other meaning which is the author's real design, his *one* and true intention. In allegories, for instance, the apparent meaning is not what the author intends; this is a mere covering under which is concealed the true meaning. The sense is still but one, and the interpretation one. Allegories, therefore, form no exception to our Canon. Nor are Parables an exception. These are either *allegorical*, and subject to all the laws which apply to allegories; or they are *historical* and designed to illustrate and enforce some important moral truth or duty, and in this case, are susceptible of only one meaning like any other historical narrative or fictitious story. And yet perhaps there is no portion of Scripture to which the principle of a double sense has been more frequently applied than to the parables. Thus Dodd and others tell us that by the priest and levite in the parable of the Good Samaritan, are intended natural religion and the Mosaic dispensation, and by the two pence given to the Innkeeper are meant the two Christian Sacraments. Others tell us, that the man travelling from Jerusalem to Jericho who fell among thieves, represents Adam and his posterity travelling through the wilderness of this world, who are robbed and wounded by Satan; that the priest and levite who passed by without helping him, represent the law which cannot save the sinner, and good works and ceremonial observances, which cannot help him; that the Good Samaritan is Christ; that the oil and wine are the forgiveness and grace of the Gospel; and that the gratuitous work of helping the wounded man is a lively emblem of the Redeemer's gratuitous work in respect to sinners. Now all this may be very evangelical, but is it the true sense of the parable?

Ambiguity is not a double sense. A passage may be equivocal in its terms, and even designedly so, and yet have but one real meaning in the mind and intention of the speaker or writer. We find this designed and studied ambiguity in some of the heathen oracles, which were so framed that the event, whatever it might be, would verify the pretended prediction, and thus sustain the character of the oracle. The well-known Delphic oracle "Aio te Romanos vincere posse," is an example of this, which may be rendered, with equal propriety, that the Romans would conquer Pyrrhus, or Pyrrhus the Romans. The words of our Saviour addressed to the Jews (John 2: 19,) were equivocal, and admitted of two different interpretations. "Destroy this temple, and in three days I will raise it up." This is alleged by Olshausen, Bush and others, to be an instance of a double sense. But such is not the case, if the inspired apostle is to be regarded as an authoritative interpreter of his Master's language. The language is unquestionably equivocal and designed to be so by our Saviour, because it is a prophecy, and, therefore, like most prophecies, veiled in obscurity, the exact meaning and full import of which could only be learned from the event which was a fulfilment of it. It is not by any means surprising, under the circumstances, that the Jews misinterpreted the declaration, and supposed that our Lord referred to the destruction of the Jewish Temple. For even the disciples did not fully apprehend its meaning till after his resurrection. The passage in Gal. 3: 20, "A mediator is not a mediator of one: but God is one," it is said has been interpreted in fifty different ways. Shall we then adopt the Cocceian principle and say that it actually has fifty different senses? Or shall we adopt the Swedenborgian theory and choose out of these fifty meanings, three which may appear to be the most probable? Or, shall we say, with many others, that it has two meanings? Because a passage of Scripture is capable of being understood in two or more senses, this is no proof that it was *designed* to be taken in all these senses.

The fact that certain persons or things mentioned in the Old Testament are typical of certain persons or events recorded in the New, furnishes no exception to our Canon. Types are not *words* but *persons* or *things*, which under the

Old Dispensation, were designed in certain respects to prefigure corresponding persons or things called the antitypes, under the New Dispensation. There is no typical sense in the words which relate to these persons or things distinct from the obvious sense, any more than there is in the words of Scripture relating to any other subject. The words, for instance, which describe the rites, sacrifices, or occurrences, of the ancient dispensation, are to be interpreted in their plain, usual, historical sense. And although many of these rites were undoubtedly typical of future events under the Gospel dispensation, no secondary, typical or mystical sense is to be attributed to the language employed in speaking of them. David was undoubtedly in some respects a type of Christ; but it does not hence follow that all which he uttered or wrote, even under divine inspiration, has a typical import.

It is no violation of our Canon to attach especially to the words of our Saviour, a deeper and profounder sense than that which lies upon the surface, and would first suggest itself to the mind of the careless and indifferent reader. This πληρώσις or ὑπόνοια, as it is called, is not a διλογία, or double sense, though it has often been confounded with it. It is the real and only sense intended by Christ,—the only sense which corresponds to the character and office of Christ and the spiritual nature of his religion. Nor is it an *occult* or hidden sense any farther than that it requires more thorough examination and thoughtful attention, and a deeper and more truthful insight into the spirit of Christianity, to bring out to view the real meaning, than is necessary in regard to historical passages. For example: by the expression "to be born again," as used by our Saviour in his discourse with Nicodemus, a Jew, according to the particular usage of his nation and of the time, would naturally understand by it, to become a proselyte to the Jewish religion; and many Christian interpreters regard it as identical or nearly so with baptism. But our Saviour employed the expression in a peculiar sense, in accordance with the whole nature and spirit of his religion, as denoting a radical change of heart or affections and will—a complete moral and spiritual regeneration, of which baptism or the public profession of religion and initiation into the Christian Church is but an outward sign, symbol, and indication.

Again: it is no violation of our Canon to employ the Scriptures in an accommodated sense for devotional purposes, or for moral and religious instruction and improvement, provided it is understood that the accommodated sense is not the real one intended by the writer, but only an adaptation of the passage to a particular use. In this way we accommodate the Psalms, when we employ them for devotional purposes in public or private worship, rather than for instruction. We adopt the language of the Psalmist as our own and employ it as expressive of our circumstances and feelings as far as by accommodation we can do so.

The question of a double sense is not the same with the question whether any prophecy is so constructed as to admit of a gradual fulfilment, not confined to one precise object or time, but extending through a considerable period and

designedly applicable to more than one event. It is very probable, that there are prophecies which extend through a long course of years and point out a succession of events, all tending to one point, or all centered in one person. It is doubtless to such prophecies as have this gradual accomplishment and completion, that Lord Bacon refers when he speaks of "a springing and germinant accomplishment." The simple point is, whether a prophecy fulfilled in *one sense*, looks forward to another accomplishment in a sense entirely new and diverse, altogether independent of the former sense, not bearing on the same point, not forming a part of the same dispensation, nor referring to the same general design.

That there are difficulties in regard to the use made by the New Testament writers of certain passages in the Old Testament, which the theory of a double sense is supposed to solve, will not be denied. But it would seem to be better to leave these difficulties unexplained, than to resort to a method of solution, which violates the established laws of language.

CANON III.

A word which has more meanings than one, cannot, at the option of an interpreter, be understood as combining any two of them.

This canon is no less self-evident than the one last considered. An interpreter has no more right to combine two distinct meanings of a word, than he has to create a third meaning. It is at his option to select either of two meanings belonging to a word, which he may regard as most suitable; but he is not at liberty to combine the two and thus virtually to form a third not authorized by usage, nor required by the exigency of the passage. This law is not perhaps so frequently or systematically transgressed, as Canon 2, but is nevertheless often disregarded even by eminent biblical expositors. The following are examples of this. The phrase translated in our standard version *evil conscience* in Heb. 10: 22, is rendered by Prof. Stuart, "a consciousness of evil," or "a conscience oppressed with evil or sin." "Perhaps," he adds, "both senses are included; for both are characteristic of Christian sincerity and full faith." Thus this distinguished commentator makes the same word signify both *conscience* and *consciousness* in combination. Undoubtedly the original word has both these significations, but not at the same time, and in the same place. Besides it is quite doubtful whether the phrase has in this passage, either of the two meanings ascribed to it by Prof. Stuart. The phrase "consciousness of evil," or "consciousness of being evil or sinful," i. e. of intrinsic demerit, is certainly not removed either by the pardoning or sanctifying efficacy of the blood of Christ; for this remains with the Christian till death. He will ever feel that he is a guilty sinner, i. e. a transgressor of the Divine law, and consequently *deserving* of punishment, though by means of a pardon no longer *liable* to punishment. It is no part of the Saviour's work or of the Spirit's work to remove this conviction of sin and of its ill desert, but to deepen it, in order to magnify the grace of God in the pardon of the self-condemned soul. The rendering of our standard version is much to be preferred, and is not difficult of explanation. By *conscience* is understood that faculty of the mind by which we either justify or condemn ourselves, in view of our conduct regarded as good or evil according to a known law. An *evil conscience* is a *guilty*, *accusing*, self-condemning conscience. See John 8: 9. Tit. 3: 11. 1 John 3: 20. It is opposed to a *good conscience*, i. e. an *approving* conscience, one which commends instead of blaming us:—that which gives a favorable testimony to the sincerity and uprightness of a man's conduct. See Acts 23: 1. 2 Cor. 1: 12. 1 Tim. 1: 15, 19. Heb. 13: 18. 1 Pet. 3: 16.

A *purified conscience*, or an heart sprinkled from an evil conscience, is one from which the accusations and terrors of a guilty conscience are removed by means of a pardon, so that the sinner, though fully conscious of his sinfulness and ill-desert, is enabled by faith in Christ Jesus, to rejoice in hope of the bliss of heaven. See Heb. 9: 14; 10: 2. It is to such a conscience that the Apostle here refers.

The Greek verb παιδεύω in the New Testament, like the corresponding Hebrew word in the Old Testament, signifies both to *instruct* and to *chastise.* 2 Tim. 2: 25. Titus 2: 12. Heb. 12: 6, 7, 10. In 1 Tim. 1: 20, the Apostle speaking of Hymeneus and Alexander, says, "whom I have delivered unto Satan that they may *learn* not to blaspheme." Now Parkhurst in his Lexicon of the New Testament has invented a meaning for the word in this place, which combines both instruction and correction. But this is as arbitrary and unauthorized as if he had assigned to the word a meaning at random. It is true that it was through the medium of chastisement or ecclesiastical discipline, the instruction to which the Apostle alludes was given: this, however, is not expressed in the words, but is ascertained from the context.

The Hebrew word rendered in our standard version to *deal prudently*, in Isa. 52: 13, signifies both to *act wisely*, and to *prosper*. Some commentators understand it in this passage in the former, and others in the latter sense. But Prof. Hengstenberg in the first edition of his Christology, undertakes to combine the two. "It is better," he says "to join both significations together; *he shall in wisdom reign prosperously;* or more briefly, *he shall reign well.*" Now these two significations are entirely distinct; and though national prosperity may be and often is the result of a wise administration of the government, the word never has, and by our Canon never should be made to have both significations in the same occurrence. Prof. H. subsequently perceived his error, and in the last edition of his valuable work he has corrected it, and adopts the rendering *shall act wisely*, though he erroneously asserts that the verb always has that meaning and never *to be successful*. The Greek noun translated in our standard version *volume*, Heb. 10: 7, Dr. Owen explains as uniting the signification of *volume, roll*, and that of *head* or *beginning*. "As the book itself," he says, "was one roll, so the *head* of it, i. e. the *beginning* of it—among the first things written in it, is this recorded concerning the coming of Christ to do the will of God. This includes both senses of the word; in the roll or volume itself, and in the head, or in the beginning of the roll, i. e. of the part of Scripture which was written when

David penned this psalm:"—alluding to the first promise of the Saviour in Gen. 3: 15. But neither does the Greek word nor the Hebrew word to which it answers in the Psalm from which the passage is quoted, ever signify the *beginning* of a book, but, as our translation has it, a *volume* or *roll*. And if the Greek word from its etymology could be supposed to signify the *head* or *beginning*, it cannot have both significations at the same place. The word translated *judgment* in Heb. 10: 27, Dr. Owen observes, "is sometimes taken for the *sentence* and sometimes the *punishment* suffered according to the award." "I doubt not," he adds, "but in the word here used both these are included, viz., the righteous sentence of God *judging* and determining on the guilt of this sin, and the *punishment* itself which ensues thereon." But though the sentence of condemnation and the punishment awarded as the penalty of the violated law are connected as antecedent and consequent, there is no reason whatever for uniting them in any case, and in this particular instance such a combination is entirely out of place, for the reason that the punishment consequent on the sentence of condemnation is explicitly alluded to in the expression *fiery indignation*, which immediately follows. The Hebrew word translated *to wither* in Psalm 1: 3, signifies also to *fall*, to *fall off*, and the Septuagint renders it in this place to *fall off*. But Prof. Bush combines the two and translates it *fall withering off*—remarking, that "the primary sense of the verb is doubtless *to dry up*, *to wither*, and connected with this to *flag*,, to *droop*, to be *exhausted*. But as the leaves of trees when thus *withered* and *dried up* fall to the ground, we shall probably do most justice to the original by retaining both ideas." Such an interpretation as this is a violation of our Canon.

The Greek noun υπόμονη, is translated in our standard version in Rom. 2: 7, *patient continuance.* Now this word signifies sometimes *patience*, viz., under trials and afflictions, and sometimes *constancy* or *perseverance*, viz., in the performance of good works. But in our version the two meanings are combined. The context shows that the proper meaning in this place is *constancy* or *perseverance*, and denotes continued activity and steadfastness in the Christian life. The passive virtue of *patience* does not seem to be at all alluded to.

The Greek verb δικαιοω, signifies in the New Testament, 1. to *make just* or *holy*, intrinsically. 2. to *declare* or *pronounce just* judicially, i. e. to acquit, to clear. 3. to *regard and treat* as *just* or *holy*, extra-judicially, i. e. to pardon, to absolve from guilt or liability to punishment. But Faber and some other theological writers combine the second and third significations, and regard the cognate noun *justification* in its evangelical sense as a complex term denoting both *acquittal* and *pardon.* But the ideas severally conveyed by these two terms are incompatible with each other. A man cannot be both acquitted and pardoned in relation to the same act or acts. For *acquittal* implies *innocence*, and *pardon* implies *guilt.*

Our Canon does not forbid us to regard certain terms and expressions in the Scriptures as used in an *intensive* sense. Thus the Greek word 'αποκαραδοκια, has in Rom. 8: 19, and in Phil. 1: 20, an intensive force, which is well expressed in our standard version by *earnest expectation.* This is evident both from the composition of the word and the nature of the passage. So also the Hebrew word in Psalm 2: 1, *rage* appears to be intensive, and may be rendered as in our Prayer Book translation *furiously rage*, or better still with others, *tumultuously assemble.* The word rendered in the same Psalm, v. 4., *sore displeasure*, is intensive and denotes *hot displeasure*, violent anger. See also Psalm 6: 1.

Again: our Canon does not forbid us to attach to a word or passage as full, comprehensive and fertile a sense, as the usage of the sacred writers justifies or the context, nature of the subject, and the spiritual and comprehensive character of Christ's religion seem to require. A feeble, jejune and frigid sense so commonly attached to the Scriptures by rationalistic commentators, is derogatory to the Word and Spirit of God. As the Scriptures were appointed by God to enlighten, reform and sanctify the human race, it is to be presumed that those books and passages in which weighty religious and moral truths are propounded, contain an important, rich, and comprehensive sense, worthy of their Divine Author, and adapted to accomplish the great end for which they were given.

CHAPTER XV.

DIFFERENT SENSES IN WHICH WORDS ARE USED.—FIGURATIVE LANGUAGE.

Before proceeding further to exhibit the Principles and Canons of Interpretation, it is necessary, in order to the right understanding of our subject, that some attention should be given to the different senses in which words are employed, and the uses to which they are applied. The most common and by far the most important division or distinction of words in respect to their meaning, is into *literal* or *grammatical*, and *figurative* or *tropical*. The terms *literal* and *grammatical* refer equally to the ELEMENTS of a word, and in reference to our present subject are used precisely in the same sense. *Literal*, from the Latin *litera*, denotes the meaning of a word, which is according to the letter, the proper or primary meaning; and the same is indicated by the term *grammatical*, in this connexion, a word of Greek derivation for what is according to the γράμμα, or *letter*. But when a word originally appropriated to one thing, comes to be applied to another, which bears some real or fancied resemblance to it, as there is in such a case a turning of it to a new use, we say a *trope* is employed. (Greek τρόπος, *inversio*, *conversio*) and the transferred meaning is called *tropical*: or we say in language derived from the Latin, (*figura*, *image*) that a *figure* is then used, because in such cases the meaning of the word assumes a *new form*. When other meanings become by usage attached to a word, besides the primary and principal meaning, they are all denominated *improper* or *secondary* senses, of whatever number or kind they may be. But to make a sense *figurative* in the proper acceptation of that term, there must be not only a departure from the primary sense, but there must at the same time be excited something like an *image* in the mind. Thus when the property of *hardness* is applied to a stone, the expression is used literally in its proper and natural sense; but when it is applied to the *heart*, it is used figuratively, or in an improper or tropical acceptation. The sense, however, allowing for the change of subject, is virtually the same, its application only being transferred from a physical to a moral quality. In the phrases *rosy face*, *snowy skin*, the epithets *rosy* and *snowy* are used tropically, because the properties indicated by those terms cannot be literally and properly applied to the face or skin. The Greek verb προσκόπτω properly signifies *to strike* one substance *against* another: as, for example, to strike the foot against a stone. Matt. 4: 6, and then *to stumble*,—the natural and frequent consequence of thus striking the foot. John 11: 9, 10. But it is transferred from material to spiritual objects, and then signifies tropically *to stumble at* any thing, i. e, *to take offence at it.* Rom. 9: 32,—1 Pet. 2: 8.

Tropes and figures abound in all languages. They originate in some instances from necessity: as when the language furnishes no appropriate term to express the idea, or in order to avoid the indefinite multiplication of new words. Accordingly we find tropical language in use in the first ages of mankind, and abounding most in languages, the vocabulary of which is most limited. That which constitutes the beauty of language thus arose from its very poverty. But necessity is by no means the sole cause of their introduction. They are more frequently employed merely for the sake of *variety* in expression, in order to avoid the too frequent repetition of the same word; for in all human operations gratification is studied even more than necessity. Still more commonly they are introduced for the sake of *ornament.* In proportion as an author is desirous of adorning his style, the more does he abound in tropes. The frequency of tropes depends much, also, on the genius of the writer, or the nature of his subject, and on the state of his mind at the time of writing. Men of warm and vivid imaginations, delight in tropes, even of the boldest character. This arises from the fact that they easily perceive and form similitudes, and by their peculiar temperament are excited to make comparisons. Indeed the least excitement of feeling impels a man of ordinary fancy to express his thoughts, not by the words directly appropriated to them, but by some accessory idea, suggested to his mind by the principle of association, and preferred on account of its greater vivacity and beauty. It is easy to see therefore, among what people, and in what species of composition, we are especially to look for tropical language. The nations which inhabit tropical climates are from their ardent temperament, more addicted to its use than those which dwell in cold regions; and poetry is particularly the field in which tropes most abound. Eastern nations indulge in figures, also, far more than Western. The common language of the Arabs of Western Asia, for instance, abounds in imagery of the boldest character. These remarks will explain why the language of Scripture is so highly figurative, especially of the Old Testament. The Hebrews were Orientals, and like other inhabitants of the East, possessing warm and lively imaginations, and living in a warm and fertile climate, surrounded by objects equally beautiful and agreeable, they delighted in a figurative style of expression; and sometimes fancied similitudes which seem to us farfetched, and to the chastened taste of Western readers do not always appear the most elegant. Another reason why the Old Testament abounds in imagery is, that much of it is poetry. Now it is the privilege of a poet to illustrate and adorn the productions of his muse, and to render them more animated and attractive by figures and images drawn from almost every object that presents itself to the imagination. "Hence David, Solomon, Isaiah, and other sacred poets, abound with figures, make rapid transitions from one to another, everywhere scattering flowers, and adorning their poems with metaphors, the real beauty of which, however, can only be appreciated, by being acquainted with the country in which the sacred poets lived, its situation and peculiarities, and also with the manners of the inhabitants, and the idioms of their language." The language of the New Testament, and especially the discourses of our Saviour, are not less figurative.

A close attention, therefore, to the nature of figurative language in general, and especially of the tropical language of the Scriptures, is of the highest importance to the Biblical Student; for while on the one hand, almost all the peculiar doctrines of the Gospel have been resolved by one class of interpreters, into Oriental metaphors, numerous mistakes on the other hand, have been made by another class, in consequence of a literal application of what was figuratively meant; important doctrines in theology have been made to rest on tropical expressions interpreted literally, and even grave dogmatic errors have originated in the same way, and are persistently maintained on this ground alone. As an illustration of this remark, the following example is taken from the admirable Lectures of Bishop Marsh:

"When our Saviour at the Last Supper took bread, and blessed it, and brake it, he gave it to his disciples, saying, 'Take, eat, this is my *body!*' In like manner, when he had taken the cup, and given thanks, he said to his disciples, 'Drink ye all of it, for this is my *blood* of the New Testament.' In the same figurative language he had spoken on a former occasion, when he said, 'He that eateth my flesh and drinketh my blood, dwelleth in me and I in him.' And then, comparing his body with bread, he added, 'This is that bread which came down from heaven.' The Jews, indeed, as well on this occasion, as when he spoke of the *temple* of his body, understood him literally, and asked, 'How can this man give us his flesh to eat?' though our Saviour himself, when he said of his body, that it was the bread which came down from heaven, plainly indicated, that he was only *comparing* his body with bread. The Church of Rome has followed the example of the *Jews*, and has *likewise* ascribed a *literal* meaning to words which were purely *figurative*. But the difficulty which pressed upon the *Jews*, in regard to *literally* eating the body of Christ, is not felt by the Church of *Rome*. The mistake of the Jews consisted in supposing, that our Saviour literally offered them his *body* to be eaten; whereas he *literally* offered his body as a *sacrifice*, and what he offered in *remembrance* of that sacrifice was literally *bread* and *wine*. But the Church of Rome, regarding the ceremony of the Lord's Supper as an actual *representation* of that sacrifice, not as a *commemoration* of it, supposes, that the body and the blood of Christ are *literally* presented to the view of the communicant. And believing, that Christ himself, by the consecration of the bread and wine at the Lord's Supper, had literally converted them into his own body and blood, before he said to his disciples, 'This is my body,' and 'this is my blood,' they conclude, that the miraculous conversion, thus ascribed to Christ himself, (a conversion, which, had it been *necessary* lay undoubtedly within the reach of *almighty power*,) is equally performed by the *human* power of an officiating priest. But the Church of England [and the same is true of the Protestant Episcopal Church in the United States,] with due attention to that figurative style, so frequently employed by our Saviour on *other* occasions, has interpreted his words on that *solemn* occasion by the rules of analogy, and by the dictates of common sense,—we eat the bread in *remembrance*, that Christ died for us; we feed on him only in our *hearts* by faith with thanksgiving. We believe that the blood of Christ was *shed* for us, and will preserve us to everlasting life. But the cup, which we drink, we drink only in *remembrance* that Christ's blood was shed for us. The same interpretation of our Saviour's words was adopted by the Reformers in general, with the exception only of Luther. He firmly indeed resisted the doctrine of Transubstantiation, or an actual change in the *substance* of the elements, as maintained by the Church of Rome. He *so far* took the words of Christ in a figurative sense, as not to believe that the bread and wine, even after the consecration, meant the *same things* as the body and blood of Christ. He believed that the bread and wine still retained their proper qualities. But he was perplexed by this expression: 'This *is* my body!' and though conference after conference was holden on the subject, he could never be persuaded to construe that expression consistently with the figurative language which is used throughout; and he persevered to the last in so strict an interpretation of that expression, as if it meant, This is *really* and *literally* my body. Having rejected, however, the doctrine of transubstantiation, or an actual change in the elements, he endeavored to remove the difficulty, in which he had unnecessarily involved himself, by supposing that, after the consecration, the body of Christ was *united* with the bread; and this *union* (not conversion) of substance was called *consubstantiation*. But there was a difficulty still remaining, which occasioned a controversy of long duration after Luther's death. The divines of Switzerland objected to the Lutherans, that our Saviour could not be everywhere *corporeally* present, which the doctrine of consubstantiation implied; while the Lutherans, on their part, endeavored to remove that objection, by accounting for the hypostatic union on the ground of what they technically termed 'communicatio idiomatum,' or the communication of properties. And since Christ, as God, must be omnipresent, in respect to his *divine* nature, they hence inferred, that as this *divine* nature had been united to his *human* nature, there existed a communication of properties from the former to the latter, which made him *corporeally* present, where he was *spiritually* present. The argument, however, did not satisfy their opponents, who thought it wiser to *prevent* the difficulty, by an uniformly consistent interpretation of figurative language."

It is strange that any sensible man should fail to perceive that the expression of our Saviour here referred to, which has occasioned so much bitter controversy and even bloodshed in the Christian Church, is simply a metonymy of the sign put for the thing signified. This is a figure common to all languages, and the idiomatic expression under consideration is of frequent occurrence in the Hebrew, because there is no word in that language which properly means *to signify* or *represent*. In the absence of such a word the substansive verb is employed in a tropical sense, and is either expressed or understood, as in the following example: "The three branches *are* three days." Gon. 40: 12; and "the three baskets *are* three days," i. e. the branches and the baskets *represent* three days. (See also ch. 41. 26. Ezek. 32: 11.) The same metonymical expression is found in the service for the celebration of the Passover among the modern Jews; in which the master of the family and all the guests take hold of the dish containing the unleavened bread, which had been previously broken, and say, "Lo! this *is* the bread of affliction which all our ancestors ate in the land of Egypt." The same idiom occurs frequently in the New Testament. Thus, "the field *is* the world," "the harvest *is* the end of the world," etc. Matt. 13: 38. 39. "I *am* (represent) the vine—ye *are* (represent) the branches." John 15: 5. "That rock *was* (represented) Christ." 1 Cor. 10: 4. This tropical meaning is required in reference to the words of our Saviour not only by biblical usage, but also by the context and the scope of the passage, not to mention the demands of reason and common sense. And yet in consequence of Luther's failing to see this, and persistently refusing to yield his opinion, a large and important branch of the Protestant Church has had incorporated into her creed a doctrine scarcely less unscriptural and incomprehensible than that of transubstantiation; while in the Church of Rome many a valuable life has been sacrificed to expiate the sin of rejecting a dogma, originating in the dark ages, and founded on a misconception of a figure of speech.

The Hebrews were exceedingly fond, as we have already remarked, of a style of composition abounding with tropes and figures of various kinds and of the boldest character, amounting in many instances to the most startling exaggeration. Their poets in particular indulged greatly the luxuriancy of their imagination in the employment of figurative language, for by presenting a kind of picture to the mind, it afforded delight as well as instruction. Treating, as the Bible does, also, of supersensuous objects and of beings who move in a sphere beyond our observation, much of the language of Scripture is necessarily analogical. It is highly important to the correct understanding of the Scriptures, therefore, that the Biblical student should be familiarly acquainted with the different kinds of figures employed by the sacred writers, and the proper method of distinguishing figurative from literal language. Without this knowledge, it will be impossible for him to make much progress in ascertaining the true meaning of the Scriptures; and he will be constantly liable to mistakes, which may lead to an erroneous belief, or to wrong practice. We proceed, therefore, to enumerate and briefly explain some of the more common and important figures which occur in the sacred volume.

There are figures of *diction* which relate merely to the addition or subtraction of letters or syllables. There are also figures of *construction;* but these relate to grammatical arrangement and not to the meaning of words. Neither of these has any relation to the interpretation of the language of Scripture, with which alone our subject is concerned. It is *rhetorical* figures only which affect the sense. These for the most part are founded either on *conjunction* or on *resemblance.* By conjunction is meant the mutual relation subsisting between two things; and this relation may be either *physical* or *intellectual.* When the conjunction is physical, the trope is technically called a *synecdoche.* This occurs when there is a substitution of *the whole for a part,* or *a part for the whole.* Thus the *world* sometimes denotes the *Roman Empire,* which was a very small, though a very remarkable portion of it. Luke 2: 1. The *soul* is put for the entire *person.* Acts 2: 41, 27: 37: the *flesh* is put for the *body,* Ps. 16: 9. *Many* put for *all*, Dan. 12: 2, where the prophet certainly does not intend to describe a partial resurrection. Rom. 5: 19, who the many are in this place we learn from the preceding verse. The *container is* sometimes *put for the thing contained.* Thus *a table* is employed to denote *the food* placed on it. "Let their table become a snare." A *cup* stands for the liquor it contains. "The cup of blessing which we bless," 1 Cor. 10: 16; just as we say of the intemperate man that he is fond of the bottle. *House is* put for *household*—the family residing in the house. Gen. 7: 1. *Heaven* is put for *God himself.* Hence the often recurring phrase "kingdom of heaven," applied to the new dispensation of the Messiah, and the Christian Church. There is no allusion in it to the heavenly state of that dispensation or church, but simply to their divine origin.

Where the conjunction is *intellectual* or supposed, the figure is called a *metonymy,* in which there is the substitution of one word for another, where the thoughts are closely conjoined and rise up together in the mind, though there is no proper resemblance between them. Thus where the *cause is put for the effect:* as when the *Holy Spirit* is put for the *gifts* and *influences* of the Spirit. "Quench not the Spirit," 1 Thes. 5: 19, Luke 11: 13. Christ is called *our life*, because he is the author of our spiritual life. *The sign is* frequently *put for the thing signified.* Thus a *sceptre* is put for *power,—to bow the knee* is *to do homage,*—to *lift up the hand* is to *sware. Circumcision* is called in Acts 7: 8, a *covenant,* because it was the *sign* of *the covenant.* In like manner *Baptism* is denominated *regeneration,* Tit. 3: 5, because it is the visible token and symbol of inward moral regeneration. The neglect of this figure led the ancient fathers, who are followed by many in the present day, to hold that baptism is itself a moral and spiritual regeneration. Frequently a *sentiment* or *action* is used for the *object with which it is conversant.* Thus *faith* sometimes signifies not the *belief* itself, but objectively the *doctrines* which are addressed to our faith —the Christian truths believed. "Contend earnestly for the *faith* once delivered to the saints." Jude 3. *Hope* stands for *Christ* the great *object* of hope: "Which is Christ in you, the hope of glory." Col. 1: 27. *Desire* is put for the *thing desired*: "I take away from thee the desire of thine eyes," i. e. the prophet's wife. Ezek. 24: 16.

That numerous class of tropes which is founded on the *resemblance* or similitude which exists between objects, is called *metaphor*, which consists in the substitution of one thing for another which in some respects is like it. When I say 'God is my protector,' I express the thought in its simplicity. When I say, 'He is my shield,' I clothe the thought in metaphorical language. In a metaphor the writer substitutes some image for the thought which that image is intended to express. This substitution takes place in consequence of a tacit comparison which the mind makes between the *image* and the *thought*, so that the metaphor is nothing else than a virtual *comparison* between the image and the thought which is illustrated by the image. A metaphor is not the same thing as a *simile*, though they are both founded on resemblance, and are very nearly allied to each other. The simile and the metaphor differ in this respect, that the metaphor is an *implicit* and *virtual* comparison between two things, while in a simile the comparison is *express* and *formal*. The difference may be illustrated by the following example: If a person should say of Alexander the Great that he was *a lion*, it would be a metaphor; but if he should say that he is *like a lion*, it would be a simile. In the former case the word *lion* is not used in its proper and natural sense for the animal designated by that name; but it is turned from it and made to designate a brave and courageous person: while in the latter it is obviously employed in its natural and customary signification. Hence the simile is not classed among tropes.

In connection with metaphors it is important to notice a numerous class of words and phrases which are derived from human objects and used to express something in or concerning God. Upon a proper understanding of these depend all correct apprehensions of the character of the Supreme Being as revealed in the Bible. In the language of Seiler, "As a finite being can have no intuitive knowledge of an infinite, so no language of rational creatures can completely express the nature of God, and render it capable of being comprehended. Only one thing can be *immediately* made known concerning him, HE IS. Even of this we should have no idea, if we had not an *immediate* consciousness of what is meant by the expressions *I am*, *I work*, *I act freely*," &c. All farther knowledge of God must be communicated in words invented to express ourselves intelligibly concerning human and other terrestrial objects. All words which we use in human language, in order to speak with others concerning God and divine things, have their foundation in a *resemblance*, which, according to our conceptions, exists between the Deity and human beings, and must also exist in a certain measure between causes and effects. This resemblance is either essential or non-essential. The essential is such as regards the pure *perfections* of our minds, i. e. such perfections as are not necessarily accompanied by any imperfections,—as *Reason*, *Liberty*, *Power*, *Life*, *Wisdom*, *Goodness*. These human expressions, applied to the Deity, afford an *analogical* knowledge. Hence arise analogical phrases, which are absolutely necessary whenever we speak of God, and would ourselves acquire, or would communicate to others, some knowledge of his perfections. All these analogical expressions must be received *properly*, although they give no immediate and intuitive, but merely a symbolical knowledge of the Deity. God possesses indeed reason, wisdom, goodness, liberty, although it is not *human* reason, human liberty, &c. There is between God and finite minds a natural resemblance, inasmuch as they have been formed after his image; while without reason and liberty, wisdom and goodness, neither virtue nor happiness can possibly exist. These then are *proper* expressions of that which exists in God."* In reference to such language, therefore, we are to interpret literally and not tropically. But besides these analogical expressions, there are many others of a different character which must be regarded as *improper* or *tropical*. They are, 1. those in which *human affections*, *passions*, and *sufferings* are ascribed to the Deity. The figure in

* Biblical Hermeneutics, by Seiler.

this case is called *anthropopathy.* 2. those in which God is spoken of as if possessed of a *human form*, *human organs*, and *human members*, and as if performing *human actions.* In this case the figure is called *anthropomorphism.* "A rational being, such as man is, who receives his impressions through the *senses*, can only form his knowledge of God by what he finds in himself,—from his own powers and properties. Anthropomorphitic modes of thought and expression are therefore unavoidable in the religion of men; they are absolutely necessary. Although such expressions can give no other than corporeal or sensible representations of the Deity, they are necessarily founded on the nature of things, and consequently true and just, when we proceed no farther than the point of resemblance and guard against transferring to God qualities pertaining to the human senses. God it is true *thinks;* but that God possesses *human* thoughts is untrue. That God *knows* all things is a proper expression: but it is improper or tropical to say, God *sees* all things. One is equally true with the other. But the man who should imagine that God sees in a proper [literal] sense, would be under a complete misapprehension."† In explaining passages therefore which are of an anthropopathic or anthropomorphitic character, we must be careful to understand them in a way suitable to the infinite majesty of God and free from every thing which may savor of impurity or imperfection. 'His eye' is his infinite knowledge; 'his arm,' is his almighty power; 'the sounding of his bowels' is his tender love and compassion;

† Seiler.

'his repentance' is his purpose to change the course of his providence for good and sufficient reasons, springing out of the moral conduct of his creatures; he is 'angry,' when he punishes the sinner; and his 'fury' paints the severity of their doom.*

Among tropical expressions should likewise be classed the figure *Prosopopœia*, or *personification*, in which sometimes in order to add force and beauty to the discourse, and sometimes for other purposes, properties, actions and character, are ascribed to fictitious, irrational or even inanimate objects, which properly appertain only to rational subjects or persons. The Personification evidently partakes of the nature of the metaphor, and is by far the boldest of that class of figures. Examples of this will be found in Job 12: 7, 8; Ps. 85: 10; Rev. 8: 27–31; Matt. 3: 9; Luke 19: 40.

The Allegory is another figure employed in the Scriptures, and like most others, is founded on resemblance. Indeed by many writers on Rhetoric it is regarded as and frequently called a continued, or extended, metaphor. But it differs materially from a metaphor in this respect—that while in the metaphor the tropical sense expressed is the only one intended,—in the allegory one meaning is expressed while another is intended, under cover of the words. The metaphor therefore admits of but one interpretation; the allegory, on the contrary, admits of two, viz. the literal or grammatical and the allegorical or the interpretation of that sense which underlies the natural and obvious sense. The meta-

* McClelland on Interpretation.

phorical interpretation is an interpretation of *words;* the allegorical is an interpretation of *things.* Other figures occur in the Scriptures, such as *Irony*, in which we say one thing and design another, in order to give the greater force and vehemence to our meaning. Examples of this figure may be found in 1 Kings, 18: 27; 22: 15; Job 12: 2. By some commentators the advice of Job's wife to her husband, Job 2: 9—"Curse God, and die," which they render "Bless God, and die," is regarded as ironical; see also 1 Cor. 4: 8. Under this figure belongs also the *Sarcasm*, which is irony in its superlative keenness and asperity. Matt. 27: 29; Mark 15: 32. This figure, however, is of rare occurrence in the Scriptures as not well suited to the character and design of that sacred book.

CHAPTER XV.

FIGURATIVE LANGUAGE.

It is of the highest importance to the Biblical student to be able in the first place to distinguish the literal from the figurative language of Scripture and then rightly to interpret what is tropical. Otherwise he will be very likely in many instances, on the one hand, to mistake the figurative for the literal, as was sometimes done by the Jews, and even by the disciples of our Lord in their interpretation of his discourses, (*e. g.* John 6: 52, 4: 11; Matt. 16: 6, 12), or on the other hand, to pervert literal forms by forcing upon them a tropical sense. In relation to this subject it is proper to remark that those words are not to be considered figurative which have altogether lost their original and proper signification and are used no longer in any but a secondary sense; or which have become so connected by usage with the objects to which they have been transferred, as that the applied has become their usual and perhaps only signification; *e. g.*, when we predicate *luxuriousness* of a crop, and when we speak of the *wing* of an army, the *foot* of a mountain, the *head* of a river, or the *bed* of a stream. The words *luxuriousness*, *wing*, *foot*, &c., were all originally proper nouns used in a very different sense, but now they have become proper as thus used by transfer. Again, there are certain kinds of composition in which a florid style and figurative language would in a good degree be out of place, and are therefore not to be looked for. Tropical language is not usually to be expected in legal instruments, statutes, history, didactic, philosophical and scientific works, Creeds and Confessions, &c. In writings like these, perspicuity and literal exactness are chiefly to be aimed at, and not elegance of diction. At the same time allowance must be made for the temperament, character and usages of the people among whom the writer or speaker lived. The prose compositions of Eastern nations abound much more in metaphor and imagery than those of Western nations, and hence we may expect the more frequent occurrence of figures in the historical and didactic portions of the Scriptures, than in the works of occidental writers of a similar character. It is also proper to remark, that words, when employed to denote moral or mental phenomena, are used in a secondary and tropical sense, because in their original and proper signification, they were designed to express material and physical phenomena. *e. g.*, to perceive, regeneration, illumination, sanctification, purity, purification, straight, path, way, &c. The following Canon will assist us in determining whether a word is used figuratively or not. *Where the subject and attribute, whether assumed or affirmed, are heterogeneous, incongruous, and incompatible with each other, the predicate should be interpreted figuratively.* In applying this rule, we should examine the object spoken of, either by the external or internal senses, or by recalling the external or internal perception. *E. g.* The phrase *inflamed mind* we understand tropically by repeating the perception of the idea of mind, and observing that the literal meaning of inflamed is incompatible with it. In interpreting the phrase *snowy locks* we appeal to the external senses, which determine that the meaning of *snowy* here must be tropical. The subject and predicate are heterogeneous when the one is material and the other immaterial; the one rational, the other irrational; the one animated, the other inanimate; as, also, when they are different species of the same genus. Because things, which, from a natural incongruity, cannot co-exist in the same subject, cannot logically, and therefore cannot *properly* be predicated the one of the other: for logical truth is the foundation of propriety of expression. Hence if they are predicated at all, it must be figuratively: *e g. the fields smile, the stones cry out, the floods clap their hands, day unto day uttereth speech.* Jahn expresses the above rule substantially in the following words: "If the subject and predicate (or adjunct) be such, that in their proper sense, they are inconsistent, we must conclude, that one or the other is tropical, provided that both be clearly known, and the repugnance be manifest." "From the rule," which we have given, "must be excepted," says Ernesti, "those texts in which divine and infinite attributes are predicated of Jesus, equally with those in which spiritual attributes are ascribed to man. For as both corporeal and spiritual qualities may be predicated of man, who is a being compounded of soul and body; so both divine and human attributes may properly be predicated of Christ, on account of the union of the two natures in his person."

In order to determine whether language is figurative or not, it is necessary in many cases to have recourse to the nature of things; *e. g., the mind is inflamed.* Here by resorting to the nature of the mind, we determine that the sense of the predicate *inflamed* must be tropical. So when God is said to *ascend*, to *descend*, to *walk*, &c., we must resort to the real nature of the subject spoken of to ascertain the nature of the language employed. Our appeal may also be made to the dictates of common sense and the plain elements of knowledge; *e. g.*, *Pluck out the right eye*, *Cut off the right hand*, *Put a knife to thy throat.* In considering expressions like these, our views of the worth of life, and of our corporeal members, which were given to us for the most important use: our views of duty as to the preservation of life and usefulness: and our knowledge of the nature of the Christian Religion in general, all conspire to lead us to reject the literal sense, and give to them a figurative meaning. When our Saviour says, "I am the vine, ye are the branches;" "I am the door," "I am the good shepherd," no one thinks of understanding him literally. Common sense teaches us to interpret these expressions figuratively, because taken literally they are utterly unintelligible. And does not common sense teach the same thing in regard to another declaration of our Lord respecting the sacramental bread, namely, "This is my body?" When this language was first uttered, Christ's body had not been broken nor his blood shed: the bread and wine used *then* at the institution of the sacrament could not have been a part of Christ's real body and blood, and the apostles could not have understood him as so affirming. And the supposition that the sacramental elements, are now after consecration converted into the real body and blood of Christ is utterly repugnant to reason and common sense, for not only is such a miraculous change improbable in itself, but it is contradicted by all our senses: for our sight, our taste and our smell testify that the consecrated elements have none of the properties of flesh and blood, but all the properties of bread and wine which they possessed before consecration. "Let the dead bury their dead," Common sense teaches that this declaration must be understood tropically, because a literal interpretation involves an impossibility. The connexion shows that a metaphor is employed in the subject of the proposition and that the meaning is, Let those who are spiritually dead (the worldly-minded, who are concerned only about the things of the present life.) attend to the burial of those who are corporeally dead. Christians are called "living stones." They are exhorted to "put on the armor of light," and to gird up the loins of their minds." In all these places the connexion of each word shows that a figure has been employed. Taken alone, disconnected from the context and subject of discourse, the language of the predicates might be figurative or it might be literal; but in the connexion in which they stand, the literal interpretation would be incongruous. This leads to the remark that words may be ascertained to be tropical not only by the incongruity of the subject with its adjuncts, but by the general context and parallel expressions. Thus Jeremiah 9: 7, "Behold, I will *melt* them and try them." Here the latter verb determines the former to be figurative in its signification. Different terms, moreover, are frequently employed in different passages to express the same ideas. This greatly facilitates the distinction between tropical and literal. In deriving assistance from this source, it is an important principle in regard to parallels, *that we must compare their homologous parts.* If they be simple propositions, we should compare subject with subject, copula with copula, predicate with predicate; if syllogisms, antecedents with antecedents, and consequents with consequents. Where similar expressions are employed in different places, however, if the one is plainly literal, it does not necessarily follow that the other is, for the context, or nature of the subject treated of, may show that such is not the case; *e. g.*, in Heb. 9 : 20 we have th· expression, "this is the blood of the covenant," and in Matt. 26 : 28 "for this is my blood of the new covenant." In the former passage there is no doubt that the word *blood* is to be taken in its proper and literal sense, for it refers to that which the Jews, by all their bodily senses knew to be blood, and nothing else; but it does not follow that when the same word was applied by our Saviour to the *eucharistic wine*, it was used in its proper sense, or that the disciples who by all their senses, knew it to be wine, and nothing but wine, must have understood it in that sense. The *rock* which Moses smote in the desert, was literally what the term imports, and in speaking of it he used the word rock in its proper sense; but when St. Paul (1 Cor. 10: 4) applies the same word to the anti-type Christ, no one would maintain that anything more is asserted than typical similarity. Once more: God gave the Israelites *bread from heaven*, and Christ gives his disciples *bread from heaven*. But the latter is a very different thing from the *manna;* indeed the word is plainly used in that case figuratively.

As it regards the language of Scripture employed to portray the realities of the invisible world and of a future state, it has been a question how far it is to be taken literally and how far figuratively, and some writers have been guilty of gross inconsistency in admitting that the language which describes the heavenly world and its felicities is figurative, while that which describes the world of woe and its punishments is literal. But "in examining whether language be tropical or not, we necessarily carry along with us those ideas which spring out of innate tendencies in the mind. Thus in reading the Scripture language concerning the nature of Deity, we instinctively separate from it whatever is material, or appropriate to humanity. The spirituality of his character leads us at once to understand tropically the descriptions of his character; so also the invisible realities of futurity, as heaven and hell, the state of the righteous and that of the miserable are delineated in tropical diction. Such things could not have been described otherwise than in language borrowed from sensible, material things, else it would have been unintelligible. Had abstract phraseology been employed, we should not have been able to attach to it definite conceptions. A spiritual vocabulary of this sort is not in use among us. We are accustomed to borrow the language of external nature, and to adapt it to incorporeal agents with their acts and operations. The wisdom of God is quite apparent in describing his own nature, as also the heavenly and infernal worlds, in tropical diction. Hence we explain such expressions as *their worm dieth not and the fire is not quenched*, *everlasting fire*, &c., metaphorically to denote intense torment. The imagery is taken from the death and corruption of the body. Carcases were destroyed by fire or eaten by worms. Now this is transferred to the soul, with the superadded idea of perpetuity. The state of the miserable, who shall be excluded from the presence of God, is one of active, intense and corroding torment forever and ever. The "lake of fire," (Rev. 20 : 15) and "furnace of fire," (Matt. 13 : 42, 50) express the same idea, viz., *intensity of suffering*. Of the same nature is the phraseology employed respecting the judgment seat of Christ, before which assembled millions of human beings stand. The opening of the books out of which they are judged, the right and left hand of the judge, are tropical also. Thus attention must always be given to the nature of the subject, in regard to which it is inquired whether language is figurative or otherwise."*

The student of the Bible should be able not only to *detect* figurative language, but rightly to *understand* and explain it. His progress in this direction will be greatly facilitated, 1. By becoming intimately acquainted with the *sources* from which the Sacred writers principally drew their imagery. These are four, viz., *nature*, *common life*, the *political and religious institutions of the Hebrews*, and *their history*. In borrowing imagery from *natural objects*, the Hebrew writers generally and the poets in particular, selected such as were well known and familiar to their readers. The perspicuity of language, indeed, will be found in a great measure to depend on this, for a principal use of metaphors is to illustrate the subject by a tacit comparison; but if, instead of familiar objects and ideas, an author introduces such as are new, or unfamiliar and imperfectly understood, in order to shed further light on what is already in a good degree plain; instead of making the subject clearer, he only renders it more involved and obscure. Thus the familiar images of *light* and *darkness*, are very frequently employed in Scripture to denote respectively good and evil, joy and sorrow, prosperity and adversity, knowledge and ignorance. Christ is called "the *light* of the world," and "the *sun* of righteousness." The Psalmist says, "God is a *sun* and shield." The apostle St. Paul describes the new moral creation of the Gospel in highly figurative terms drawn from the creation of the

*Davidson's Sacred Hermeneutics, p. 286—288.

material world. "God who commanded the light to shine out of darkness, hath shined in our hearts, to give the light of the knowledge of the glory of God in the face of Jesus Christ." Images are also derived from rivers and fountains, and the earth recreated with rain. The scarcity of water, the paucity of showers, and the extreme heat of the summer, together with the remarkable fertility of the soil, rendered these much more elegant and jocund comparisons in the East than with us. Hence, to represent distress, such frequent allusions among them to "a dry and thirsty land where no water is;" and hence, to describe a change from distress to p osperity, th ir metaphors and comparisons are founded on the falling of showers, and the bursting forth of springs in the desert. Thus we find the blessings of the Gospel spoken of by the Sacred writers under the images of fountains of water, rivers and copious showers. The numerous figures derived from the mountains of Palestine must be familiar to every reader of the Bible. Lebanon and Carmel, in particular, the one remarkable for its height, magnitude and the abundance of the cedars which adorned its summit, exhibiting the appearance of strength and majesty; the other, rich and fruitful, abounding with vines, olives and delicious fruits in a high state of cultivation, and displaying the attractive appearance of fertility, beauty and grace, furnish the Hebrew poets with the most appropriate similes and beautiful metaphors. In the images of the awful and terrible with which the writings of the inspired poets abound, they plainly drew their descriptions from that violence of the elements and those concussions of nature, with which their their climate made them familiar. Earthquakes were not unfrequent, and sometimes were accompanied with land slides. To these the Psalmist alludes, when he speaks of "the mountains being carried into the midst of the sea," (Ps. 46 : 3,) and of their skipping like lambs, and the little hills like young sheep," (Ps. 114 : 4, 6.) Tornadoes, followed by thunder, lightning, rain, and hail, were also very common during the winter season in Judea and Arabia, far exceeding anything of the kind which occurs in more temperate regions. To such phenomena Isaiah alludes when he says of the wicked, "The whirlwind shall take them away as stubble," (Isa. 40 : 24), "Chased as the chaff of the mountains before the wind, and like a rolling thing (*stubble*) before the whirlwind." (Isa. 17 : 13), (Ps. 83 : 13.) The illustrations drawn from the *manners, cusoms, arts, occupations and circumstances of common-life* among the Hebrews, are innumerable. . Simplicity and uniformity characterize these in the greatest degree. There existed not that variety of studies and pursuits, of arts, conditions and employments, which may be observed amongst other nations who boast of superior civilization. Separated from the rest of makind by their religion and laws, and not at all addicted to commerce they were contented with the few arts which were necessary to a simple and uncultivated, or rather uncorrupted, state of life. Their chief employments were agriculture and the care of cattle and sheep; they were a nation of husbandmen and shepherds. Hence not even the greatest among them esteemed it mean or derogatory to be employed in the various occupations of rural labor, the products of which constituted the wealth of each individual. In the Scripture history we accordingly read of eminent persons called to the highest and most sacred offices, heroes, kings and prophets, from the plough and from the stalls. (see Judg. 3 : 31, 6 : 11 ; 1 Sam. 9 : 3, 11 : 5 ; 2 Sam. 7 : 8 ; Ps. 78 : 72, 73 ; 1 Kings 19 : 19, 20 ; Amos 1 : 1, 7 : 14, 15.) Frequent allusions are made to pastoral and agricultural occupations. Thus Jehovah is described as a *shepherd*, (Ps. 23 : 1), and is represented as threshing out the heathen as corn, trampling them under his feet and dispersing them. In the New Testament, the world is compared to a field; the children of the wicked one, to tares; the end of the world, is the harvest; the angels are reapers; the preacher of the Gospel is a sower; the Word of God is the seed; the heart of man is the soil; the cares, riches and pleasures of life are thorns; the preparation of the human heart by penitence, is ploughing and breaking up the fallow ground. An abundance of metaphors occur in the Sacred writings drawn from the *religious institutions of the Hebrews*, The Epistle to the Hebrews abounds with imagery drawn from this source, from which it is apparent that the entire system of ritual institutions under the Mosaic law, while it subserved other important ends, was symbolical of the future dispensation of the Gospel and the sacrifices and expiations typical of the one great sacrifice and expiation for the sins of mankind offered upon the cross. As examples of the use of historical facts to represent spiritual truths, we may instance the following: The moral renovation of the human heart is represented under the figure of a new creation, in allusion to the original physical creation described in Genesis. The lifting up of Christ on the Cross is compared to, if not typified by, the lifting up of the brazen serpent in the wilderness. The miraculous supply of manna in the desert, is made a symbol of that true bread which came down from heaven and which is the life of the soul. The wanderings of the Israelites in their journey to Canaan, are represented as emblematical of the pilgrimage of the people of God to the heavenly Canaan. Thus we see that in order to perceive the significancy, force and beauty of the sacred imagery, the Biblical student must transport himself in imagination to the theatre of Scripture events, and familiarize himself with the physical geography of Palestine, the antiquities of the Jews, their arts, manners and occupations, their political and religious institutions, and their history. 2. Assistance may often be obtained in determining the meaning of Scripture tropes by *consulting the proximate context.* Sometimes we discover by this means, that the speaker or writer has himself made known his intention by furnishing an explanation of his language. Thus when Jesus admonishes his hearers (Matt. 11 : 29) to take his *yoke* upon them, he adds, and *learn of me*, by which he clearly shows that by the figurative term *yoke* he meant the moral precepts which he taught. The Apostle St. Paul, after inquiring of those who had once been devoted to the practice of vice, (Rom. 6 : 21) "what *fruit* had ye then ?" shows by immediately adding "for the end of these things is death," that *fruit* here signifies figuratively *result, advantage* or *reward.* The same inspired

Apostle in Phil. 3 : 2, says, "Beware of dogs," and the tropical application of the word *dogs* to false and audacious teachers is made evident by what follows, "beware of evil-workers." Comp. Rev. 22 : 15. In like manner in James 4 : 4, the words "adulterers and adulteresses," refer not to actual *adultery*, but to an undue attachment to worldly things, as appears, not only from the context generally, but also from what immediately follows: "Know ye not that the friendship of the world is enmity with God." When Jesus compares (Matt. 27, 28) the Pharisees to whited sepulchres, making a fair show outwardly, but internally full of bones, filth and corruption, he himself immediately adds an explanation of the figure, "so ye also without appear," meaning evidently that they put on the external appearance of probity and virtue, while their minds were full of improbity and injustice. So the apostle Paul, in his valedictory address to the presbyters of the Ephesian Church, (Acts 20 : 28) shows in the prop r and tropical terms which he alternately employs, that by the *flock* which he commands them to watch over, he means the church of Christ, the associated organic body of Christians; and hence the verb *to feed* must be interpreted in the sense of *to rule, to instruct,* and *to provide for* the spiritual wants of the church. In 1 Pet. 3 : 21 the *baptism* which saves us is defined to be "not the putting away of the filth of the flesh, but the answer of a good conscience towards God." In Hosea 4 : 12, a spirit of lasciviousness is said to have drawn the Israelites astray; but then it is immediately added "They sacrifice upon the tops of the mountains, and burn incense upon the hills," to show that it is spiritual unfaithfulness of which the prophet is speaking. When Christ said, "He that eateth me, even he shall live by me," John 6:57, the Jews misunderstood his meaning, but he had himself already explained it; for in the same discourse he had repeated the truth in literal terms, "He that *believeth on me* hath everlasting life," v. 47. This text is understood literally by most Roman Catholic writers, though our Lord expressly gave it this figurative interpretation, and the ordinance of the Supper, to which they suppose it to refer, had not then been instituted and was entirely unknown to his hearers. Where no direct and explicit interpretation of tropical language is furnished by the author himself, we may sometimes ascertain the meaning by the help of contrasted expressions. Thus, Matt. 7:9, our Saviour does not expressly say what he means by a *stone* instead of *bread*, and *serpent* instead of a *fish*. But at v. 11, he explains bread and fish as meaning generally *good gifts*, things useful and salutary; hence we may conclude from the opposition, that by the stone and the serpent are meant objects either useless or pernicious. It is not uncommon for the Sacred writers to subjoin to tropical expressions proper ones of similar import, so as to explain the imagery they have just employed. Especially is this the case in the parallellisms of sentiment or thought—rhythm which is a proinent characteristic of Hebrew poetry. Thus Ps. 97:11, "Light is sown for the righteous and gladness for the upright" Here the first member of the couplet is tropical, and the second which is literal, explains it. Isa. 46:11, "Calling from the east, the *eagle*; from a distant land, the *man of my purpose.*" Here the *eagle* in the former member, a term figuratively applied to Cyrus, is explained in the latter by the *man of my purpose.* Sometimes the sense of tropical expressions may be gathered from the antecedents or consequents. We have an example of the former in Matt. 7 : 3, 4, where the figures *mote* and *beam* occur without particular explanation. If we refer to vs. 1, 2, and consider that the object of the divine teacher was evidently to warn men against forming rash or uncharitable judgments of others, it will at once appear that the *mote* is used for the minor offences of others, and the *beam* for the greater faults of ourselves. We have an example of the latter in Matt. 9 : 38, where Jesus exhorts his disciples to pray, that God would send laborers into his *harvest*, he immediately shows by selecting twelve apostles from among them, and commissioning them to preach the glad tidings of the kingdom, (ch. 10 : 1, 7) that by *harvest* he means figuratively not as some suppose, the propagation of his religion, but the multitude of persons who listened attentively to him, and thereby gave a reasonable ground to hope that they were *ripe* for conversion.

3. In discovering the meaning of tropes assistance may often be derived from *parallel passages.* Thus in Mark 10 : 38, 39, the *cup* and the *baptism* which were to be received by the Apostles John and James, are the privations and sufferings which they were to undergo, as clearly appears from a comparison of the parallel texts, Matt. 26 : 39, John 18 : 11, Luke 12 : 50. There is, moreover, another class of texts, which though they cannot be considered as strictly parallel,

may still be advantageously employed in discovering the sense of tropes. Thus the denunciation of St. Paul to the High Priest, (Acts 23: 3) "God will smite (*i. e.* punish) thee thou *whited wall*, may have light thrown upon it from Matt. 23:37, where our Saviour compares the Pharisees generally to *whited sepulchres*. Here it appears that the idea intended in both passages is that of the worst hypocrisy.

4. It is necessary also to a right understanding and interpretation of tropes, to consider the particular points of similitude existing between the sign and the thing signified and specially alluded to by the speaker or writer. Examples of comparison are not to be taken entirely and in all possible relations, else they would cease to be examples and become the things themselves. They should not be extended beyond the point or points of resemblance evidently intended by the speaker or writer, as shown by the context, and technically called the *tertium comparationis.* Thus, if Christians are represented under the figure of *lambs* or *sheep*, the points of comparison are *innocence, patience* and *gentleness.* God is frequently styled a *king* and a *shepherd*; the points of similitude in such cases are *guidance, protection, authority*, and accordingly we may substitute for them the proper terms, governor, guide or protector. St. Paul, (Rom. 12: 1) exhorts the Roman christians to present their bodies a *living sacrifice* to God. Here, the qualifying term *living*, the context and common sense show, that he is speaking of self-immolation. We must, therefore, exclude the idea of sacrifice in any proper sense, and substitute the notion of *dedication* and *presentation to God.* A tropical expression may,

indeed, have several meanings and suggest various comparisons, but such only are pertinent in a particular locality as harmonize with the context. When Jesus says (John 6 : 35) "I am the *bread* of life," adding by way of explanation, "he that cometh to me," &c., he plainly indicates that he would make provision for all the spiritual necessities of men : so that whoever should be united to him by faith and obedience, would enjoy true happiness, together with all necessary safeguards to his salvation, and would neither require nor wish for anything else. The point of comparison lies, therefore, in tho property of bread to nourish men, preserve life and support the sinking strength.

Again, when the apostle Paul (I Thes. 5 : 2) says that the second coming of the Lord will be "like a *thief* in the night," the words which follow, "when they shall say peace and safety, then sudden destruction cometh upon them," show that it will come unexpectedly upon men, who are not thinking of it, just as a thief glides by night into the houses of those who sleep securely and anticipate no evil. Comp. Matt. 24 : 43, Luke 12: 39. When Jesus, in his address to the pious women who followed him (Luke 23 : 31), after denouncing a miserable fate on the city and inhabitants of Jerusalem, adds, "for if these things be done in a *green tree*, what shall be done in a dry ?" it is clear from Ezek. 20 : 47 and 21 : 3, and comparing for the sense 1 Pet. 4 : 17, that by the *green tree* is meant an *innocent and righteous person*, the cause of safety to others; and by the *dry*. a *wicked person*, the cause of injury to others. And if we examine more carefully the passages in Ezekiel, we shall readily discover what is the point of comparison between men and trees, and will find that it lies in their good or bad qualities, as being the cause why we think a dry and barren tree ought to be cut down, and why a worthless and hurtful man is deserving of destruction. The sense of the passage in St. Matthew thus becomes clear. "If the innocent and righteous be thus cut off, what may be expected to befall the wicked and disobedient in the day of visitation which impends over you."

While the figurative meaning of a word has doubtless some reference to its literal signification, it must not be supposed to include in the figurative use all that is included in the literal: similitude in some one respect, as we have seen, is sufficient to justify the metaphor. Sin is called in Scripture a *debt;* atonement, the payment if a debt; pardon, the forgiveness of a debt. But we would err if we should interpret these terms so rigidly as to maintain that, because Christ died for man's sin, therefore all will be saved, or have a legal claim to forgiveness and eternal life, for this would be opposed to the analogy of Scripture. Again, men are represented figuratively as *dead in sins*, but it would be erroneous to infer that they are dead in such a sense as to be exempted from the duty of repentance, or are guiltless if they disregard the divine call, for this would be contrary to the whole tenor of Scripture, as well as the dictates of common sense. More errors, perhaps, have arisen from pushing analogical expressions to an extreme, far beyond what the speaker or writer intended, than from any other single cause. Against this tendency the sober, earnest student of the Bible needs to be be specially upon his guard.

5. Ernesti and other writers on Interpretation have laid down the following rule for determining whether figurative language is understood or not, viz., *to substitute proper words for tropical ones.* "Not," says Ernesti, "that a person who can do this always rightly understands the words, but if he cannot do it, he certainly does *not* understand them." Undoubtedly the very attempt to do this may lead to greater discrimination in our ideas; and in many cases we may thus succeed in coming at the exact meaning and force of the metaphor. But in a multitude of instances the substitution of proper diction for figurative in the Scriptures is impossible. When the Sacred writers employ metaphorical language to convey to our minds some conception of spiritual things, of the realities of the invisible world and a future state, they do it not from choice and for the sake of ornament, but from the necessity of the case, because there are no literal terms of equivalent import, in which to express such spiritual truths. We may indeed, change the figure, but this is only like turning liquid from one vessel into another. No doubt each word and phrase of Scripture employed in relation to spiritual truths, sets forth a definite sentiment with precision and certainty. No tropical word is entirely destitute of meaning, or serves as a mere expletive. Each has its use and performs its appropriate office as far as human language can, though we may not be able to discover the one or to perceive clearly the other.

6. We may remark further, that important aid towards the understanding of the figurative language of the Scriptures as well as discovering

its beauties, may be derived from the cultivation of the imagination. "Imagination is that power by which we form images or pictures to be seen by the eye of the mind, as the objects of the outward world are seen by the bodily eye. It was through the imagination that a large part of the revelations recorded in the Bible were made to those holy men, who have transmitted them unto us. Divine revelations were addressed to the minds of the prophets by symbols set before them in visions and dreams, and the events of their daily life. Now it is imagination alone that can reproduce these symbols to the mind of the reader, so that they may be clearly apprehended, and stand out before his mind as they did before the mind of the prophet. Moreover, imagination looks into the soul and living principle of things, discerns those moral ideas, or spiritual truths, which they are fitted and designed to express. The poet and the clown may both look at the same outward object, *e. g.* the western sky at the time of some brilliant sunset; but the one sees in it only what strikes his bodily eye, while the other may see in it the emblem of the gateway to the celestial city."* These remarks apply with peculiar force to the poetic books of Scripture.

7. Finally it is important in the interpretation of figurative language, to remember the inadequacy of figures of speech, or of any sensible symbols, fully to express spiritual truth. Without comparisons and figures indeed we could have no ideas at all of spiritual, invisible, and heaven-

---

*Robie on Figurative language of scripture in Bibliotheca Sacra. vol. 13 p. 321.

ly realities. At the same time it should be remembered that the image of invisible things is at best, but very imperfectly and inadequately represented by language borrowed from material things. And not only so; there are many spiritual truths which require many different figures, in order rightly, in some measure, to express their fullness and greatness. Thus all our language with regard to the Supreme Being is figurative. "God is a spirit," "God is a rock," "God is a high tower," "God is a dwelling place," "God is a sun and shield." Yet no one of these figures, nor all possible figures put together; can adequately represent God to us. In all such cases, therefore, we must rest satisfied with the general idea arising from the particular comparison or comparisons employed, and neither on the one hand, seek for a perfect agreement in the object compared, nor, on the other, imagine that we fully comprehend that object, because we may be able to understand to some extent the import of a particular image employed to picture it to our minds.

CHAPTER XVI.

HEBREW IDIOMS.

Every language has some forms of expression, some characteristic modes of clothing ideas, peculiar to itself, and called the idioms of the language. The Hebrew language abounds in peculiarities of this sort, and it is impossible even for the English reader to attain to a correct understanding of the meaning of Scripture without some knowledge of them; for in our standard English version, instead of being exchanged for equivalent expressions in our own language, they are to a considerable extent translated literally. Such expressions are consequently to be interpreted not according to the English, but according to the Hebrew idiomatic usage. This Hebraistic style pervades the New Testament no less than the Old, because though the New Testament writers composed their Sacred books in Greek, yet being native Jews they naturally expressed their thoughts in the Hebrew style and manner in which they had been educated, and with which they were most familiar. The following are a few examples of the Hebraisms which occur in the Scriptures, and which for the most part have been transferred in our English Bible.

One striking instance is the use of the limiting noun (the genitive) in regimen with another noun. The relations which the former bears to the latter are much more various in Hebrew than is customary in English. Sometimes the genitive denotes the *possessor*, sometimes the *object*, and at others the *agent*; and not unfrequently it qualifies the governing noun as an adjective. Thus the phrase "the love of God," when employed in relation to man, according to the English idiom would signify the love which *God* bears to *us*; but in the Bible it frequently signifies the love which *we* bear to *God*. In 1 Cor. 1:5, St. Paul says "the sufferings of Christ abound in us." He does not mean by this expression the sufferings endured by Christ himself in our behalf, but those which are endured by Christians *for* or *on account of* him. The corresponding English expression would be sufferings for *the sake* of Christ. The same is intended by the apostle when he calls himself "a prisoner of Christ." He was a captive *for* or *on account of* him In his Epistles he frequently speaks of "the righteousness of God," denoting thereby not subjectively an attribute or property of the divine nature, but objectively the righteousness by which the sinner is pardoned, or the method of justification through the perfect righteousness and all-sufficient merits of Christ. This is called God's righteousness, because he graciously provided and accepts it. In Col. 2: 11, "the circumcision of Christ," means not the circumcision which he himself endured, but the circumcision of the heart *enjoined* by him. The phrase "horn of salvation" signifies a horn (the emblem of power among the Hebrews, borrowed from their pastoral life,) which is the *procuring cause* of salvation; or it may be equivalent to the expression, "a powerful Saviour." The custom of employing nouns in regimen for adjectives was very common among the Hebrews, in consequence chiefly of the paucity of qualifying and limiting terms in their language. Thus the apostle, addressing the Thessalonians, (1 Thes. 1: 3) speaks of their "patience of hope," meaning their *patient hope* or *expectation*. The expression "glory of his power" occurs for *glorious power*, "newness of life," for *new life*, "spirit of promise," for *promised spirit*, " bond of perfectness," for *perfect bond*.

Sometimes two nouns are joined by a copulative, apparently indicating two distinct things when only a single thing is really asserted (*Hen*.

diadys), one of the nouns being employed as a limiting term. Thus in Acts 23 : 6, the apostle Paul says, "Of the hope and resurrection of the dead I am called in question," by which he means the hope of the resurrection of the dead. The phrase "kingdom and glory" is used to denote a glorious kingdom. We are informed in Acts 14: 13, that the priests of Jupiter brought "oxen and garlands," to their gods. The oxen were decoratad with the garlands, and the precise idea is indicated by the phrase oxen crowned with garlands. Many Commentators explain by this grammatical figure, the expression in Matt. 3 · 11, "He shall baptize you with the Holy Ghost and with fire," *i. e.* a burning spirit—a spirit who is a power penetrating and all-purifying as the element of fire. The context, however, strongly favors a different interpretation, based on the supposition that the connective particle should be taken in a disjunctive sense ; thus, "He shall baptize you with the Holy Spirit *or* with fire," *i. e.* he will copiously imbue you with the influences of the Holy Spirit, if you yield your hearts to him; or else, if you reject him, he will overwhelm you with the severest punishment. The word *name* is frequently used as synonymous with *person*. Thus to believe on the *name* of Christ (Jo. 1; 12) is to believe *on him*. *Soul* also is put for *person*, as being the more important part of man. In Acts 2 : 41. it is said, that there were added unto them about three thousand souls," *i. e.*, *persons*. In consequence of there being no superlative in their language, the Hebrews employed the additional words *of* or *to God*, or *of the Lord*, in order to denote the greatness or excellency of a thing. Thus in

Gen. 13 : 10. a *beautiful garden* is called the garden of the Lord"; very *high mountains* are called "the mountains of God." In Ps. 80: 10. the *tallest cedars* are termed in the original "the cedars of God." In Ex. 9 : 28. *loud thunderings* is in the original "the voices of God." In Jonah 3 : 2. Nineveh is termed *an exceeding great city*, which in the original is "a city great to God." In Acts 7 : 20. Moses is said in the original to be "fair to God," *i. e.*, as it is correctly rendered in our version, *exceeding* fair. In the last four examples our Translators have departed from their usual custom of giving a literal rendering and thus transferring idiomatic expressions, and have expressed the sense in language accordant with our own usage. In 2 Cor 10: 4. The weapons of the Christian's warfare are declared to be "mighty to God," *i. e.*, exceedingly powerful, not mighty through God, as in our standard version.

It is in the use of verbs, however, that the Hebraic style of the Scriptures is most strikingly manifest. These verbs frequently indicate not the action itself which the word signifies, but something approaching or allied to it, the desire or endeavor to perform it, its commencement merely, or the giving occasion to it, its permission, or the obligation to its performance. For example: Things are said to be done where there is only the *endeavor* or *intention* to do them. Thus Reuben is said (Gen. 37 : 21) to have delivered Joseph from the hands of his brethren. He indeed intended the deliverance of his brother, and attempted it but with only partial success. Thus too, in Ex. 6 : 18. the magicians are said to have done so with their enchantments, *i. e.*, they attempted to do so. "Whoso findeth his life," says our Saviour "shall lose it," *i e.*, he who seeks to find, is unduly anxious for its preservation.

Sometimes verbs only intimate that the subject *gave occasion* to the action. Thus in Jere. 38 : 53. God says to King Zedekiah by the prophet, "Thou shalt be taken by the hand of the King of Babylon : and thou shalt cause this city to be burned with fire;" *i. e.*, the conduct of the unhappy monarch would lead to this catastrophe. Our Saviour said, "I came not to bring peace on the earth, but a sword." *i. e.*, my advent in the flesh will be the occasion of sharp persecution and bloodshed. "This child," said Simeon, "is set for the fall and rising again, (or rather *rising*) of many in Israel." (Lu. 2 : 34) He will be the *occasion* of the fall, the ruin and misery of many who will reject his message ; and the rise or restoration to spiritual life and happiness of many who shall embrace his religion. "The wrath of man says the Psalmist, "shall praise God" :—not actually utter his praise, but be the *occasion* of praise being rendered to him. In Acts 1 : 18. St. Luke says, that Judas "purchased a field with the reward of iniquity," while St. Matt. states (ch .27 : 6. 7.) that the field was bought by the priests and elders with the thirty pieces of silver which Judas Iscariot had returned to them. The fact is that Judas was no further concerned in the transaction, than that he gave *occasion* for it. The two statements are thus satisfactorily harmonized. The word *cannot*, which properly denotes a *physical* inability is frequently employed to signify merely a *moral* inability, or indisposition to do a thing. Thus in Ruth 4:

6. the near kinsman of Elimelech says, "I cannot redeem his inheritance." Now he could have done so, had he been disposed; for he was evidently a man of property; but he was unwilling to do it, on account of the pecuniary sacrifices it involved. The householder in our Lord's parable into whose house a friend solicited admission at midnight, replies that the door is shut, that the children are with him in bed, and that he *cannot* rise. All that he meant by this expression is that it was extremley inconvenient to rise and therefore he was unwilling. It is said of our Saviour in Mar. 6 : 5. that "he could do no mighty works" (perform no miracles) in a particular district because of the unbelief of its inhabitants, *i. e.*, he could not with pleasure and satisfaction to himself or profit to others. It was *painful* to him, as well as useless to throw pearls before swine. Joseph's brethren it is said "hated him, and *could not* speak peaceably unto him." (Gen. 37 : 4.) "I have married a wife, and therefore I *cannot* come." (Lu. 14 : 20.) In all these instances there was obviously no lack of capacity, or natural power. The inability was wholly of a moral nature, the inability of the will. This idiom however, is not peculiar to the Hebrew. We find it in all languages, ancient and modern. In our own language for instance we find the word *cannot* frequently used in two different senses; the one expressing what is termed a *moral*, the other, a *natural*, inability; the one a mere inability of disposition and will; the other an inability extraneous of the will, and over which the will has no power. Thus we ask a pious friend to lift up for us a thousand pounds. He replies; "I cannot do it." We ask him to

go to some place of amusement on the Sabbath; he replies again; "I cannot do it." In both cases he pleads an inability. But it is easy to see that here there are two kinds of inability. Our friend has no natural power to lift a thousand pounds. He could not do it if he would. He has all the physical power necessary to comply with the other request, and only lacks the willing mind.

Sometimes verbs are used in a *declarative sense*, denoting the recognition of the thing spoken of as having been performed or as being about to be. "Behold," says Isaac to Esau, "I have made Jacob thy lord, and all his brethren have I given him for servants." (Gen. 27: 37). The only agency which the venerable Patriarch had in the transaction consisted in announcing it. He designed to say, I have declared, (or have declaratively made,) Jacob thy lord. So Jeremiah was set up by God over the nations, to root up, pull down and destroy. The Prophet was not a military conqueror; but as a divine messenger he declared what would be accomplished by the hand of Nebuchadnezzar. When a priest saw on a man signs of leprosy, he was required by the law "to pollute, or make him unclean," *i. e.*, to *pronounce* him unclean, as our common version, casting off the Hebraisim, rightly expresses it. In Ps. 2: 7, we have another example of the declarative use of the verb. The Lord hath said to me, Thou art my son; this day have I begotten thee." The import of the language undoubtedly is; "This day do I *declare* thee to be begotten by me; comp. Romans 1: 4. "What God hath cleansed, call not thou common," *i. e.*, what God has *pro-*

nounced clean, that call, &c. Verbs have sometimes a *permissive* sense. Thus, Ps. 119 : 31, "I have adhered to thy testimonies, put me not to shame," *i. e.*, permit or suffer me not to be put to shame, and reproach. Again, Isa. 62 : 7. "O Lord, why hast thou made us to err from thy ways, and hardened our heart from thy fear"? This does not mean that by a positive, immediate agency God produced the moral evils complained of by the prophet; but that he had simply permitted them in his providence.

In a similar manner we may explain the petition in our Lord's prayer, "Lead us not into temptation," *i. e.*, suffer us not to be brought under the power of temptation. The declaration that God hardened Pharoah's heart is susceptible of a like interpretation. Misapplication of this idiom at one time led some New England metaphysical divines to assert as an article of their belief the monstrous and revolting doctrine that unholy as well as holy volitions were the immediate effect of divine agency. Such are only a few specimens of the very numerous and various idiomatic expressions which occur in the Scriptures. But these are sufficient to show the great importance of a careful study of them to the right understanding of the sacred volume.

CHAPTER XVII.

GENERAL LAWS OF INTERPRETATION.

We now propose to exhibit and illustrate some of the general laws of Biblical Interpretation. And first: *The Bible should be interpreted in harmony with the clear deductions of reason.*

Reason and Revelation have the same author, and proceed from the same source of infinite intelligence and truth: they must therefore coincide in their decisions. They can never really come into contrariety. And yet it is well known that in some parts of Christendom the attempt has been made under cover of the phrase "pure reason" to get rid simply by way of interpretation, of the plainest facts and doctrines of Revelation, nay of Christianity itself. And some of the most plausible and mischievous of all attacks on revealed religion in recent times, have been made under the pretence that its distinguishing doctrines as deduced from the plain and obvious meaning of its language, are repugnant to reason. Hence recourse has been had to violent and forced interpretation, to metaphor and figure, to the doctrine of accommodation and various other false schemes, in order to eliminate these doctrines from the pages of the Bible. But notwithstanding this gross and palpable abuse and perversion of Reason, it still remains unquestionably true, that our chief weapon for the defence of Scripture truth is our reason, rationally, legitimately and properly used. We may be sure that the Spirit of God speaking in and through the Scriptures does not in a single instance design to assert for truth what is evidently contrary to the clear and acknowledged decisions of reason properly enlightened and rightly employed. But it must ever be borne in mind, that human reason is limited and finite. Its sphere of operation is circumscribed by certain boundaries which it cannot pass. It is possible, therefore, that there may be statements in the Bible which reason cannot explain, because they lie beyond the domain of human comprehension, and are, therefore, inscrutable to the mind of man. Nor is this merely possible, but from the very nature and design of a supernatural Revelation, it is highly probable: nay; in point of fact, it is absolutely certain. But to assert things which human reason cannot comprehend in their modes, is one thing; and to assert things contrary to the innate dictates of reason, is quite another thing. The latter, we may boldly affirm, the Scriptures have never done. There is a class of texts which, if construed according to the strict letter, might seem to oppose the dictates of reason. Thus in Heb. 12: 29, we have the declaration "God is a consuming fire." The literal import of this passage asserts the ancient doctrine of the Persians that God is literally the principle of fire. But such an interpretation would not only contradict the whole tenor of Scripture, but be at war with reason and common sense. The language therefore, must be taken figuratively as descriptive of God's power utterly to destroy. Jere. 23: 24. "Do I not fill heaven and earth, saith the Lord?" This passage taken literally would appear to teach Pantheism, than which nothing is more repugnant to reason. John 6: 53, "Except ye eat the flesh of the Son of Man and drink his blood, ye have no life in you." The literal interpretation of this passage is contrary to reason: it must, therefore, be rejected, and the text understood in a figurative and spiritual sense.

There is another numerous class of texts which when literally explained, as they manifestly should be, assert nothing contrary to reason, but which involve doctrinal truths which lie beyond and above the range of the human faculties, and are therefore incomprehensible. Take for example the doctrine of Divine Omnipresence. The doctrine that God is everywhere and at all times present, beholding the evil and the good, is everywhere asserted in the Bible, and as a fact is perfectly consonant with the decisions of reason. But we are no where told *how* he can be thus every where present, and the *manner* of his omnipresence is beyond the reach of our comprehension. Shall we then reject the plain and obvious meaning of the passages which teach the doctrine, and put upon them a forced and unnatural interpretation? Certainly not. Again: the Scriptures clearly teach in their literal and obvious sense, that the Father, the Son and the Holy Ghost, all possess divine attributes and perform separate offices in the economy of human redemption. At the same time they as clearly and unequivocally assert the divine unity. Upon these two facts the Church doctrine of the Trinity in Unity in the godhead is based. Now the proposition that in the godhead, these three persons, so called for the want of a better term, are one in precisely the same respects in which they are three, and three in the same respects in which they are one, cannot be true, because it is repugnant to reason. But the proposition that the Father, Son and Holy Spirit, are three in certain respects, and one in certain other respects, is not contrary to reason, and therefore may be true. That there is numerically but one God is a fact which we believe on the clearest testimony of Scripture. That the Father, Son and Holy Spirit are each partakers of the divine nature, and therefore are equally entitled to, as they justly claim our homage, is also a fact abundantly established on the same testimony.—These two facts we fully receive on the authority of the word of God. And we are sure that however inexplicable they may be to us, there is in them no contradiction. But of the *mode* of the divine existence, as a Trinity in Unity, beyond the simple fact, we know and can know nothing. This is one of those mysteries which the Bible has not solved, and about which we are not at liberty to speculate. If reason begins to cavil and ask, how the Deity can be three and one at the same time, it forsakes its proper sphere, and would be wise above what is written. Of one thing we may be certain, that in the statements of Scripture in relation to this or any other doctrine there can be nothing contradictory to right reason. The two must harmonize, because they both proceed from the same author.

It is also of the highest importance to remember that human reason is not only *finite* but *fallible.* "Man is liable to err. He finds himself deceived in his judgments of things that take place around him. He draws conclusions which he afterwards finds to be wrong. The fallibility of his reason constitutes him a fallible being.

Since, therefore, his nature is such, he may form wrong opinions respecting the truths of revelation. He may fail to perceive what is propounded for his reception. Finite and imperfect as he is, it is not marvellous that he should frequently go astray in his sentiments. Rather would it be a cause of wonder, if he should never tax himself with error, or acknowledge that his mind does not judge accurately on all topics which come before it. Every thing connected with him partakes, at present, of imperfection. His soul is tainted with sin, and alienated from God. His body is liable to decay. The Bible is infallible, because its author is so; but reason is fallible, because man has corrupted his ways, and deteriorated his constitution. He is not what he once was. The candle of the Lord shines not within him in its original brightness. The lamp of reason has been dimmed by his infatuation. Its beams are not shed forth with the same lustre or loveliness as when Jehovah himself first lighted up the luminary of the soul. Let us always, then, bear in mind this truth, that reason is fallible; while the Scriptures cannot err, either in their propoundings of doctrine, or expositions of duty, or statements of eternal truth. Of reason's liability to err we have ample proof in the fact, that there are important differences in the conclusions at which its extravagant encomiasts arrive. Far from coinciding, the results of their researches are widely at variance. Reason, it is said, teaches some to believe that Christ was not a true man, consisting of a human soul and a mortal body; but that the *Logos* supplied the place of a soul in the man Christ Jesus; others are conducted by the same guide, to the opinion, that he was nothing higher than a man, with a real body and a reasonable soul. The innumerable varieties of creed among such as call themselves by the common appellation of Unitarians, prove the fallibility of the guide to which they abandon themselves. The folly of extending the province of reason beyond what is written, is abundantly evident. All contradictions between Arians and Socinians owe their origin to a dissatisfaction with the amount of Scripture revelation. They begin to exercise their reason in matters beyond what is written; and thus lose themselves in speculations no less presumptuous than unprofitable. If reason were contented to abide by the plain exposition of the written word, no perplexity would ensue. Unreserved submission to the dictates of Heaven is the right and righteous exercise of reason. Partial homage, on the contrary, is the sin of such as do not cause it to bow with implicit reverence to all utterances proceeding from the sanctuary of heaven. It is the source of the fallacies and the follies of those who permit reason to go beyond the limits assigned to it by Infinite Wisdom. If every doctrine and precept which it cannot fathom are to be set aside on the ground of their obscurity, the Scriptures will be reduced to a very meagre compass. If man were possessed ef a pure and perfect reason, by which he could discern the relations of the universe,—if he could discern the connexion subsisting between things natural and moral,—if he could understand the ways of the Lord unto perfection, and the reasons of his dealings with men, he might then employ a reason, which could accomplish so much, to search out the things which are only hinted at in the Bible; bnt if he must be contented with knowing in part here below, reason must acquiesce in many circumstances as right and true, although it cannot tell *why* or *wherefore* they are so."*

Second law: *The Bible should be interpreted in harmony with the well-established facts of natural science.* Truth is always in accordance with herself. The book of nature and the book of Revelation proceed from the same author, and have a common origin. There can never, therefore, exist any absolute and irreconcilable discrepancy between the laws of nature and the disclosures of Divine Revelation. If there seems, in any instance, to be a real discrepancy, it must be owing either to a misinterpretation of the written record, or to some error in regard to the alleged facts of science. With regard to the latter, there may have been too hasty a generalization, or a position may have been assumed on insufficient evidence, and further discoveries on the subject may rectify the erroneous conclusion. Especially is this remark applicable to the comparatively modern, and, as yet, imperfectly developed science of geology. "A natural science, while in its infancy, when but partially developed, while some of its main features are still under discussion, is not to be placed on the same footing with sciences whose laws have been long established. Its earliest revelations, though seemingly adverse to Biblical truth, need not occasion alarm or anxiety. The laws of philology are to be admitted as unhesitat-

* Davidson's Sacred Hermeneutics.

ingly as those of any physical science. There is the same certainty that the Bible came from God as that the solar system did. It would be no greater mark of folly to reject the evidence on which the facts of the material sciences rest, than that by which Scripture truth is supported."* One thing is certain, no absolute contradiction between physical and Biblical truth has yet been established, notwithstanding the prating and dogmatizing of some sceptical and half-fledged sciolists. It should be constantly borne in mind that it is not the design of the sacred writers to teach the natural sciences, but moral and spiritual truth. Whenever they have occason, therefore, to allude incidentally to physical phenomena, they describe them according to apparent truth, in conformity with the usage and imperfect knowledge of the times in which they lived, and not with philosophical accuracy. Had the language of revelation been scientifically accurate, it would have defeated the object for which the Scriptures were written; for it must have anticipated the scientific discoveries of a later age, and therefore have been unintelligible to those for whose benefit they were written, and who were ignorant of such discoveries. Professor Maury, indeed, undertook to show that the Psalmist anticipated the modern discovery in geography with respect to the spherical form of the earth. And in proof of this, he appealed to Psalm 98: 8, as rendered in our Prayer Book version—"Let the sea make a noise, and all that is therein; the *round world*, and they that dwell therein." Now the fact is,

* B. B. Edwards.

there is no qualifying word in the original corresponding to *round* in this translation; the only Hebrew word used signifies simply *world*, considered as the habitation of man: a fact which he might have ascertained, had he merely consulted the authorized version, where it is correctly rendered. Sometimes an apparent contrariety exists between the Bible and natural science, in consequence of an imperfect or inaccurate translation, even in our common version. Take the following examples in chemistry: In Prov. 25: 20, we find it said that, "as vinegar upon nitre, so is he that singeth songs to a heavy heart." We should infer from this statement, that when we pour vinegar upon the substance which we call nitre (nitrate of soda) it would produce some effervescence, or other disturbing influence; but on trying the experiment, we would find no such result to follow. So Jere. 2: 22—"Though thou wash thee with nitre, and take thee much soap, yet thy iniquity is marked before me, saith the Lord." Here, too, we should expect that the use of *nitre* or *saltpetre* would increase the purifying power of soap; but the experiment would prove the contrary. There is a well-known substance, indeed, viz: *Carbonate of Soda*, which if substituted for the nitre, would effervesce with vinegar, and also aid the purifying power of soap. Now on recurring to the original we find that the Hebrew word נתר, (nether, *nitrum* or *natrum*) does not signify the salt which we call nitre, but a fossil alkali, the *natron* of the ancients, and the *carbonate* or rather *sesqui-carbonate* of soda of the moderns.

"Scarcely any truth," says President Hitchcock, "seems more clearly taught in the Bible than the future resurrection of the body. Yet this doctrine has always been met by a most formidable objection. It is said that the body laid in the grave is ere long decomposed into its elements, which are scattered over the face of the earth, and enters into new combinations, even forming a part of other human bodies. Hence not even Omnipotence can raise from the grave the identical body laid there, because the particles may enter successively into a multitude of other human bodies. I am not aware that any successful reply has ever been given to this objection, until chemistry and natural history taught us the true nature of bodily identity: and until recently the objector has felt sure that he had triumphed. But these sciences teach us that the identity of the body consists, not in a sameness of particles, but in the same kinds of elementary matter, combined in the same proportion, and having the same form and structure. Hence it is not necessary that the resurrection body should contain a single particle of the matter laid in the grave, in order to be the same body; which it will be if it consist of the same kind of matter combined in the same proportions, and has the same form and structure. For the particles of our bodies are often totally changed during our lives; yet no one imagines that the old man has not the same body as in infancy."

Until the time of Copernicus no opinion respecting natural phenomena was supposed to be more firmly established, than that the earth is fixed immovably in the centre of the universe, and that the heavenly bodies move diurnally around it: And this opinion was attempted to be established incontrovertibly on the authority of Scripture in opposition to the Copernican system. In proof of it the appeal was made to those passages which speak of the sun as moving in the heavens, and as rising and setting. (Ps. 19: 5. 104: 19. Eccles 1: 5.); to the alleged fact that the sun, by a miracle, stood still in the time of Joshua. (Josh. 10: 12–14), and by a miracle went back in the time of Hezekiah. (Isa. 38: 8); and to the assertions respecting the immovability of the earth, (Ps. 93: 1; 104: 5; 119: 90, 91.) But if we only admit that the sacred writers did not intend to teach scientific instead of popular truth, but that they spoke of astronomical phenomena, according to appearances, and in conformity to common opinion, then their language is seen to be perfectly proper and consistent with the facts; it conveyed no error, and is as well adapted now as ever to the common intercourse of life. Hence its use has never been laid aside, notwithstanding its apparent contrariety to the true system of the universe. It is no impeachment of the inspiration of the sacred writers to admit that in common with their countrymen they were ignorant of the true principles of astronomy, for upon this point they had received no information from above, and had no oracle to utter. With respect to the discrepancies which are alleged to exist between the statements of the Bible and the modern discoveries in Geology, space will only permit me to refer to the admirable work of President Hitchcock, entitled "The Religion of Geology and its Connected Sciences." "Science," says McCosh, "has a foundation, and so has religion; let them unite their foundations, and the basis will be broader, and they will be two compartments of one great fabric reared to the glory of God. Let the one be the outer and the other the inner court. In the one, let all look, and admire, and adore; and in the other, let those who have faith kneel, and pray, and praise. Let the one be the sanctuary where human learning may present its richest incense an offering to God; and the other the holiest of all, separated from it by a veil now rent in twain, and in which, on a blood-sprinkled mercy-seat, we pour out the love of a reconciled heart, and hear the oracles of the living God."

3. The Bible *should be interpreted in harmony with our intuitive moral judgments.* It cannot be at issue with any of these. If, therefore, it recommends "the cutting off a right hand, and plucking out a right eye," it must not be taken literally to mean bodily mutilation. Our life and members are a sacred trust committed to us, which must not be trifled with. The declaration of our Saviour, "If any man hate not his father and mother, and wife and children he cannot be my disciple," if interpreted literally, would be revolting to our moral sense, and no exposition which would sanction the feeling of hatred to parents would for a moment be tolerated. We must regard it, therefore, as a strong hyperbole denoting the greater love which is due to himself.

In St. Luke 10: 4, Christ commands his seventy disciples while in the performance of their missionary tour, "not to salute any by the way." We cannot suppose that our Lord here intended to inculcate rudeness and incivility. Their mission required haste; he therefore enjoins upon them not to waste their time in merely complimentary or courteous addresses, and in holding unnecessary intercourse with their friends to the neglect of the weightier concerns of their sacred vocation Matt. 5: 39. "Whosoever shall smite thee on the right cheek, turn to him the other also." That the commands in this and the following verses are not to be taken literally, as enjoining the particular actions here specified, and forbidding self-defence, but rather as inculcating the *disposition* of forgiveness and benevolence, is apparent not only from its being usual in the East to put the action for the disposition, and from the manner in which the precepts are introduced, but also from our Lord's own conduct (John 18; 22, 23), and that of his Apostles, (Acts 23: 3) Not *slavishly* and *literally*, but *truly* and in the *spirit*, our Redeemer obeyed this precept; for "He gave his back to the smiters, and his cheeks to them that plucked off the hair, and hid not his face from shame and spitting," (Isa. 50: 6); and his Apostles also did the same, (see 1 Cor. 4: 9–13.) The precept requiring us "not to revenge ourselves," forbids indeed the taking of private revenge, but it was not designed to forbid judicial punishment. Our Saviour in Matt. 5: 33, commands us to "swear not." Now it is evident from the context, that our Lord is here not to be understood as forbidding *judicial* oaths, or oaths on solemn occasions and for the satisfaction of others, for that would be a mere technical Pharisaism wholly at variance with the spirit of the Gospel, and inconsistent with the example of *God himself.* (Heb. 6: 13–17; 7: 21); of *our Lord when on earth*, and of *his Apostles.* (Gal. 1: 20. 2 Cor. 1: 23. Rom. 1: 9. Phil 1:

8. and especially 1 Cor. 15: 31); but such oaths as are introduced into common conversation, and on ordinary occasions, which are not only unnecessary but highly irreverent.

On a similar principle are to be explained those passages, which exhibit the prophets as doing by the command of God things inconsistent with natural propriety. Hosea, for example, is commanded to marry two impure women, and Ezekiel to lie on his left side a year and a month, looking at an iron pan—and then to turn over to his right side, on which he must lie forty additional days,—eating during the whole period, a composition of vegetables and grain prepared in a manner most decidedly disagreeable. These are not to be taken as real transactions, for that would both dishonor the word of God and betray an utter want of taste. They were doubtless symbolical representations, which passed before the prophet's mind in his inspired ecstacy.

4. The *Bible should be interpreted in harmony with universal experience and observation.*

This principle requires us to take universal terms and expressions in a modified and limited sense. Thus absolute expressions often denote only what *usually* takes place—what is accordant with *general* but not universal experience and observation. Solomon tells us, for example, in Prov. 22: 6, "train up a child in the way he should go, and when he is old he will not depart from it." This we know does not always hold true. Strange as it may appear, Solomon himself at one period of his life, was an exception to it. Nevertheless it is true generally. And the precept loses nothing of its value and importance because we are compelled to limit somewhat its application. The exceptions only proves the rule.

Sometimes such expressions only denote the *natural tendency* of a thing. Prov. 15: 1: "A soft answer turneth away wrath," i. e., it is evidently calculated to produce this happy result. St. Paul declares that the "goodness of God leadeth to repentance." Such is doubtless its natural tendency, and such we should reasonably expect would be its consequence; but we know that sometimes it produces the very opposite effect; it corrupts and hardens. At other times such expressions merely indicate *duty—right—official obligation.* Thus, Prov. 16: 10, "a divine sentence is in the lips of the king, his mouth transgresseth not in judgment." St. Peter, in like manner says of the civil magistrate, "he is the minister of God for good, a terror to evil workers, and a praise to them that do well." Such declarations show what he ought to be in the exercise of his official functions—what he is *de jure;* but not what he always is *de facto.* Sometimes we find assertions broadly made that refer only to *external character* and *profession.* Thus all credible professors of the Gospel are called "saints," and "holy"; and the sacred writers treat them as being what they profess and ought to be.

5. The *Bible should be interpreted in harmony with the testimony of our senses.*

Thus when David says that "he is poured out like water, and all his bones are out of joint, that his heart is melted in the midst of his bowels," it is manifest that a literal pouring out and melting cannot be intended, as nothing of the kind has ever been witnessed. Again, when our

Saviour, in the institution of the Supper, declares of the bread then in his hand, that it is his body, and of the wine, that it is his blood, his disciples must have necessarily understood him to be speaking not literally, for that would have contradicted the clear testimony of their senses, but figuratively and symbolically.

And when Christians in accordance with the command of their Lord celebrate this Supper, their senses distinctly see, taste, smell, and feel, that the sacramental elements are nothing but real bread and wine. The Romish doctrine of Transubstantiation, therefore, is most clearly and unequivocally refuted by the evidence of the senses, and hence cannot be true. To believe a doctrine in direct and palpable opposition to the clear evidence of the senses, is destructive of all evidence, and can be required of no intelligent being.

6. *The Bible should be interpreted in harmony with itself.*

Viewed in all its relations, this is by far the most comprehensive and important principle of Biblical interpretation; and it is a principle of constant application. It requires not only that each individual writer should be explained in harmony with himself, but also with every other sacred writer. Let us apply the principle, in the first place, to the composition or compositions of a particular writer. It is to be presumed that no judicious and sensible writer will contradict himself, or introduce in the course of his argument what is entirely irrelevant to his immediate purpose, or inconsistent with his general design and object. When a passage, therefore, is obscure, ambiguous or of doubtful import, the first care of the interpreter should be to *consult the immediate or proximate context, both preceding and following.* The *context* is in the Scriptures as well as in all other writings, the primary means of discovering the true sense. The legal maxim on this subject is thus expressed: *ex antecedentibus et consequentibus fit optima interpretatio,* "a passage will be best explained by referring to that which precedes and follows it." A single sentence plucked rudely from its connexion in an argument, it matters not from what writer, may often be made to express a sentiment which was not only not in the mind of the writer and foreign to his intention at the time, but which is in contradiction to his real sentiments elsewhere expressed, and wholly irrelevant to his course of reasoning. And yet this is the manner in which the word of God is very frequently treated in homiletics and didactic theology. In sermonizing nothing is more common than to select a text and deduce a sentiment from it as the foundation of a discourse, not only in utter disregard of the context, but in perfect contradiction to it. Many popular preachers, in giving scope to their fancy and imagination, allow themselves to be captivated with the mere phraseology of the English version, or with the mere sound of an expression without any regard to its real meaning in the particular connexion in which it occurs. In the departments of didactic and polemic theology, it is very frequently the case that isolated passages are quoted as proof texts of doctrines, which when taken in their connexion are found to be quite irrelevant to the subject. What should we think if we heard any other book discoursed upon in this way? or what should we think of a judge on the bench expounding in this way a legal instrument or statute? The civil law has laid down an express canon on this subject in which the practice alluded to is strongly rebuked. *Turpe est de lege judicare tota lege non inspecta.* "It is disgraceful to judge of a law, by examining only a part of it." It is certain that many of the controversies which have been carried on with acrimonious zeal in the Christian Church, have arisen in consequence of their authors having overlooked this rule. Had the texts which thay hurled against their antagonists, with, as they verily believed, overwhelming force, been first examined in their connexion, these theological combatants would have found themselvәs deprived of many a weapon with which they carried on their wordy warfare. Some indeed there are, who are far from being lawless interpreters, that do not hold the rule under consideration in very high estimation; but conceive its use to be confined within very narrow limits. But this is by no means an accurate view of the subject; for, as Professor Stuart has justly remarked: "the immediate context, either preceding, succeeding, or both together, is a rule for judging of the meaning of words [and sentences] of the very broadest extent. In very many cases, indeed, the evidence of the *usus loquendi* is itself built upon the context. We adopt the opinion, that the *usus loquendi* sanctions this or that particular sense, because the context clearly shows that such a meaning is to be assigned to it, and that no other can be given without rendering the sense frigid and inept. Moreover, the *general scope* of an author does not forbid the admission of a great variety of arguments, illustrations and episodes, into the immediate parts of a discourse; so that one is far more certain of giving a sense that is congruous, by consulting the *immediate context*, than by immediately consulting the general scope of the whole. Both, no doubt, are to be regarded; but of the two, the former is by far the more important means of assistance. Indeed I should doubt whether there is any one rule in the whole science of hermeneutics so important, and of such practical and actual use as the one in question. Great care, indeed, is necessary to decide with certainty, what sense the context requires that a word should have, especially when the immediate subject is briefly stated. But this care is as easily practised as any other rule is, which hermeneutics prescribes in different cases. Violence must not be done to words, by forcibly subjecting them to the context, against etymology, analogy, the rules of grammar, and the nature of language. But in every thing short of this, all good lexicographers and commentators adapt the meaning of words to the context, in cases too numerous to need any specification."* The remarks of the Professor with special reference to the signification of particular words, are equally applicable to the sense of words in combination. The examination of the context is as important to the meaning of sentences as of words. The manner in which our Bibles are commonly printed is unfavorable to a proper examination of the context. The fracture of great coherent masses into sepa-

* Ernesti: Elements of Interpretation.

rate verses, is an unhappy arrangement in this respect, though attended with advantages for reference, which, however, could as well be secured by placing the figures in the margin as is done in some editions. The reader's attention is diverted from the flow and current of thought and fixed on an isolated proposition. Thus the logical connexion is overlooked and revelation is apt to be treated as a vast collection of proverbial sayings or independent propositions. The following examples will illustrate what has been said. The declaration of our Saviour, Matt. 22: 14. "Many are called but few are chosen," is supposed by many to refer to sovereign election; but the context shows that he is only stating the fact that while all are invited to the Gospel feast, there are comparatively few admitted to the participation of it in consequence of neglect on their part to secure the necessary qualifications. Universal grace for the purpose of salvation is attempted to be proved from 1 Cor. 12: 7: "the manifestation of the Spirit is given to every man to profit withal." But the whole argument shows that the Apostle is speaking of supernatural gifts of the Spirit, and is addressing Church members exclusively. In 1 Cor. 15: 22, the Apostle says, "For as in Adam all die, so in Christ shall all be made alive." From these words there has been deduced by some the doctrine of universal salvation, and by others the legal identity of the human race with our first parent and their spiritual death in him. But the context shows that it was not the design of the Apostle in the passage to teach either of these doctrines. He is proving the resurrection of our Lord as a demonstration of the resurrection of all men. After citing the testimony of witnesses to our Lord's resurrection, he proceeds to an argument distinct from that of testimony, in the gracious design of God in this matter. He says, "for since by men came death, by man also (according to the design of God) came the resurrection of the dead. For as in Adam," &c. That is as *physical* death (not *spiritual* death as is shown by the antithesis) came by Adam and was the consequence of his sin, so the physical resurrection from the dead will come by Christ; as in the providential arrangement of God man brought in death, so by the same arrangement man would bring in the resurrection. The passage then relates solely to the resurrection, and there is in it not the faintest trace of universal salvation, nor of mankind's oneness with Adam. In James 5: 14 the elders of the church are commanded to anoint the sick and to pray over him, "and the prayer of faith shall save him." The Church of Rome founds on this one passage the doctrine of extreme unction, which they say is to save the soul of the dying. But from verses 15, 16, it is plain that by "save" in this passage is meant "heal," so that, whatever the practice may have implied, it was to be observed, not with the view of saving the soul, but in the case of one already a Christian, with a view of restoring his health.

The Canon applicable to this branch of our subject is, *Every passage must be interpreted in harmony with the context.* In other words, No explanation must be admitted which is opposed, or unsuited to the context. We haye an instance of the direct violation of this canon, on the part of the Church of Rome, in regard to Matt. 18:17. "Tell it unto the Church, but if he neglect to hear the Church, let him be unto thee as a heathen man and a publican." This passage is interpreted by the Romanists as referring to the infallible decisions of all doctrines by the (Roman) Catholic Church. But what says the Evangelist? By reading the passage carefully in its connexion, the obvious meaning will be found to be this; "if a man have done you an injury, first admonish him privately; if that does not avail, tell the Church,—not the universal Church dispersed throughout the world, but the particular church, to which you both belong. Through the whole of the context there is not one word said about disobeying the determination of the Catholic Church respecting a disputed doctrine. Where no connexion manifestly exists between what immediately precedes or follows, none of course should be sought. This observation applies to the Proverbs of Solomon, and chiefly to the 18th and following chapters, which form the second part of the Book. This portion of Scripture consists almost entirely of isolated propositions connected by no principle of association. In reference to parenthetical clauses, also, our rule must be applied with caution. Where the parenthesis is short, it creates no special difficulty, and can hardly be said to interrupt the flow of the argument; but when it is long, it sometimes materially affects the continuity of the discourse, and occasions considerable difficulty. e. g. Eph. 3: 2–14. The connexion is also sometimes interrupted by the introduction of a covert dialogue, in which objections, responses, and replies are not distinctly marked.

The Scope.—It sometimes happens, however, that the context fails to remove all doubt as to the exact meaning of the writer. Recourse, in that case, should be had to the *scope*, or design of the writer, either in regard to the entire book, or some large section in which the passage occurs. Every intelligent author proposes to himself some definite object or objects which he seeks by his writings to attain; and not only may it be presumed that he will say nothing inconsistent with that design, but also that what he does say will coincide and harmonize with it. The scope, therefore, is the soul—the *vis vitæ*—of a work, which lives and breathes through the whole, giving order, force, consistency and beauty to every part. As an illustration of the importance of regarding the scope of a writer, take the passage in James 2: 14, where the Apostle says, "Ye see how that by works a man is justified, and not by faith only." St. James here appears to express a sentiment at variance with the declaration of St. Paul, when he says that "a man is justified by faith only." Luther, to whom the doctrine of justification by faith only, or gratuitous justification, was most precious, as being, in his estimation, the crowning excellence of the Gospel, perceiving no way of reconciling the statements of the two Apostles with each other, rashly pronounced the letter of James an epistle of straw, and refused to acknowledge its inspired authority. The Romish Council of Trent, on the contrary, relying exclusively on the passage in James, enacted the following decree and anathema, in opposition to the Protestant doctrine, "Whosoever shall affirm that the good works of a justified man are, in such sense, the gifts of God, that they are not his worthy merits, and that he really does not deserve increase of grace and eternal life, let him be accursed." Had the Romanists, on the one hand, and Luther on the other, directed their attention to the respective designs of the two Apostles, and the scope of their epistles, both would probably have come to a different and harmonious decision. St. James' object was to warn converted Jews of the danger of relying on the mere profession of faith. He would have them understand directly, that obedience must accompany the Christian faith; and that a man who was satisfied with merely saying he believed, to the neglect of holy living, was like a body without a vital spirit. An inoperative faith is a dead faith, and without avail. It must be a living principle in the soul, or it is nothing. In all this St. James has no reference to the question on what ground is a man justified (i. e. pardoned and accepted) in the sight of God? It was St. Paul's object to answer that question. St. James had another point, wholly distinct, before his mind. He intended to enforce practical piety, and maintained, not, in opposition to St. Paul, that men are not pardoned by faith, but that an alleged faith, unaccompanied and unevidenced by obedience, was no faith at all. In this sense the declaration of St. James is to be understood; and so interpreted, it does not contradict, but confirms the doctrine of St. Paul.

The scope of a writing may be ascertained by examining into the particular *occasion* and *circumstances*, which led to its composition, and the *class* of *persons* addressed or had specially in view. Sometimes it may be learned from the *express mention* or *clear intimation* of the writer or speaker himself. See John 20: 31. Lu. 1: 1-4. 2 Pet. 3: 1. 1 Jo. 2: 14. Prov. 1: 1-4. In several of our Lord's Parables we find their design expressly announced, so that there could be no mistake as to their particular application. See Lu. 12: 15. 18: 1. With respect to the scope, two canons are to be observed:—

1. No *argument from scope is allowable, when the scope is not ascertained with certainty.* Writers frequently make a scope to suit their own purpose. When the design of the writer or speaker is known with certainty, too much stress cannot be laid upon it in interpretation.

2. In the argument from scope, *the alleged scope must necessarily demand the alleged interpretation.* It is not sufficient that the interpretation should harmonize with the scope, and that it should serve to promote it. For it might do both without being the true interpretation. That which is in opposition to the scope, cannot, indeed, be the true meaning, but a false meaning may be in harmony with the scope. All parts of a discourse have not invariably a strict connexion with its general scope; many things being often introduced which are merely *obiter dicta.* These are to be interpreted not by the general scope of the discourse, but agreeably to the subject treated of, in the place where they occur.

Next to the context and scope, the most important aid in the investigation of the usage of words and the meaning of sentences, is *the comparison* of *similar* or *parallel passages.* By these are meant passages, whether occurring in the writings of the same author, or of different authors, which contain substantially the same idea, expressed either in the same or equivalent terms. Where the same words occur, whether in the same or a different sense, the parallelism is said to be *verbal;* and where the same idea is expressed, though the words may be different, the parallelism is *real.* There is therefore a parallelism of *words,* and a parallelism of *ideas;* or of both words and ideas. The comparison of passages, between which the similarity is only verbal, is highly important for ascertaining the usage of the language. For this purpose the student should make diligent use of such works as The Englishman's Hebrew Concordance, and Greek Concordance; Robinson's Greek Lexicon of the New Testament, and his Translation of Gesenius' Hebrew Lexicon. When the same words, however, are used in a different sense, or in relation to a different subject, the passages are not really parallel and throw no light upon each other. It is only the parallelism of ideas that is of much importance to the interpreter, and those passages only are to be placed in juxtaposition either for exposition or illustration, which relate to the same subject, and convey substantially the same sentiment. It is in reference to such passages that the Canon applies: *Compare Scripture with Scripture; "spiritual things with spiritual."* It is by the observance of this comprehensive rule alone that we become sure of the true meaning of particular passages. In the examination of parallel passages a certain order should be observed. We should seek for parallels 1. in the writings of the same author. 2. in the compositions of other sacred writers.

1. Every correct writer is accustomed to use the words he employs in one and the same

sense, when treating of the same subject. That sense may be peculiar to himself: hence we find that Paul, Peter and John use the same words in a different sense from each other, as well as adopt a different style of expression. We have a strikirg instance of this, as it regards St. John, in the use of ὁ λόγος, *the Word*, as denoting the Godman Christ Jesus. (Comp. Jo. 1: 1. 14. 1 Jo. 1: 1. Rev. 19: 13.) Consequently a difficult passage of an evangelist or apostle is best explained by a comparison of parallel passages in *his own* writing. The style of a writer in treating of the same subject will at one time be more concise and obscure, at another, more diffuse and clear; and as consequently both easy and difficult passages may be expected to occur in his writings, when treating of the same subject, so it is a dictate of sound reason to explain the obscure and doubtful passages by the clear and unequivocal, the difficult by the easy, and to employ the more diffuse in eliciting the sense of the briefer propositions, e. g. In Heb. 1: 3. the phrase "by himself" is an elliptical form of expression, and the meaning is uncertain. But if we compare it with Heb. 9: 26. where the full form occurs, "by the sacrifice of himself," the meaning is made plain. Some expositors assert that the phrase "all things" (τά πάντα) in Col. 1: 16, signifies the *new moral creation*. But in 1 Cor. 8: 6. the same phrase is employed in the sense of *all created things*,—the material world—and the act of creation in this sense is ascribed to the Father and the Son. The doctrine of justification by faith, or gratuitous justification, is discussed by St. Paul, both in his Epistle to the Romans, and in that to the Galatians; but it is elaborated more fully in the former than in the latter. They should be studied, therefore, in connexion. There is great similarity between the Epistle to the Ephesians and that to the Colossians in regard both to the words, style and sentiment. Hence they shed mutual light on each other, and should be studied concurrently.

2. But we may go beyond the compositions of the same writer, and refer to parallels in any part of Scripture. It is manifestly proper, however, that the works of *contemporary* writers should be consulted before those of others. In the Old Testament this mode of conducting parallel investigation is particularly important, because the nature of the Hebrew language varied remarkably at different periods. The later Hebrew of Kings and Chronicles is very different from the earlier of the Pentateuch. But the component parts of the New Testament Canon were written almost contemporaneously. Again: it is obviously the dictate of common sense, that writings of the same general character should be brought together for mutual illustration rather than such as belong to different classes of composition. Hence prophetical passages should be compared with prophetic, historical with historical, and poetical with poetical. The Books of Kings and Chronicles should be read in connexion, because they relate to the same periods of Jewish history, and reflect mutual light on each other. In like manner, and for the same reason also, should the Gospels be read, particularly the first three, or synoptical Gospels, as they are termed.

The poetical compositions of the Hebrews are

characterized by another kind of parallelism, called the parallelism of members, which is deserving of special attention. Each verse or short period usually consists of two members, between which there exists a certain relation of thought, by virtue of which one corresponds with the other, so as to produce a beautiful proportion. This peculiarity runs throughout the books of Job, Psalms, Proverbs, Canticles, and most of the Prophets. Sometimes the parallelism is *synonymous* or *gradational*, giving precisely the same thought, or the same thought with some extension. Sometimes the parallelism is *antithetic;* containing opposite terms, and not unfrequently opposite sentiments. The Book of Proverbs abounds in antithetic parallelism. This peculiarity of Hebrew poetry is occasionally to be met with in the New Testament, and penetrates even the prosaic compositions of the evangelical writers. The late Bishop of Limerick (Dr. Jebb) has given some happy illustrations of this in his Sacred Literature. In regard to parallelisms of this class, the principal idea which lies at the ground of both parts of the distich should be first ascertained; and then the several parts or members should be subjected to a minute examination.

The foundation of the parallelisms occurring in the sacred writings is the perpetual harmony of Scripture itself, which, though composed by various writers and in different ages, yet proceeding from one and the same infallible source, cannot but agree in the sentiments it expresses. This is called *the analogy* (similarity) of *Scripture,* and upon this is based its self-interpreting power.

The principle of illustrating an author by comparing him with himself, or with other authors, who write on the same subject, or were formed in the same school, seems so natural and so obviously just, that even Roman Catholics have not refused a qualified admission of it Thus Father Lami, an enlightened but zealous disciple of the Romish Communion, in his Apparatus Biblicus, where he is delivering rules for interpreting Scripture, writes as follows: "When the same thing is expressed obscurely in one place and clearly in another, that which is clear must serve as a rule by which to explain that which is obscure, and the light in one passage must be employed to dispel the darkness of another." But this rule is laid down in connexion with another in which is enjoined a strict adherence to the interpretation of the Church, whatever that interpretation may be. Thus the analogy of Scripture is admitted as a principle of interpretation but in subordination to the dogmatic law, that, "it belongs to the Church, to judge of the true sense and interpretation of Scripture."

The following directions are important to be observed in the comparison of parallel passages, whether historical, doctrinal, or ethical:

1. The interpreter should satisfy himself that the passages which he brings into comparison; are *real*, and not merely *verbal*, parallelisms. In many instances this cannot be done without consulting the Scripture in the original, because in our standard version different Hebrew or Greek words are often translated by the same English word, and as frequently the same Hebrew or Greek words are represented by different Engligh words.

2. A passage which is more concise should be explained by one which is more full and particular, and consequently less open to doubt and dispute from ambiguity. The maxim applies here in its full extent. "*Pauciora exponi debent per plura.*" e. g. Lu. 6: 20. "Blessed are ye poor." This passage should be interpreted by the aid of Matt. 5: 2. "Blessed are the poor in Spirit." The explanatory adjunct "in Spirit," shows very clearly who are meant by "the poor." Ma. 10: 11 and Lu. 16: 18 should be explained by Matt. 5: 32. where we find the exception "fornication" introduced as a just ground for divorce; which is omitted by the other two Evangelists. Comp. also Lu. 12: 20. with Matt. 12: 32.

CHAPTER XVIII.

ANALOGY OF SCRIPTURE—ANALOGY OF FAITH.

The Harmony of different passages of Scripture, relating to the same subject, which form the subject of the preceding chapter, belongs to what is denominated the *Analogy of Scripture.* This principle of analogy is based on the Inspiration of the sacred writers, and is a logical sequence from the position, that the entire volume of revealed truth is substantially the emanation of one infallible mind. This Analogy is consistent with apparent discrepancies, but incompatible with the admission of real contradictions, in the sacred volume. The old Protestant canons on this subject were, *Scriptura sua in-*

terpres, "Scripture its own interpreter," and *Non nisi ex Scriptura Scripturam potes interpretari.* "You cannot interpret Scripture except from Scripture" A portion of the Rationalistic school of interpreters, however, rejecting the inspiration of Scripture, have recently substituted for the principle in question, the following rule: *Interpret Scripture from itself*: by which they mean, that each passage is to be explained apart from, and independently of, any connexion with other portions of a different age or writer. According to this rule, the Biblical student has simply to make himself familiar with that part of Scripture which he attempts to explain, regardless of other passages relating to the same subject to be found in other portions of the sacred volume. He may put upon it such a construction as he thinks it will bear, without troubling himself to inqure whether that meaning agrees or disagrees with the clearly ascertained sense of other passages.

The principle of Scriptural analogy admits of a much more extensive application, and a much wider scope, than parallel passages. It embraces the entire scheme of revealed religion and the general tenor of Scripture in regard to all material facts, doctrines and precepts. In this wider application it is usually denominated the *analogy of faith*, or of Scripture doctrine. The Bible contains but one and the same religion throughout, though existing under different and successive dispensations. Hence there must exist a correspondence and harmony between its several doctrinal statements and the general scheme of revelation, so that one class of texts relating to a particular doctrine or moral duty, cannot conflict with the true sense of another class, relating to kindred doctrines in the scheme of religion, by which the truth of those doctrines is established to the satisfaction of the interpreter.

Illustrations.—No truth is asserted more frequently in the Bible, and consequently none is more certain in religion, than that God is good, not only to some individuals, but also towards all men. See Ps. 145 : 9. Ez. 18 : 23. Frequently, in the Old Testament, as well as in the New, does the Almighty declare how earnestly he desires the sinner's return to him. See, among other passages, Deut. 5 : 29. Ez. 18 : 32 and 33: 11. Matt. 23 : 37. John 3 : 16. 1 Tim. 2 : 4. Titus 2 : 11. 2 Pet. 3 : 9. If, therefore, any passages occur, which at first sight appear to contradict the benevolence of God, in such case, the clear and certain doctrine relative to the divine goodness is not to be impugned, much less set aside by these obscure places, which, on the contrary, ought to be illustrated by such passages as are more clear and indisputable. One such passage is alleged to exist in Prov. 16 : 4. where, according to our authorized English version, we read, that "the Lord hath made all things for himself; yea, even the wicked for the day of evil." This passage, thus translated, has been supposed by several eminent writers to refer to the predestination of the elect, and the reprobation of the wicked. Interpreted in this way, it would seem to express a sentiment at variance with the general benevolence, as well as justice of God. But the sentiment which the passage contains, according to the common rendering, is simply this, that there is nothing in the world which does not contribute to the glory of God, and promote the accomplishment of his adorable and gracious designs. A more correct translation of the passage, however, and one which frees it of all appearance of contradiction, is this: "Jehovah hath made everything for its end" (or purpose,) "yea, even the wicked for the day of evil." i. e. Jehovah in the administration of his natural and moral government, has ordained an inseparable connexion between cause and effect, so that piety and uprightness will surely receive their appropriate reward; while punishment, sooner or later, will certainly follow the commission of unrepented sin. John 4: 24. "God is a Spirit." This *locus classicus* is explicit and indisputable in support of the doctrine of the Spirituality and immateriality of God; and if there were no other passage in the Bible in which the same truth is affirmed or implied, no one would be disposed to call it in question. It is a fundamental article of belief among all who admit the existence of a Supreme Being at all. Now the analogy of faith demands, that we interpret all those passages which seem to represent God as material, as possessed of a human form, human organs, human limbs, and human passions, agreeably to this clearly revealed and universally admitted truth. The language, in such cases, is regarded very properly as figurative and analogical.

The same remark applies to all those passages which appear to represent God as local or limited in knowledge, in power, in righteousness. They must be explained consistently with those clear passages, in which he is set forth as omniscient, omnipotent, holy and just. Again: in the beginning of St. John's Gospel, Jesus Christ is called *God.* The question arises, is the appelative here used in its highest sense? Or does it import merely one personally or officially exalted or venerable, (godlike): just as magistrates and angels are sometimes called gods? Unitarians maintain the latter opinion; but to refute it, and remove all doubt as to the meaning of the Apostle, we collect all the passages which relate to Christ, and we find divine works and attributes ascribed to him, divine names given to him, and divine honors paid to him. The conclusion, therefore, to which the unprejudiced mind involuntarily comes is this, that He who is said to have created the world, who sustains it, who is omniscient, possesses all power in heaven and on earth, must be the Supreme God, and not merely godlike, and consequently that there need be no hesitation from the analogy of faith in understanding the term as here used in its highest sense. "And their works do follow them." Rev. 14: 13. This clause by itself will fairly bear the interpretation, that the good works of the pious dead follow them into eternity, as the ground of their acceptance and happiness there. But this interpretation is refuted by the analogy of faith. For we find that, not only is such a sentiment not avowed by any sacred writer, but it is directly opposed to the doctrine of salvation by the alone merits of Jesus Christ. We conclude, therefore, that it cannot be the real meaning of the words, intended by the writer. The works of the righteous do, indeed, follow them into eternity, and undergo the scrutiny of omniscience there, as furnishing a test of their faith and fidelity; but it is not for these good works, that they are saved. Salvation is the gift of God, conferred by grace through faith, and not the purchase or reward of good works.

James 5: 20. "He who converteth the sinner from the error of his way, shall save a soul from death, and shall hide a multitude of sins." This text will bear two distinct constructions. 1. The soul saved and the multitude of sins covered, may refer to the person who reclaims his erring brother; or 2. The words may refer to the brother reclaimed. Now if the appeal be made to the general system of revealed truth to determine which of these is correct, we shall find that the first is wholly at variance with it. We are saved by faith in Christ, not by acts of kindness done to an erring brother. Hence we conclude the meaning of the passage to be, that he who reclaims a backslider is the instrument of saving that backslider's soul and procuring the pardon of his sins.

Again: *The kingdom of God is moral and spiritual.* So the Saviour has most explicitly declared. "The kingdom of God cometh not with observation; neither shall they say, Lo, here! or lo, there! for behold, *the kingdom of God is within you.*" Lu. 17: 20, 21. So also says St. Paul: "The kingdom of God is not meat and drink, but righteousness, and peace, and joy in the Holy Ghost." Rom. 14: 17. So said Jesus to Pilate: "My kingdom is not of this world—my kingdom is not from hence." John 18: 46 These explicit declarations are in accordance with the whole tenor of the Bible. This truth lies on the face of all its requisitions, commands, and promises; and on the face of the qualifications demanded of all who would belong to this kingdom. To enter it man must undergo a *spiritual* change. To remain faithful to his allegiance, he must combat and conquer his *spiritual* enemies. To attain its highest rewards, he must profess *holiness* and purity of heart. It is manifestly, therefore, not a material kingdom; it is not a politico-ecclesiastical kingdom. It is internal, having its outward manifestations in the life. The reign of God is in and over the soul. It is so in this life; it is so in the life to come. It is so now, and it will continue to be so, till the end of time. The analogy of Scripture doctrine, therefore, requires, that those passages which seem to speak of Christ's visible reign upon earth at some future period, and of his establishing a visible and politico-ecclesiastical kingdom on earth should be interpreted figuratively and spiritually, not literally.

The analogy of faith requires that, when, after a full examination of Scripture, a doctrine is proved to entire satisfaction by the consent of passages, or by clear and explicit statements, no passage should be understood as contradicting this; and further, that when any passage is ambiguous or susceptible of more than one interpretation, that meaning should be preferred, which is most accordant with the whole scheme of revealed religion and the general current of Scripture. It is in this way that philosophy interprets natural phenomena; when once a general law is established, particular facts are placed under it, and any appearance that seems contradictory is specially examined; and of two explanations of the apparent anomaly, that one is chosen which harmonizes best with the general laws.

If we would comprehend the sense in which God speaks to man, we must contemplate revelation, not in its fragments, but as a whole. We may not be able to frame a system from the Scriptures, which will be logically complete in all its parts. Links may be wanting in the chain, which we may be unable to supply. But the grand outline of Christian doctrine cannot be easily mistaken. where the heart is duly prepared to embrace the truth. The essential doctrines and precepts of revealed religion are presented so frequently on the pages of the sacred volume, that none truly desirous of knowing the will of God, can well fail to discover them. In regard to these the voice of Scripture is uniform, and this uniformity constitutes the analogy of faith, and becomes a law of interpretation of very frequent and extensive application. It is not necessary, that a doctrine, in order to come within the scope of this analogy, and be received with the utmost assurance, should be uncontroverted; for almost every truth of God has been controverted. But it must be proved to the conviction of all who appeal to this analogy, before the rule can be applied as a principle of interpretation. This analogy is a rule to the expositor himself. If others dispute what he believes to be concurrently taught in the Word of God, and by the aid of which he rejects one meaning of a passage, and adopts another, the principle will be useful only to himself. But should they agree with him in acknowledging the inculcation of revelation, this analogy then becomes a rule not only to the individual himself, but also to those who coincide with him in opinion. Neither systems of philosophy, or of

Divinity, nor the Creeds and Confessions of different churches, constitute this rule of analogy, although nothing is more common than the substitution of such systems and Creeds for the Word of Life. The utility and even necessity of some formulary of faith, either written or unwritten, to the maintenance of an outward ecclesiastical organization, and to the promotion of Christian communion and fellowship, cannot be successfully controverted. Such a formulary, in order to accomplish the ends contemplated by it, and to accord with the genius and design of the Gospel, should evidently consist, like the Apostles' Creed, of a brief statement of the principal facts and essential doctrines of Revealed religion, expressed in simple and perspicuous language, and divested as much as possible of all metaphysical subtleties and distinctions, foreign to the Bible. Creeds more or less sharp and circumstantial have existed in the Church throughout all its branches from the Apostles' age down to the present time. A few modern sects, it is true, claim that they have no creed except the Bible; but the only difference in this respect between them and others is, that their creed is unwritten. At the same time, it must be remembered that human creeds are not a rule or standard of interpretation; for if they were, the rule would vary with every existing dogmatic formulary, and every system of theology, which the ingenuity of man has devised, and consequently would be worthless. "Whatever is not read therein" (in the Bible) says the Protestant Episcopal Church in her Articles of Religion, "nor may be proved thereby, is not to be required of any man, that it should be believed as an article of faith."

On the contrary, it is a dogmatic law in the system of hermeneutics, received by the Romish Church, that "*there is in the Church of Christ* (meaning the Church of Rome) *a certain standard of interpretation distinct both from the Scripture itself, and the private judgment of the reader; to which standard all interpretation of Scripture must be conformed.*" This standard of interpretation thus extrinsic both to the Bible and to private or individual judgment, is claimed to be "that body of doctrine of which the *Apostolic teaching* was composed." This apostolic teaching, independent of Scripture and furnishing the rule for its interpretation, is alleged to be found in the writings of the Christian fathers, which have preserved the traditions of the Church. This standard, we are told, has positively declared the meaning of some parts of Scripture, and in regard to such passages this meaning must be given to the sacred text. And as to the other parts of Scripture, which are not positively explained by this standard, we must take care not to give to them any interpretation which would be opposed to it. According to the Romish Church, then, the analogy of faith is not the harmony of Scripture with itself, but the harmony of Scripture with tradition, and the traditional teaching of the fathers is made by this law the touchstone to which the word of God must be brought, and tried and explained.

Thus an arbitrary law, having no foundation or authority in reason, and recognized no where else in the domain of Literature, is made to override and supersede to the broad extent of its application, all acknowledged hermeneutical principles; and the whole science of interpretation, by the powerful spell of this magic wand, is circumscribed within such narrow limits, as to be practically useless. Holding such a law, is it surprising that the Romish Priesthood should look with disfavor on the general circulation of the Scriptures, and positively forbid the reading of them by the people except in their own authorized translation and accompanied with notes and comments in support of the dogmas of their Church.

CHAPTER XIX.

LAWS OF INTERPRETATION.

CANON IV.

The same words when they stand in the same connexion, are to be interpreted in one and the same sense.

The object which an author in his discourse or writing has in view is to communicate his ideas to others by the aid of words. These, however, would not express his thoughts intelligibly, if the same words when occurring in the same connexion, were used sometimes in one sense, and sometimes in another. He would be constantly liable to be misunderstood. Nothing can be more unreasonable and more likely to mislead than an arbitrary variation without notice in the meaning of important words in the same passage. This canon is not, however, of universal application. Sometimes the same word is designedly repeated in the closest connexion in a different sense even in serious discourse. In such cases, however, which are not very numerous, the difference is generally rendered so obvious by circumstances, that there can be no reasonable doubt of the change of meaning.

Illustrations.—Matt. 8 : 22. "Let the dead bury their dead." Here the word *dead* is used first in a figurative or *moral* sense, as in Rev 3 : 1. and then *literally.* Rom. 9 : 6. "They are not all Israel (i. e. Spiritual Israel) who are of Israel." (i e. the literal Israel.) 2 Cor. 5 : 21. "He hath made him to be *sin,* (i. e. a sin-offering) for us who knew no *sin,* (i. e. who was conscious of having never committed sin.) The figure employed in such cases is called antanaclasis.

CANON V.

Universal terms are often employed in a limited sense, as signifying only a very large amount in number or quantity.

Illustrations.—Ex. 9 : 6. "All the cattle of Egypt died." The connexion in which this passage occurs, shows that this clause refers to some of *all kinds*, rather than the *absolute totality* of the number spoken of; for in subsequent parts of the same chapter, the cattle of the king and people of Egypt are mentioned in such a way as shows that a considerable part of the nation's property of this description still remained. Again: Ex. 9 : 25. "The hail smote every herb of the field, and brake every tree of the field." A few days after this, we find the devastation of the locusts thus described: "They did eat every herb of the field, and all the fruit of the trees, which the hail had left." Ex. 32: 3. "All the people brake off the golden earrings which were in their ears, and brought them unto Aaron." That the phrase "all the people," here simply denotes a large number, and not the whole, or even a majority of the people, may be reasonably inferred from the circumstance, that the stroke of punitive justice, for this act of idolatry, fell only upon 3000 persons, while the totality of Hebrew men at that time capable of bearing arms, was 600,000. Matt. 3: 5. "There went out to him Jerusalem and all Judea, and all the country about the Jordan." A large number only can here be intended. We find the phrase "*under heaven*," employed by the inspired writers to signify an extent of country large, indeed, but falling far short of a geographical universality. Acts 2: 5. "There were dwelling at Jerusalem, Jews, devout men, out of every nation *under heaven*." With this passage is combined a geographical enumeration, which points out the extent of country intended by "every nation" —as being from Italy to Persia, and from Egypt to the Black Sea. (See also Col. 1: 23.) Rom. 11: 26. "Then all Israel shall be saved." i. e. the greater part, and not every individual. Deut. 28: 63, 64. "Ye shall be plucked from off the land whither thou goest to possess it, and the Lord shall scatter thee among *all people*, from one end of the earth even unto the other end of the earth." This is a poetic description of the dispersion of the Jewish people, as the punishment of their apostacy from God, and their rejection of the Messiah: but no one can regard the expression as denoting a proper geographical universality. The expressions "all lands" and "all nations" in 1 Chron. 14: 17. cannot be taken as reaching beyond the range of Syria, Armenia, Mesopotamia, Arabia, and Egypt. 1 Kgs 10: 24 "And *all the earth* sought the presence of Solomon to hear his wisdom." This must be supposed to refer merely to the resort of embassies and complimentary visits from sovereigns and States within such a distance of the metropolis of the Hebrew monarchy, as might have appeared immense in those times, but which was quite small as compared with the then inhabited parts of the earth. Our Saviour says of the Queen of Sheba, who was one of the principal of these visitants, and whose dominions were on the eastern side of the Red Sea, only about 12 or 1400 miles south of Jerusalem, —that she "that came from the *uttermost parts of the earth* to hear the wisdom of Solomon." The language employed in instances such as these is in fact a natural hyperbole belonging not to artificial rhetoric, but to the dialect of common life.*

CANON VI.

It is a common usage in Scripture to express a disparity between two objects by a rejection of the less.

Thus in Hos. 6: 6. Jehovah says, "I desire mercy and *not* sacrifice," i. e. rather than sacrifice. Both mercy and sacrifice are important, and both are therefore commended; yet the former is to be regarded as of superior excellence. Moral duties occupy a higher ground

---

* See J. Pye Smith's Lectures on Geology.

than ritual observances. John 6: 27. "Labor *not* for the meat which perisheth, but for that which endureth unto everlasting life," by which our Lord doubtless meant that we should labor chiefly for the latter, and give it the preeminence in our thoughts and efforts. St. Paul declares (1 Cor. 1: 17) that Christ had sent him *not* to baptize, but to preach the Gospel. i. e. the preaching of the Gospel was to be his main business, and baptizing, though important, was to occupy a subordinate place. Eph. 6: 12. "We wrestle *not* against flesh and blood;" i. e. our struggle is not only, or not chiefly, against human beings, but against superhuman adversaries. In Ex. 16: 2. it is said that "the whole congregation murmured against Moses and Aaron;" while in ver. 8. it is said "your murmurings are *not* against us, but against the Lord." The criminality of the people in murmuring against God was so flagrant, as to make their offence against their human superiors unworthy of notice. Acts 5: 4. "Thou hast *not* lied unto men, but unto God," i. e. not so much unto men as unto God.

CANON VII.

The natural and obvious meaning of a passage or sentence is usually the true meaning.

A man of sense will speak or write in order to be understood, unless he has a particular object to gain by employing ambiguous terms and expressions. It is, therefore, to be presumed that he will express himself by the use of well-chosen and appropriate words, as clearly and intelligibly as possible. Hence the more easy and natural interpretation—that which lies plainly on the surface, and which would ordinarily first occur to the mind of the hearer or reader as the meaning, should be preferred to one which is difficult and less obvious. This law does not imply, of course, that every word in the sentence or proposition should be employed in its primary or literal sense: for the figurative meaning of a word may be just as plain and intelligible to the most common apprehension as the literal meaning. But it has reference to the entire thought contained in the passage. This canon, however, has several exceptions and limitations.

1. When the literal or apparent meaning asserts that which involves a known impossibility, or a strong improbability, it must be given up.

Illustration.—Ps. 58; 3. "The wicked are estranged from the womb; they go astray, as soon as they are born, speaking lies."

The meaning of the letter here is, that the wicked sin from the moment in which they are born; and that from the same moment, they both walk, and speak lies, which is a natural impossibility. Ps. 51: 5. "Behold, I was shapen in iniquity; and in sin did my mother conceive me." Interpreted strictly according to its literal and apparent meaning, this passage would impeach the chastity of David's mother—a supposition unwarranted by history and having no probability in its favor. Such passages as these belong to the domain of rhetoric, and are to be interpreted by poetic license, as the strong language of hyperbole. They are not the material with which dogmatic theology should be constructed.

2. When the literal and apparent meaning contradicts any positive precept of Scripture, it

must be abandoned. The principle of self-consistency attributed to the Bible forms the basis of this exception.

Illustration.—Eph. 4: 26. "Be ye angry, and sin not." This appears to be inconsistent with v. 31. in which all anger is forbidden How then are we to reconcile the two passages? Various methods have been adopted to remove the apparent discrepancy. All agree that it is not a command to be angry. The whole tenor of Scripture forbids such a construction. Some render both clauses of the verse interrogatively: "Are ye angry? and do ye not sin?" But the context forbids such a construction. Others render only the first clause interrogatively: "Are ye angry? yet sin not." Others interpret the passage hypothetically: "If, or though, ye be angry, sin not." Others still, take the imperative in a permissive sense: "Be angry," (viz. when the occasion properly authorizes anger): "yet sin not." (viz. by yielding immoderately to the emotion, and thus cherishing a harsh and unchristian temper.) These interpreters allege that anger is not in itself necessarily sinful, and that it is only *causeless*, (Matt. 6: 22.) or *excessive* anger which is forbidden. The emotion described by the word "anger" (ὀργή) is complex, and consists in a sense of personal wrong, unjustly inflicted, and a feeling more or less intense towards the author of the supposed injury. The first is doubtless a feeling entirely proper: for it is involuntary and necessary to keep alive in our minds the distinction between right and wrong in human conduct. The sinfulness of the other depends upon its degree and character. If it rises to the height of a desire for revenge, it is a wrong feeling and expressly forbidden. But if it terminates in mere displeasure, or just indignation, it is not sinful. Both feelings, or the two combined, are expressed in Scripture by the term anger. Thus when our Saviour is said to have looked "round about" on the perverse Jews "with anger," nothing more is intended than that he was filled with virtuous indignation at their conduct. (Ma. 3: 5.) It is in this sense also that anger is attributed to God. But even when justifiable, the feeling is not to be cherished and perpetuated. "Let not the sun go down upon your wrath." i. e. your anger must not only be moderate and entirely free from the spirit of revenge, but it must be of short duration; it must not be allowed to have any continued influence in the mind.

3. The obvious meaning is not the true meaning, when there is an express limitation of it elsewhere affirmed.

Illustration.—John 1: 11, 12. "He came unto his own, and his own received him not." We should infer from this passage taken by itself, that not a solitary Jew believed in Christ. But the very next sentence contains the necessary limitation. "But as many as received him, to them gave he power," &c. A very slight examination of St. John's writings, whose style is the most simple and direct of all the Evangelists, will supply many more illustrations. See also Judg. 9: 5. Matt. 26: 60. Jo. 1: 8. comp. with ch. 3: 9. In 1 Chron. 23: 13. it is said that the Aaronic priesthood is established forever. But from Jere. 31: 31–34. and Heb. viii. and ix. we learn that the continuance of the priesthood, and indeed of the whole Levitical dispensation, is limited to the appointed time, when that dispensation should pass away and be succeeded by another more perfect and more enduring.

4. When the apparent meaning is frigid, inept, forced or trifling, it cannot be the meaning intended. Such a meaning is to be rejected as unworthy of inspiration, and of the dignity and gravity of the subject. By *inept* is meant when a sentiment is imputed to a writer, which is alike foreign both to his constant manner of thinking and speaking, and to his intention and object. That interpretation which does violence in any way to the true meaning of another's words, is called a *forced* interpretation. A *forced* interpretation is opposed to that which is *facile*, and differs from *false*. An interpretation which is foreign to the *words themselves*, or ungrammatical, is *false*: whereas an interpretation may be entirely grammatical and yet forced. That is a *forced* interpretation which is contrary to the ordinary usage of the writer, or at variance with a due regard to the persons, times and places in and for which he wrote, or incongruous to the series of the discourse.

CANON VIII.

When any doctrine elsewhere clearly taught, is omitted in any passage, that passage is to be interpreted in harmony with the doctrine omitted

The occasional omission of an important doctrine in the course of an argument, is easily accounted for by a well known principle of the mind. The legal maxim expresses it thus: " It is impossible to think of every thing, to foresee everything, to express every thing." The omission of a doctrine, where we should expect to find mention of it, is, therefore, no proof that the doctrine is ignored.

Illustration.—Mark 16: 16. "He that believeth and is baptized, shall be saved." Here is an omission of repentance, as a condition of salvation. Matt. 28: 19. "Go ye, therefore, and teach all nations, baptizing them," &c. In this passage there is no expressive mention either of repentance or faith as a pre-requisite to baptism.

1 Tim. 2: 5. "There is one God, and one mediator between God and man, the man Christ Jesus." In this passage there is affirmed the unity of God and the mediatorship and humanity of Christ. But to quote this passage to prove that Christ is simply a man, would be a violation of our canon, because his divinity is elsewhere clearly and abundantly taught. The passage undoubtedly teaches the humanity of Christ; but it does not disprove his divinity. Just as in the sentence "man is mortal," there is an important truth omitted and the meaning of the sentence is to be determined in harmony with it. It does not disprove directly, or implied, the immortality of the soul. In Eph. 5: 23. it is said that "Christ is the Saviour of the body." Surely the apostle does not mean to assert that he merely saves the body, and leaves the soul to perish.

CANON IX.

Of two or more possible meanings of a passage, that is to be preferred which exhibits the most full and fertile sense.

The Holy Scriptures were appointed by God to enlighten and improve mankind in all ages and under all circumstances. It is, therefore, to be presumed that those books and passages, in which weighty religious truths are propounded, contain an important, rich, and comprehensive sense. It is not unfrequently the case that a passage of Scripture is grammatically susceptible of several meanings, all of which accord with the context and the analogy of Scripture; but one of them contains a fullness, (πληρωσις), richness and fertility of sense, not possessed by the others, which render it more instructive, and admits of a wider application than the others. This is to be preferred, because it answers best the end for which a revelation was given, and is, therefore, most likely to be the meaning intended by the inspired author.

This Canon is not intended to afford the least sanction to the practice of putting a sense into a writer's words, which he cannot be supposed to have himself attached to them. A certain class of expositors are in the habit of pressing each word of the sacred text, until every idea, which by mere possibility it might etymologically contain, is forced out, and alledge as a reason for this violent and singular method of treating the inspired volume, that by this operation the *pregnant sense*—'pragnantes sensus Scripturæ'—as they call it, and the holy emphasis of its expressions can alone be received in all their fullness. This method is pursued without the least regard to connexion, design, character of the writer, and coherence of his ideas. By this means they hope to make the sense of Scripture more edifying than it is likely to become by a mere grammatico-historical interpretation.

CANON X.

The Old Testament should be interpreted in the light of the New.

Much of the New Testament consists of exposition of the Old. The true intent and spirit of the latter are unfolded in the former. The discourses of our Saviour, and especially his sermon on the mount, are emphatically of this character. In these the falsity and carnality of the traditional interpretation are exposed, and the spiritual and comprehensive import of the Mosaic law are fully exhibited. It is true that the New Testament writers often quote the Old Testament by accommodation for the purpose merely of illustrating their subject. But it should also be remembered that very frequently, when they quote or refer to Old Testament texts, they cite them as proofs: and not only so, but they authoritatively interpret and apply them, drawing out their proper and full meaning as developed in the latter revelation. From their interpretation and application of the Old Testament there is no appeal; for the Divine inspiration of our Lord and his apostles, being received as an axiom in the science of Biblical hermeneutics—as a dogmatic law of interpretation, which must be constantly kept in mind; it follows that their expositions of the Old Testament must be regarded as infallible. By this rule we learn the import and fulfillment of the Old Testament prophecies respecting the Messiah, and the typical character of the Jewish sacrifices and of many historical personages and events under the ancient dispensation. The principle in question, however, should be applied only to such passages and events as are particularly referred to by the New Testament writers; and it prohibits us from interpreting a passage in the Old Testament in a different sense from that which is declared by Christ or his apostles, to be the true meaning. We may refer to the 2d and 16th Psalms in illustration of our rule. These Psalms are expressly declared by the New Testament writers to refer prophetically to Christ and the latter especially, both St. Peter and St. Paul affirm to apply to him exclusively. Hengstenberg, however, adopting the idealistic hypothesis, regards the 16th Psalm as generic and designedly descriptive of the whole class of pious sufferers; thus setting aside altogether its proper Messianic and prophetic character. In this he is followed by Dr. Alexander in his commentary on the Psalms. But with singular inconsistency, the same learned commentator in his valuable work on the Acts of the Apostles, maintains on the authority of the two apostles already named, that the psalm is messianic, and that the express and argumentative denial by both of them, that the words can be applied to David, "excludes not only the typical, but also the generic method of interpretation."*

CANON XI.

The revelations of God in their doctrinal and perceptive parts, have been adapted to the age, character, moral and intellectual development and circumstances of man; in other words, they have been progressive.

The race, like the individual, has its period of infancy, of childhood, of youth, and of maturity;

* See Alexander on Acts 2: 29, and 13: 35 37.

and the light communicated must be adapted to each of these periods respectively. The former, as well as the latter, requires to be educated; and this education is carried on partly by the ordinary providence of God, and partly by his extraordinary and special interposition. In respect to the supernatural process, Jehovah, after the flood, selected a particular family to be the favored depositors of his revealed will. Next a nation was chosen,—the descendants of that family;—and at last, the door of the Temple of Truth was thrown open to all mankind, and the Gospel was directed to be preached to all nations. The entire Bible, indeed, contains but one and the same doctrine, so far as respects the essential truths of revealed religion; yet the communication and development of these truths and of the corresponding duties which they involve, were gradual and progressive; and not immediately and at once complete. The notions which were entertained by men at various periods, or, in other words, the subjective ideas of religion, were far from being uniform, and the expression or exhibition of religious truths was necessarily proportioned to the more confined, or subsequently to the more enlarged views, the less refined or more rational knowledge which prevailed at separate periods, and among various successive generations of mankind. The moral weakness of the Hebrews in the time of Moses, and the strength of their sensual affections, and evil propensities, rendered it necessary to make some allowance to that people, and not to strain the divine law to too high a pitch of moral perfection. Thus our Saviour declares that it was on account of their "hardness of heart," that certain practices were permitted to continue among them, which are inconsistent with the higher law of Christianity. On this accouut polygamy, and concubinage, divorce on the most frivolous grounds, slavery, the avenging of blood, and several other things were not entirely prohibited, but only had limits assigned to them. Nothing can be more evident than that God has acted in his dealings with men on the principle of adapting his requirements to the capacity of the human race, and of raising the standard of duty in proportion to the intellectual and moral advancement of mankind, and the progress of a true civilization, and that he has regarded good men and their acts in a different manner under different degrees of light. Hence what has been tolerated in one age, ceases to be so in another, and even comes to be regarded as criminal in a third. Both the ignorance of man and the hardness of his heart, are elements which seem to have entered into the calculations of the Supreme Intelligence, (if the expression may be permitted) whenever he has vouchsafed a revelation of his will. In thus educating mankind step by step, the Creator has advanced the standard of piety and virtue, as men have become more capable of understanding the principles on which they rest. And it is not easy to see how this could have been otherwise; unless the Deity had hastened the progress of society by an overpowering and miraculous impulse. This, however, we know to be altogether alien from the general character of his providential government. The Mosaic institutions and laws were doubtless the best that could have existed at the time they were promulgated, among a people, who were yet at so low a degree of civilization. And is a demonstrative proof of the divinity and immutability of Christianity, that it lays down principles in religion and ethics adapted to the very highest state of moral culture to which man can attain in this world. In view of this great principle in the moral government of God, the interpreter in explaining the doctrines contained in the books of the Old Testam nt, should carefully guard against transferring to a former age the superior knowledge of subsequent periods—against obtruding upon ancient times and earlier dispensations that which only belongs to more recent times and to a later and more perfect dispensation.

CANON XII.

The com nands of God addressed to one man, or one generation of men are binding on other men and other generations only so far as their respective circumstances and conditions are similar.

This principle, which more properly respects the application than the interpretation of Scripture, is doubtless liable to evasion and perversion; but its truth cannot well be denied, and it is acted upon constantly by the Christian world. "So far," says Prof. Stuart, "as our circumstances and relations are like those of the persons to whom the Scriptures were originally addressed, so far what was said to them, is binding upon us; but no further." In consequence of the progressive character of Revelation, and its adaptation to the particular condition of man at certain periods of his intellectual and moral growth, some laws which were once required to be rigidly observed according to their literal exactness, have ceased to be obligatory in their strict sense; but inasmuch as in their *spirit* they were adapted to future periods and equally important and useful at all times, they are in that sense still in force: while other laws being intended only to be temporary, local, and confined to a particular dispensation, have passed away with that dispensation, and are no longer in force. It is so with human laws; and hence the legal maxims, "*Manente ratione manet ipsa lex*," and, "*cum cessat ratio legis, cessat ipsa lex.*" The *letter* of the injunction to hallow the Sabbath day, was in its utmost strictness, applicable only to the Jews; but the Supreme authority from which it proceeded—the solemnity with which it was inculcated—the position it occupies in the tables written by the finger of God—its admirable adaptation to the necessities of man both temporal and spiritual in every age,—all these and various other considerations which might be mentioned, combine to make it certain that this was no transitory institution. The *spirit* of the ordinance, therefore, survives the Mosaic economy, although the mere letter of it may have been abolished. It has lost nothing by the destruction of the Jewish polity, except those incidental circumstances, such as the precise day of the week, the prohibition to travel, etc., which have unavoidably dropped away from it in consequence of a change of dispensation, but which are not at all essential to the attainment of the ends contemplated by the law. Other laws have ceased altogether to be operative and obligatory. Such is the case with the sacrificial rites, the Levitical institutions and the ceremonial ordinances of the Hebrew ritual. Though prescribed by Jehovah, they have accomplished their purpose, and are no longer in force. They received their fulfilment in Christ, and by that fulfilment in the great antitype, they were abrogated and passed away.

CANON XIII.

The interpreter should endeavor to place himself in the identical situation and circumstances of the individual whose writings he interprets, and of those to whom they were immediately addressed.

Every man has some peculiarity, according to which his thoughts and the expression of them, are fashioned. It is a dictate of reason, that this peculiar characteristic, or individuality, of a writer, should be, as far as possible, studied and observed in interpretation. Accordingly, the expositor should endeavor to make himself acquainted with all those circumstances, which would have an influence in giving shape to this individuality; such as the author's country and origin; his education; the instruction which he received in his youth in religious and secular knowledge; his customary vocation and habits of life; his natural temperament and previous history; his manners, opinions, and relations, so far as they can be discovered, and as they stand in connexion with some one or more passages of his writings. A knowledge of these particulars will often throw great light on an author's meaning, and render that luminous which otherwise would be obscure and uncertain. The *occasion* which gave rise to the composition of a writing, is often the cause of an author's writing just what and in the manner he does, and no other. The time, place, and circumstances of a writer frequently determine his thoughts and sentiments, and influence the choice of his words and their combinations. Men are accustomed, moreover, to express themselves in various ways, according to the several states of mind in which they happen to be at the time of speaking or writing. The interpreter, therefore, should attentively consider the particular *state of mind* in which words are spoken or written; whether in a calm and collected, or in an excited state. Hence the rule: *a writer's language should be interpreted in conformity with his known character, previous history, habits of thought, opinions, religion, situation, and circumstances; and no principle foreign to the views and habits of the writer should be allowed to exert an influence on the interpretation of his writings, whether philosophical or theological.*

Again: Every author writes immediately for his contemporaries, or at least for a certain class of them. He is consequently expected to make choice of words and phrases, to which the reader is likely to attach the same ideas as the writer. Accordingly the interpreter must pay particular attention to the usage of words which prevailed at the time, to the modes of thinking, the sentiments, the manners and customs, of those for whom the writer composed his work. "That," says Planck, "may always be considered as the true sense of the writer to be explained, which either alone, or at least as the most natural sense, would be suggested by his expressions to the men, to whom, and for whom, he wrote." This remark. however, is not intended to authorize an interpreter to allow the spirit and mode of thinking of the age to modify or do away with the evident meaning of a passage; but merely to assist him in ascertaining what the meaning is. *Illustration:* The New Testament was written by native Jews, principally for the immediate benefit of Jewish converts to Christianity, who were acquainted only with the Greek language of common life. Consequently we should expect them not only to employ the common dialect (κοινη διαλεκτος), but to use particular words and phrases on religious subjects in a Hebraic rather than a classic Greek sense. Thus the phrase "You will die in your sins," (John 8: 24) would mean, according to the Greek idiom, *You will persevere to the end of life in sinning;* but according to the Hebrew, *You will be condemned on account of your sins.* It cannot be doubted, therefore, that the latter is the true meaning. Again: No one would have thought that oaths were forbidden on every occasion, in Matt. 5: 24. James 5: 12, provided he had sufficiently considered to *whom* the interdiction was made, and the customs and opinions which were particularly reprobated. For the persons here specially referred to, were probably those who at that time neither affirmed nor denied any thing, even on the most trifling occasions, without the addition of an oath, (Matt. 5: 37); and who thought that in an oath, in which they swore by heaven or by something else than God, even falsehood might be affirmed or truth denied, *without perjury*, which they supposed could not be committed, unless by those who introduced the name of Jehovah in their oaths. There is no reference whatever to judicial oaths, and there is no reason for supposing that a *necessary* oath *taken religiously in the name of God* is forbidden.

By carrying ourselves back into the age of the writer, and making ourselves familiar with the circumstances by which he was surrounded—the geography of the country, the history of the times, the customs, manners, and prevailing opinions of the people, and all the objects, natural and artificial, which most usually engaged their attention—we shall be enabled to understand, limit and apply expressions, which otherwise might be unintelligible, or which, from the imperfection of human language, are too general and extensive to be taken in their literal sense. To this end, the most valuable assistance may be derived from the study of Biblical Archæology, in which are collected into a focus all the most important facts from travels in the East and other sources, which illustrate the Bible.

It sometimes happens, however, that a speaker or writer propounds truths, which are either not understood at all, or very imperfectly apprehended by his hearers or first readers; or truths which are at variance with their educational prejudices, preconceived opinions and cherished sentiments. In that case, the sense of the author must be carefully distinguished from that in which his hearers or readers understand him. In such instances, the sense does not necessarily consist in that meaning which the hearers or readers attach to the words, but it is *that sense which the hearers or readers ought to attach to them.* Nothing is more common in the ordinary intercourse of life than for one person to misunderstand and misinterpret the meaning of another's language, even on trite and familiar subjects; and this, not simply in consequence of the intrinsic ambiguity of human language, but from the influence of prejudice. The difficulty is often wholly subjective, and lies in the heart of the hearer. This was pre-eminently the case with the Jews in their conversation with our Saviour. He employed terms and phrases which were in common use, such as *to be born again, regeneration, kingdom of heaven,* &c.; but he attached a deeper and more spiritual sense to them, than that to which his hearers were accustomed; hence they misunderstood or perverted his meaning. Nothing is more evident than that his hearers frequently misunderstood Christ. Thus, when he spake of the leven of the Pharisees and Sadduces, his disciples reasoned among themselves, saying, "It is because we have taken no bread." Matt. 16: 6. We may sometimes choose for wise reasons to speak obscurely and ambiguously. Lu. 9: 44, 45. John 2: 19. In enunciating the doctrines of the new dispensation, our Saviour and his Apostles were necessitated to employ words and phrases in a new and different sense, though somewhat similar to that which common use had assigned to them; for they taught many truths which were new and unknown to their hearers, or which, though revealed in the Old Testament, were not understood at the time. The contemporaries of Christ, for instance, allotted to their own nation exclusively, and perhaps to every individual in it, a place in Abraham's bosom. Yet Christ employs the Jewish phrase (Lu. 16: 22) to express the general idea of blessedness and enjoyment in company with Abraham; but instead of annexing to it the false notions of the Jews, he attaches other views entirely opposed to theirs. He teaches them in express terms, that the posterity of Abraham may be excluded from that happiness, and that strangers will be admitted to it.

CANON XIV.

The Interpreter must endeavor to attain to a sympathy in thought and feeling with the sacred writers, whose meaning he seeks to unfold: or, in other words, he must possess a kindred spirit with the author whom he interprets.

Such sympathy is not required for the interpretation of the inspired writings merely: it is equally necessary in respect to any author, ancient or modern, and the possession of it to some extent must be regarded as altogether indispensible. But it is pre-eminently necessary in reference to the sacred truths of revealed religion. Those who possess the state of heart enjoined in the word of God are most likely to succeed in its interpretation, because in their case, the mind is divested of prejudice and is in a kindred state to that of its author and the thing interpreted. It is on this principle that no man is competent to re-produce the life of Jesus, who is not in sympathy with the mind of Jesus. He may possess many and high qualifications for writing such a work, but he lacks one which is indispensible. No man in the light of this principle, can fail to see that such men as Strauss and Renan were not the men to write the Life of the Saviour. It is plain, that no man can truly understand St. Paul or St. John, whose mind has not been brought into harmony with theirs: has not been elevated and purified by the same spirit, with which they were filled. This was doubtless what the pious Spener intended by his much disputed assertion that none but the regenerated could understand Holy Scripture.

CHAPTER XX.

FIGURATIVE DISCOURSE AND REPRESENTATION.

In *rhetoric* the term *figure* is employed in quite a general sense. It denotes not merely a mode of speech, in which, as in the *trope* or *metaphor*, one or more words are changed from their literal and proper sense to one which is improper; but it is applied also, to a discourse, in which two thoughts or sentences, literally expressed, are placed in opposition to each other, in order to be more strikingly presented by contrast, as in antithesis. The term is further applied in its generic import to certain forms of literary composition, and to certain objective representations and significant actions, in which the idea of resemblance or analogy, either real or imaginary, intellectual, and arbitrary, is in some shape involved, and which constitutes their distinctive peculiarity.

Under the general head of figurative discourse and representation, we shall arrange certain topics, not already discussed, which appropriately belong to the science of Biblical hermeneutics, and are entitled to the special attention of the Biblical student.

I. *The Comparison or Simile.*—In every comparison there are two elements,—a subject of discourse and an object of comparison. These are placed side by side and viewed separately; the former being supposed to be but imperfectly known or understood, and needing illustration or ornament to make it more plain, or render it more vivid, attractive, and impressive; the latter being assumed to be well known, or easily understood, and introduced for the purpose of lending its light and beauty to the former. The design of the simile (Gr. αμοιωμα) is to suggest or trace the resemblance formally existing between the subject of discourse and the object with which it is compared; and which are in themselves dissimilar. To indicate the comparison the correlative signs *as* and *so* (Gr. καθως and ουτω or ουτως) are employed; the former being placed before the object of comparison, and the latter before the subject of discourse. e. g. "He was led *as* a lamb to the slaughter, and *as* a sheep before his shearers is dumb; *so* opened he not his mouth" Isa. 63: 7. Sometimes the comparison is indicated by the adjective *like* placed before the object of comparison. e. g. Alexander was *like* a lion It is characteristic of a comparison, or simile, that every word is to be taken in its proper sense, no word being turned out of its literal and usual signification. Thus in the example, "Alexander was like a lion," the subject and attribute are both to be understood literally; and Alexander is compared to a lion in consequence of a supposed resemblance between him and that animal in respect to certain peculiarities. So in the passage, "He was led as a lamb," &c.—the words *lamb* and *sheep* are to be taken in their proper and customary meaning, while the subject of discourse (the Messiah) is compared to these animals on account of a resemblance in certain specified particulars. Sometimes the object of comparison only is expressed, and the subject of discourse is inferred or left to be supplied by the reader; in which case, the correlative signs are also omitted. See Ma. 3 : 23. Lu. 5 : 36.

II. *The Metaphor.*—The *Metaphor* or *trope*, (Gr. μεταφορα, from μεταφερω, *to transfer;* and τροπος, from τρεπω, *to turn,*) is a figure of speech by which a word is transferred from the subject to which it properly belongs, and applied to another which has some similitude to its proper subject. This transferrence or substitution of some image for the thought which the image is designed to illustrate, is grounded on a tacit comparison which the mind makes between the image and the thought illustrated by it; and hence the simile is easily converted into a metaphor. e. g. "Alexander was like a lion"; this is a simile. "Alexander was a lion"; this is a metaphor. Thus it appears that the metaphor differs from the simile *in form* only, and not in substance. In the simile the subject and the object of comparison are kept distinct in the expression, as well as in the thought; in the metaphor the two are kept distinct in the thought only, and not in the expression, in which the two are blended. The metaphor, however, always asserts what is literally false; the comparison, on the contrary, asserts nothing but what is true. In the simile the predicate or attributive is to be interpreted literally; in the metaphor it is to be interpreted figuratively and analogically. Thus in the sentence, " Alexander was a lion," the predicate noun lion cannot be taken in its natural and proper signification, because in that case, the sense of the proposition would be, that the monarch referred to was literally the animal called a lion. The word "lion" as it stands in the metaphor is consequently transferred or turned from its proper meaning and made to designate a brave and courageous person;—this animal being conspicuous for these qualities. The simile is not the language of emotion, but supposes the mind of the writer or speaker to be in a cool and tranquil state, and hence it occurs in simple description, in plain narrative, and even in didactic discourse. But, if the mind is in an excited state, and the imagination is disposed to be excursive, it will naturally omit the words indicating the resemblance, and forcibly grasping the image, at once express itself in metaphor. The metaphor is based either on a resemblance of *things*, or a resemblance of *relations*. We have an example of the former in John 1: 29. "Behold the *Lamb* of God which taketh away the sins of the world." Here the name of the object of comparison is substituted for the subject of discourse, because the subject and object, in certain respects, resemble each other. Another instance occurs in Lu 13: 32, where our Lord calls Herod *a fox*. Herod's character bore a resemblance to the disposition of this cunning and crafty animal; and hence the name of the one is substituted for that of the other. As an example of the latter, take the declaration of Christ in John 6: 35. "I am the bread of life." Here the metaphorical expression rests on the mere resemblance of relations, i. e. the relation which bread sustains to the nourishment and preservation of *physical* life, is like that which Christ sustains to the extension and growth of the spiritual life.*

III. *The Fable or Apologue.*—This is called by the Greeks λογος, απολογος, and αινος, and by the Latins *fabula*. Though belonging to the general class of figurative composition, it differs entirely from the metaphor in that the figure does not appertain to the words or expression employed, but to the *thought*. The fable is a brief story intended to inculcate some virtue, expose some vice, or administer some sage counsel and advice. It is characterised by the following particulars: 1. Into the fable inferior animals are commonly introduced, and made to act a conspicuous part. 2. Circumstances highly improbable, or even entirely impossible, are related. Irrational creatures and even inanimate nature, are represented as thinking, speaking, acting, and talking in a manner entirely unsuited to their nature. The qualities and acts of a higher class of beings, are frequently attributed to a lower. The fable rejects probability, and teaches through the fancy; it is consequently pure fiction, and claims to be nothing else. Cicero defines it to be "that in which things are contained neither true nor probable." Not that the fabulist is regardless of truth; for it is neither his *intention* to deceive, when he attributes human language and actions to trees, birds, and beasts; nor is any one deceived by him. At the same time, the severer reverence for truth which appertains to the higher moral teacher, will not allow him to indulge freely in this mode of sporting with historic truth, and this obvious

* See Fairbairne's Hermeneutics.

departure from the well known laws of nature. And this is doubtless the reason why we have no instance on record of the use of the fable by our Saviour; and indeed only two clearly defined examples of this species of composition are to be found in the sacred volume; viz. Judg. 9: 7. seq. and 2 Kgs 14: 9. seq.

3. The fable confines itself to earthly virtues, prudential maxims, or commendable human qualities. And as these have their representatives in certain classes of irrational animals, these animals may be, and are, advantageously employed in the fable for imparting instruction. And if men are introduced in this species of composition, they always appear in a character allied to the animal, and not to the intellectual world. It is therefore essentially of the earth, and never lifts itself above the earth.

4. *The Myth.*—The myth (Gr μυθος) is a kind of fable or allegory, having truth for its basis, but which is wrapped up in the garb of fiction. It is a doctrine expressed in a narrative form—an abstract moral or spiritual truth, dramatized in action and personification;—where the object is to enforce faith, not in the historical verity of the narrative, but in the doctrinal or moral truth, which, as is supposed, it is intended to convey. A myth is not a designed invention, not a mere figment of the imagination, but a popular religious conception, applied, without warrant of fact, to some particular personage. Thus the Jews expected a Messiah possessed of certain attributes or qualities; the disciples thought Jesus to be the Messiah, and accordingly applied to him all the supposed qualities of the expected Messiah. So say the mythologists.

In mythology the course of the story is set before us as *the truth;* and uneducated and unreflecting minds, in a less imaginative age, receive it as the truth. It is only the reflective mind, which penetrates to the distinction between the vehicle and the truth conveyed by it. The myth would not have been noticed here, were it not that certain continental critics, followed by a few English imitators, have recently alleged that the Penteteuch abounds in myths; and that the biographies of our Saviour, written by the evangelists, are in a greater or less degree mythological.

IV. *The Allegory.*—The *Allegory* (Gr. αλληγορια, from αλλος and αγορευω, *to say one thing and mean another,*) is a figurative description or representation, in which *one* thing is expressed or represented, and *another* is intended; or a representation of *one* thing, which is designed to excite the representation of *another* thing that in certain respects bears a resemblance to it. Allegories not unfrequently occur in the Scripture. They are mostly, however of a mixed character; and consequently their intended application is more easily discovered, because expressions are introduced which disclose the principal object. The description of old age in Eccles. xii. is of this character. The book of Canticles is regarded by the most reliable expositors as an extended allegory, but belonging to the class of pure and unmixed allegories. In the New Testament, St. Paul's description of the Christian's armor, in his Epistle to the Ephesians, is allegorical. Many of the Proverbs of Solomon, and of the New Testament adages are of this nature. Allegory is not confined to verbal description; a painting, a piece of sculpture, or some architectural work may be allegorical. Mosier's statue of Silence is allegorical. The abstract idea of silence is first personified in the mind and then represented under the image of a female figure. Peal's Court of Death is an allegorical picture. Certain human figures are delineated on the canvass to represent the personification of abstract diseases.

The allegory has been frequently described by eminent writers as an extended metaphor; but there is a marked difference between the two. In an allegory there is an *immediate representation* called the *προτασις*, and an *ultimate representation* underlying the literal description, and running parallel with it, called the *αποδοσις*. In a metaphor likewise two things are presented to view, but in a very different manner from the allegory. In the metaphor there is but *one* meaning; in the allegory there are *two*. In the metaphor the principal subject is presented prominently to view; in the allegory it is concealed, and needs to be searched out. The metaphor always asserts or imagines that one object is another, e. g. "Judah is a lion's whelp." The Allegory, on the contrary, never affirms that one thing is another; but the two are kept entirely distinct; and the more perfectly this distinction is preserved, the more perfect is the allegory. If the subject of comparison is allowed occasionally to crop out, it becomes a mixed allegory, and, as a composition, is so far defective.

Again: in tropical expressions, the words taken in their proper and literal signification, afford no sense, or a false one, e. g. "The shield of faith," "the armor of righteousness." But in an allegory, the words composing the immediate representation, are severally to be taken in their customary meaning, as literal or figurative, and interpreted according to their grammatico-historical sense; and so taken and interpreted, they afford a consistent meaning. But from the context, the occasion, the intimation or express declaration of the writer or speaker, it appears that he intended to convey another and deeper meaning. Every allegory, therefore, must be subjected to a *twofold* examination; we must first examine the *immediate* representation, and then consider what other representation it is intended to excite. The *immediate* representation is of no further value, than as it leads to the *ultimate* representation. But this is not the case in the metaphor. Here there is but one representation, and no other is to be sought. Hence it appears that the interpretation of metaphors always remains an interpretation of *words;* whereas the interpretation of allegories is an interpretation of *things* Consequently a sequence of metaphors, or a metaphor prolonged, instead of being confined to a single word, never becomes an allegory, and is not subject to the same laws of interpretation.

Allegorical Interpretation.—When we undertake to interpret a writing, we undertake as a general rule, to ascertain and unfold the sense, which the writer had in his own mind, and designed by the language he employs to communicate to other minds. This kind of interpretation, we have seen, when applied to the Bible, takes the name of historical interpretation. But there is a different method, which that collection of sacred books has been thought by many to demand, and which goes by the name of *allegorical* interpretation. This phrase requires some explanation. It does not mean the right interpretation of allegories. To explain an allegory properly as such, according to the original design of the writer, is to interpret it historically. Allegorical interpretation is no more the interpr tation of allegories, than the interpretation of any other figure would properly take its name from that figure; no more, for instance, than the explanation of a hyberbole could be properly called *hyperbolical* interpretation, or the just exposition of a metaphor, *metaphorical* interpretation. Neither is allegorical interpretation the use of the words of another, whether containing narrative, doctrine, or something else, for the purpose of illustrating in an allegorized or accommodated application, one's own idea. If, the better to convey my own thoughts, I choose to frame an allegory, I may either create a figment of my own, or I may have recourse to something which already exists. But in the latter case, I do not attribute an allegory to the writer whose words I employ; I simply adopt his words in order to construct an allegory of my own. This has been done by St. Paul in his Epistle to the Galatians, (ch 4: 22–26,) in reference to the history of the two sons of Abraham, and hence he has been erroneously supposed to give his apostolic and inspired sanction to the system of allegorical interpretation. In our English version, the Apostle is made to say "which things are an allegory." Now, since an allegory is a picture of imagination, or a fictitious narrative, it has been inferred that St. Paul in this passage has warranted by his own declaration and conduct, the allegorical method of interpretation. Such, however, is not the case. In the instance referred to, St. Paul does not employ the Greek noun signifying allegory, nor indeed does it occur anywhere in the New Testament, nor even in the Septuagint Greek Version of the Old Testament. He does not pronounce the history *itself* to which he refers an allegory; but simply declares that it was *allegorized* by him, for the purpose of illustration. Now, it is one thing to say that a history is allegorized for a particular purpose, and quite another to say that it is *itself* an allegory. Allegorical interpretation, then, is neither of these two processes. The expression is employed in relation to two processes entirely distinct from these. The term allegorical is applicable to that interpretation which, without any demonstrable or assignable ground, and without warrant or authority from the context, or from significant marks of the plan, structure and coherence of the composition, assumes a representation or description to be altogether figurative: and in consequence, entirely rejects the *literal* and *historical* sense, and supposes another and improper sense, foreign to the design of the writer. The term allegorical is also appropriately used in reference to that interpretation which arbitrarily assumes that a passage has a figurative *in addition* to its literal and proper sense. In the one case the expositor wholly discards the obvious and proper sense, and converts history into allegory, contrary to the original intention and true meaning of the writer, thus transferring the passage, or work, from the domain of history to that of fiction. In the other, he admits, indeed, the historical sense, but also attaches to the words *another* meaning, according to his own fancy.

He puts more into the words of an author than they really contain, by affixing a *mystical* and *mediate*, in addition to the *immediate* and *direct* sense. He does not *substitute* one sense for another, but, ostensibly for the purpose either of obviating objections, or of rendering the Scriptures more edifying, he supposes one sense in addition to another, where there is no valid ground for the assumption. It is in this sense that we employ the phrase *typical interpretation.* This does not import the proper explanation and elucidation of a real type; but the assumption of a type where none was intended. Hence the terms *allegorical*, *typical*, and *mystical*, are employed as synonymous, when used to represent that system of interpretation, which attaches a secondary but hidden sense to the sacred Scriptures, foreign to the design of the writers, and the intention of the Holy Spirit This is the more common application of the phrase allegorical interpretation in the history of Biblical Hermeneutics. The method of interpretation in question originated with Pagan writers, from whom it was introduced into the Jewish schools, and the early Christian writers adopted it from them.

The Proverb, or Adage—A Proverb is a short pithy sentence, which embodies a well known and admitted truth, or common fact, ascertained by experience or observation, and which passes current among the masses of society. Among the Greeks proverbs were called *παροιμίαι* (from *παρα near*, and *οιμος way*) *wayside idioms.* (= *παροδια*) because common, and adapted to meet daily wants; and also for the purpose of distinguishing them from the more logical and discriminating harangue of schools and philosophers. The Romans denominated them *adagia*, because they were *ad agendum apta*, practical maxims fitted for quickly solving the problems of daily life. *Brevity* appears to be not only one of the constituent elements, but a prime excellence of the proverb. This is indicated by the word itself—*proverbia* (from *pro* and *verbum*) *for*, or *instead* of *words*, i e. a few words. Proverbs may be divided into two distinct classes, viz *literal* and *figurative* or *allegorical*. The former class comprises those which admit only of a literal interpretation, and are to be understood according to the plain, obvious, grammatical meaning of the terms in which they are expressed. The latter comprise those in which one thing is said and another meant. In the former case the literal sense exhausts the meaning: in the latter, it is of no further use than to suggest the applied meaning. The following are examples of the first class: "Honesty is the best policy," "Right wrongs no man," etc. To the second class belong such proverbs as these: "Drink water from your own cistern," "Every one draws the water to his own mill." "There is many a slip between the cup and the lip." "Strike while the iron is hot." "Physician, heal thyself." "Those who live in glass houses should not throw stones." "The fathers have eaten sour grapes, and the children's teeth are set on edge." These and similar proverbs have a real sense quite distinct from their literal meaning, and this must be determined from the connexion in which they are employed, and the particular application which is made of them.

There are many proverbs and adages scattered through the Old and New Testament; and the

Book of Proverbs by Solomon is a collection of those which were composed by this Hebrew monarch, and current among the Hebrew people in his day. The following rules and observations will assist the student in the study and interpretation of Proverbs and particularly of the Book of Proverbs:—

1. Proverbs are manifestly not intended to have only an *individual* application. From their very nature they are designed to apply to all cases where similarity of circumstances would render them appropriate. At the same time, with few exceptions, the proverbs of Solomon have not an unlimited and *universal* application, but only that which is *general*. e. g. ch. 10: 17. 16: 7. 22: 6.

2. Nothing more is frequently intended in the Book of Proverbs that what usually occurs, and not what is good and proper in itself. Indeed a proverbial maxim may, as a sentiment, be false, while as a matter of fact it may be strictly true. e. g. "Might makes right." "The end justifies the means." Upon such false principles as these men are continually acting, and to their own minds, at least, justify, on the ground of them, oppression, slavery, and an endless variety of wicked acts.

3. In the Proverbs of Solomon a thing is sometimes represented as really *done*, in order to indicate what *ought* to be done, although too often neglected. e. g. ch. 16: 12, 13.

4. Some maxims in that book, which, taken in their broadest and most unqualified sense, and without regard to the circumstances which gave rise to them, appear to be inconsistent with the law of fraternal kindness, (e. g. the warnings

against suretyship.) are only salutary and impressive admonitions against indiscreet and imprudent actions.

5 In the study of the Book of Proverbs particular attention should be paid to the structure of Hebrew poetry, especially to the laws of Hebrew parallelism.

CHAPTER XXI.

THE PARABLE.

The Greek word παραβολη, from which our English word parable comes, is derived from the verb παραβαλλειν [παρα, *near to*, and βαλλειν, *to cast.*] which properly signifies *to throw near*, *to cast one thing before or beside another*, *to place side by side.* Hence the cognate noun παραβολη imports primarily *a placing side by side*, as of ships in battle, a juxta position. Now, as this juxta-position of two things may be for the purpose of comparing one with the other, a secondary meaning of the verb is *to compare*, and of the noun, *a comparison*, and as this comparison is commonly made for the purpose of showing the resemblance between the two, hence the signification *similitude.* Cicero defines the parable to be "a form of speech in which we compare one thing with some other on account of a resemblance between the two." By the aid of etymology, therefore, we may form some idea of the generic character of Parables, but not of their *specific* character. We learn that they belong to the class of figurative composition, based on resemblance, but we are left in uncertainty, whether they are simply metaphors, allegories, or examples. And when we come to inquire into the use of the word parable in the Scriptures, we find ourselves still more embarrassed, from the fact that the word is employed in a variety of senses, and with much greater latitude of signification, than in classic usage. In the Greek version of the Old Testament, its answer in every instance to the Hebrew noun משל, *mashal*, and as the same Hebraic usage, which obtains in the Septuagint pervades the New Testament, in order to determine the precise import of the word parable in the latter, we must have recourse to the Hebrew Scriptures. Now, the Hebrew verb משל *mashal*, signifies to *liken*, to *compare*, and the primary meaning of the kindred noun משל *mashal*, is a *comparison*, a *similitude*. Thus far, the corresponding Hebrew and Greek words coincide. But, beyond this, the Hebrew word takes a wider range. Among its secondary meanings, are *an image*, a *figure*, or word picture, a *fable*, an *apothegm*, a *proverb* or *adage*, an *obscure*, *enigmatical expression*, *an allegory*, a *gnome*, or grave sententious saying, *figurative discourse* generally, a *prophetic announcement*, expressed in figurative language, and finally, a *poem*, because that species of composition abounds in images, and figurative language. Thus it appears that the word embraces within its comprehensive scope almost every variety of figures and figurative discourse, based on resemblance. The Greek word **παραβολη**, therefore, both in the Septuagint, and in the New Testament, like the Hebrew corresponding word, is *generic* in its usage, and the specific meaning in any case must be determined by the context and nature of the composition. Overlooking this important fact, some writers have classed metaphors, fables, and proverbs, among parables. Drummond, especially, has evinced a singular lack of discrimination, by converting nearly all the metaphorical and proverbial expressions of our Lord, into parables. He thus swells the number recorded to *seventy*, while, in point of fact, they do not much exceed *thirty*. Various attempts have been made to frame a definition of the Parable, which shall be sufficiently comprehensive to cover the whole ground of our Lord's parabolic discourses. Were these parables all cast in one mould, and did they all exhibit one uniform aspect, there would be no difficulty in constructing a perspicuous and satisfactory definition. But such is not the fact; hence, when the Biblical student comes to apply the definitions with which he is provided, he finds them lacking in discrimination, or defective in comprehensiveness. They furnish no adequate key to the solution of the parables as a whole, and consequently fail to render him that assistance which he had a right to expect from them; and instead of aiding him where he most needs aid, they embarass and perplex him, The Parables of our Lord may be conveniently arranged under two classes, differing from each other, both in their outward form and design. Of these, one class is peculiar to the New Testament, while the other is common to sacred and profane literature.

1. The first class comprises those which, in their outward form and constitution, are allegorical. They are, in fact, sacred allegories, and, like all other compositions of this kind, they have an

obvious and apparent meaning, and an occult or hidden meaning, concealed under the outward and formal description, a material and immediate representation, and an ultimate representation, running parallel with it. The truth which underlies the allegorical parable, is *historical truth*; it might be the history of the past, the present, or the future; but in point of fact, it is generally the last; in other words it is *prophetic history*. With few exceptions, the parables of this class are expressly declared to be similitudes. The subject of comparison is announced at the opening of the parable by the formula, "the kingdom of heaven is like" so and so; which furnishes the key to its interpretation. In these parables, the immediate representation or similitude is of no further use than to serve as a suitable vehicle for the ultimate representation, which exhibits the real sense intended by the parable.

Our Lord's immediate design in the delivery of these allegorical parables, was, to communicate information not already possessed, and yet information of such a nature as, for some reason, he did not at the time choose to communicate to the persons whom he addressed in a clear and distinct manner, but obscurely, and disguised under the veil of imagery and allegory, which required explanation to be properly understood. On examination, these parables will be found to relate in general to the Spiritual or Moral Kingdom, which our Saviour was about to establish in the world,—to the new dispensation of grace which he was about to inaugurate,—to the outward and visible Church, which he was about to found; or else to the growth and development of true religion in the individual soul under that dispensation, and in that visible Church. They are the vehicles, therefore, not of doctrines, but of facts; and consequently are pure histories, only not simply and properly expressed. And as the facts had, as yet, no real existence, but were still in the future, consequently the history they describe, is prophetic history. Accordingly, these parables are allegorical, historical, and prophetical, or prophetico-historical..

From the very nature and structure of this class of our Lord's parables, it is evident that they could not have been understood by his auditors without explanation. It was not the expectation of our Saviour that they *would* be then understood, nor did it fall within the scope of his design, that they should be then fully apprehended, else they would have been differently expressed. For this there may have been several reasons. The facts described in them, having, as yet, no *real*, but only a *prophetic* existence, they might be such as those who heard them were not at the time personally interested in, or there might have been a present repugnance to the knowledge of the facts alluded to, and a present difficulty in making them understood and appreciated by those whose minds were enveloped in the mists of ignorance, and prejudice, as regards the true nature of Spiritual religion, and the grand purpose of our Lord's advent and mission. These circumstances would render it not only offensive and dangerous, but, perhaps, impracticable, useless, and absurd, to communicate them in clear, and simple language to the mixed multitudes who attended on his ministry. Accordingly, we do not find that any explanation was asked by, or given to them at the time. Those to whom they were addressed, were left to decipher the meaning of these parables, if at all, by the gradual development of the events themselves, which they predictively described. But the immediate disciples of our Lord stood in a different relation to them. To them the subject-matter of these prophetic parables was of the highest interest and importance; and consequently they embraced the earliest opportunity to obtain a private explanation of them. (see Matt. 13; 10-12, 18. Mar. 4: 34.) After the Saviour had fully explained to them the parables of the Sower and the Tares, they seem to have had less difficulty in understanding other parables of the same class. They were thereby furnished with a key to the interpretation of similar parables; and when afterwards he related the parables of the hidden treasure, the pearl, and the drawn net, and then enquired of them, if they understood them; they replied that they did. (Matt. 13: 54.)

Now, it was to parables of this class, that our Lord evidently alluded, when, on being asked by his disciples why he spoke to the multitudes in parables, he replied, "Because it is given unto you to know the mysteries (secrets) of the kingdom of heaven, but to them it is not given. For whosoever hath, to him shall be given, and he shall have more abundance; but whosoever hath not, from him shall be taken away even that he hath. Therefore, I speak to them in parables; because they seeing, see not, and hearing, hear not, neither do they understand." (Matt. 13: 10-13.) This remark of our Lord seems, at first view, to be repugnant to the very design of parables as commonly understood, which is to illustrate a snbject and make it plainer, not to involve it in obscurity. But, when it is understood to refer to the allegorical parables exclusively, its force and propriety are clearly perceived.

2. The second class of our Lord's parables comprises such as consist of brief stories, tales or narratives, designed in the most attractive and impressive manner to illustrate and enforce some specific duty, or to inculcate some specific doctrine. They are therefore in their scope and design *doctrinal*, *ethical* and *practical*. They occur in the midst of moral and doctrinal discourses, and often gave occasion to such discourses. Their object was to elucidate and to impress,—to simplify and to enforce. Accordingly their scope was sufficiently obvious at the time, and required no explanation; or if explanation was needed, it was given at the time, and to the persons to whom they were immediately addressed, and for whose benefit they were intended. There was no motive for concealment; and indeed concealment would have defeated the very end sought to be attained. The language in which they are clothed, therefore, is so plain that all could readily understand it, and their purport must have been quite as intelligible to their immediate hearers as it is to us. Parables of this class are *historical*, but not in the sense of being the statement of actual facts and occurrences, in opposition to fiction; but in the sense of bearing a formal resemblance to truth, by describing what might have happened, as opposed to that which is improbable or impossi-

ble. They are historical in form, also, as distinguished from allegorical and mystical, inasmuch as they have but one obvious or grammatico-historical sense. In this class of parables, the narrative or story answers to the protasis or immediate representation in the allegorical parables, while the doctrinal, or moral truth, or duty illustrated and enforced, corresponds to the apodosis. The story, or protasis, may be true in every particular, or it may be merely founded on truth, or it may be wholly fictitious. The historical verity of the tale is not at all essential; and in point of fact, most, if not all, of our Lord's moral parables are fictitious. In the employment of such illustrative examples, our Saviour is no more responsible for their literal and historical truth, than is the novelist, who, for a similar purpose, gathers flowers from the domain of fiction, responsible for the truth of the incidents which he has grouped together. Nay, more than this; a moral tale may be framed in accordance with popular ideas, even though such ideas are known to be founded in error. Our Saviour, therefore, should not be regarded as compromising in the smallest degree his character as an authoritative moral teacher, if he should be found in any instance to have laid hold of popular ideas, though groundless, for the purpose of mere illustration. The parable of Dives and Lazarus, for example, may in some particulars, have been constructed in accommodation to the prevalent, but erroneous, and essentially pagan notions of the common people, without its divine author intending thereby to commit himself to the truth of those opinions, or to vouch for their conformity to the reality of things.

The moral and historical parables of our Lord have been frequently classed by commentators among fables; and the ancients (Aristotle, Cicero, Quinctillian) place the difference between them only in the more or less ample treatment of the subject; inasmuch as the fable was regarded by them as the more finished production of the two. Some modern critics make the difference to consist simply in this, that the fable represents the single fact as *real*, the parable only as *possible*. But the specific difference between the two is much more deeply seated than this. As to form, in both the moral parable and the fable we find a story, which is designed to unfold a truth, or inculcate a duty. But the region from which these two species of inventive composition derive their imagery, and draw their materials, are not the same. While the parable sometimes avails itself of inanimate nature, (e. g. the allegorical parables of the Sower, the Tares, and the Leaven) irrational creatures are rarely introduced, and in our Lord's parables never. The parable, also, unlike the fable, derives its materials only from the territory of the possible and the real. It adheres to probability, and teaches through the imagination. When beings and powers belonging to a lower sphere, are introduced into a parable, as they sometimes are, they always follow the law of their nature, while their acts in accordance with that law are used to prefigure or represent those of a higher race. The parable declares what *might* have taken place, and deduces a moral from it; whilst the fable, with the same design, describes what *could not possibly* have happened. But the grand difference between the fable and the parable is *internal*, and relates to the substance. The ground occupied by the writer of fables is much lower than that occupied by one who teaches by parables; and the aim and scope of fables are also subordinate and inferior to those of parables. The fable, as has been already remarked, confines itself to earthly virtues, prudential maxims, or commendable human qualities. But the parable introduces us to a higher sphere of action and of duty—a purely moral and spiritual domain. Its element is preeminently in the world of mind—rational and responsible men—acting not for time only, but for eternity; while that of the fable is essentially of the earth, and never lifts itself above the earth. Unlike the fable, the parable never jests at the follies, ridicules the faults, or taunts the disappointments of mankind; it is full of righteous displeasure, of holy rebuke, and condemnation of wrongdoing; it is always earnest, affectionate, and solemn

Some writers confound the parable with the proverb; but the difference between them is evident, both in respect to form and substance. The Proverb is a pointed, sententious, moral, or prudential saying, which passes current among the people, of which brevity is an essential characteristic. The Scripture Parable is either a prophetic allegory, or a continued and well arranged narrative of some possible but fictitious event, applied to the illustration of some sacred truth. It is not, indeed, greatly extended, but by no means contracted within the brief space of a proverb. There is nothing in the proverb corresponding to the protasis of the moral parable.

A parable, however, may in some instances have been invented to illustrate a proverb already current. As to its substance, the moral parable always contains and inculcates some grave *moral* or *religious truth*, and never an error. A proverb, on the contrary, may be good or bad, true or false, important or trivial, wise or foolish. The parables of our Lord admit of no such distinctions as these.

If the distinction we have made in the parables of our Lord is well founded, then it furnishes us with a key to their interpretation by indicating the right method of procedure. As an allegory comprehends two distinct representations, the parables belonging to this class must be subjected to a two-fold examination. 1st, Of the immediate representation, and 2d, Of the representation it was intended to excite. Not so the moral parables. These have but one meaning, and were intended to be understood only in their obvious grammatical sense. In the allegorical parables all, or nearly all, the material circumstances introduced into the immediate representation, have their counterpart in the ultimate representation. But such a mode of interpretation would be unjustifiable and vicious, when applied to the moral parables. Into these many circumstances are introduced merely for the sake of ornament or verisimilitude, to beautify them, or to give an air of probability and reality to them and make them more life-like and entertaining. They were intended to have no moral significance—no recondite or occult meaning,—and to demand such a meaning is to subject them to the wayward fancy and lawless imagination of any individual who may choose to exercise his ingenuity in hunting up a meaning to suit himself. Hence the most diversified, fanciful, and contradictory interpretations have been given of these parables, while their true and only design has often been almost entirely lost sight of. The scope of the allegorical parables may generally be ascertained without difficulty. These relate to the kingdom of God viewed in some one of its numerous aspects. They describe prophetically, as has already been remarked, the establishment and spiritual nature of the Christian dispensation,—the promulgation of the Gospel and the reception it would meet with from different classes of hearers,—the planting, growth, and character of the Christian Church;—or else the rise and progress of religion in the individual soul. The scope of the moral parables may be gathered either from the preceding or subsequent context. Sometimes it is formally announced. Thus we are told in St. Luke 18: 1. that the parable of the unjust judge was spoken by our Lord in order to inculcate the duty and advantage of persevering prayer. The parable of the rich glutton (Lu. 12: 16–20) is prefaced by the following caution in v. 15. "Take heed and beware of covetousness." The parable of the Pharisee and Publican is introduced with the announcement that our Lord "spake this parable unto certain who trusted in themselves that they were righteous, and despised others." (Lu. 18: 9.) The Saviour concludes the parable of the unmerciful creditor, who would not forgive his debtor the minutest portion of his debt, though much had been forgiven him, with the following application: "So likewise shall my heavenly Father do also unto you, if ye from your hearts forgive not every one his brother their trespasses." (Matt. 18: 35.) When no declaration is prefixed or subjoined to a parable of this class, its scope may be collected from a consideration of the subject-matter, or the occasion on which it was delivered. Having ascertained the scope or design of the parable, we are to interpret it in its grammatico-historical sense in accordance with that design. But no rule has been more frequently transgressed than this; and no portion of the New Testament has been more grossly perverted, tortured and abused by hunters after allegories than the moral and doctrinal parables. A mystical or spiritual meaning has been given even to the most trivial circumstances introduced into the parable, by means of which their power for edification has been supposed to be wonderfully increased. By this process the rich man, for instance, in the parable of Dives and Lazarus, is made to denote "the high priest under the law;" the beggar means "the Gentiles;" the beggar's death signifies "the close of the Levitical dispensation;" the lifting up of the rich man's eyes in hell means "a conviction of the condemning power of the law;" his desire to have his brethren warned is "the desire of the Gentile converts to carry the Gospel to apostate Jews;" the gulph is "the time appointed for the blindness of Israel;" the five brethren are "that part of Israel broken off through unbelief." Again: what can be more simple and intelligible than the parable of the Good Samaritan, which so beautifully inculcates universal benevolence? And yet in the hands of some interpreters it turns out to be a perfect riddle. By one expositor it is made to teach the mission and example of Christ; the traveller is human nature, or Adam, the head of the race, who leaves the heavenly city and falls into the power of Satan, and is all but killed. Christ now finds him and restores him. The wine poured into his wounds is the blood which Christ shed; and the oil is the anointing of the Holy Spirit; the binding up is the Sacraments of the Church. The ring in the parable of the prodigal son is described by one as the everlasting love of God, or the seal of the Spirit; the sinner is called the younger son, because man as a sinner is younger than man as righteous; the citizen to whom he went was a legal preacher; the swine were self-righteous persons; the husks were works of righteousness; the fatted calf was Christ; the shoes were means of upright conversation, the doctrines and precepts of Scripture; the music which the elder brother heard was the preaching of the Gospel, etc. All such interpretations may exhibit the ingenuity and piety of the interpreter, but they do so at the expense of his common sense, and in utter disregard of the obvious intention of our Lord.

The following extract from McClelland's Manual of Sacred Interpretation exhibits a far more sober and correct mode of interpretation: "The parable of the ten virgins is designed to teach the folly of those who neglect preparation for their Redeemer's coming. Virgins are selected, not on account of their purity, but because virgins in those days played an important part at bridals; and a bridal feast was made the basis of the fable [parable]. The virginity, therefore, of the personages is a mere circumstance, which teaches nothing. So is the distinction into "five wise" and "five foolish." Nothing can be inferred as to the comparative number of nominal and sincere professors of religion in the world. The two classes are equalized to guard against all speculations on a subject foreign to the speaker's object. The "sleeping" of the wise virgins is another mere circumstance introduced to bring about the catastrophe in a natural way,—not to teach the dangerous doctrine that the best Christians fail in spiritual vigilance, and are very liable to be taken by surprise, when the Master calls them. The truth is, that their sleeping was designed to be rather complimentary than otherwise, as it brought out the fact that they were *provided* and *ready*. They had nothing to fear; a little refreshment, therefore, was not amiss, especially as they had no duties to perform until the arrival of the procession. The Parable of the rich man and Lazarus is another example. The angels who carry the soul of Lazarus to Abraham's bosom, probably belong, as well as Abraham's bosom itself, to the machinery, and nothing is deducible from it. The representation of the rich man and Abraham being in the same region, and within sight of each other, is an image taken from the ancient idea of Hades, and must not be listed to prove that the souls of the blessed hold intercourse with those of the wicked in another world." The interpreter should constantly bear in mind that the moral parables are intended rather for illustration than for proof; and that consequently no doctrine should be founded on the Parables, as its ultimate ground. Not that the Parable is without its doctrine; but that it is in no case the first revelation or statement of doctrine, and is merely the elucidation of a doctrine previously revealed. All doctrines of consequence are unfolded in clear, unfigurative expressions. Hence parabolic theology is not argumentative. It forms no part of the analogy of faith. On the contrary, the analogy of faith must regulate its teachings so far that they should harmonize with or illustrate it.

The following classified list of most, if not all, of our Lord's Parables will assist the student in his interpretation of them:—

CLASS I.

Allegorical and Prophetical Parables.

1. The Sower.—Matt. 13 : 3–8, 18–23. (Mar. 4 : 3–9, 14–20. Lu. 8 : 4–8, 11–15.)
2. The Tares.—Matt. 13: 24–30, 36–43.
3. The Mustard Seed.—Matt. 13: 31, 32. (Mar. 4: 30–32. Lu. 13: 18, 19.)
4. The Leaven.—Matt. 13: 33. (Lu. 13: 20, 21.)
5. The Hidden Treasure.—Matt. 13: 44.
6. The Pearl.—Matt. 45, 46.
7. The Draw Net.—Matt. 13: 47–50.
8. The Laborers in the Vineyard.—Matt. 20: 1–16.
9. The Wicked Husbandman.—Matt. 21: 33–44. (Mar. 12: 1–11. Lu. 20: 9–18.)
10. The Wedding Garment, Marriage of the King's Son.—Matt. 22: 1–14.
11. The Ten Virgins.—Matt. 25: 1–13.
12. The Talents.—Matt. 25: 14–30.
13. The Seed Growing Insensibly.—Mar. 4: 26–29.
14. The Different Servants.—Lu. 12: 39–48. (Matt. 43–51.)

15. The Barren Fig Tree.—Lu. 13: 6–9.
16. The Great Supper.—Lu. 14: 16–24.
17. The Prodigal Son.—Lu. 15: 11–32.
18. The Pounds.—Lu. 19: 11–27.

CLASS II.

Historical, Doctrinal, and Ethical Parables.

1. The Unmerciful Servant.—Matt. 18: 23–35.
2. The Two Sons.—Matt. 21: 28–32.
3. The Two Debtors.—Lu. 7: 41–43.
4. The Good Samaritan.—Lu. 10: 30–37.
5. The Friend at Midnight.—Lu. 11: 5–10.
6. The Rich Fool.—Lu. 12: 16–21.
7. The Lost Sheep.—Lu. 15: 3–7. (Matt. 18: 12–14.)
8. The Unjust Steward.—Lu. 16: 1–8.
9. The Rich Man and Lazarus.—Lu. 16: 19–31.
10. The Unprofitable Servants.—Lu. 17: 7–10.
11. The Unjust Judge.—Lu. 18: 1–8.
12. The Pharisee and Publican.—Lu. 18: 9–15.

CHAPTER XXII.

SYMBOLS AND THEIR INTERPRETATION.

Symbols are significant and representative objects, signs, or actions, employed for the purpose of communicating ideas. The word symbol (συμβολον) is derived from the Greek words συν and βαλλω, to *cast*, or *place together*, with a view to comparison or attentive consideration. The original word was anciently employed in various ways. Thus it was customary to call the Apostles' Creed a symbol, probably in consequence of the traditional, but erroneous belief, that the

Apostles had each contributed, or thrown in, his article to that formulary of faith.*

Hence the confessions of faith, catechisms, liturgies, and other doctrinal standards of the Reformed Churches of Europe, came to be styled symbolical books. The term *symbol* was also applied to military watchwords or counter-signs by which the soldiers of an army could distinguish each other. But the most frequent application of the word was to the rites of the heathen religion, where those who were instructed in its mysteries, or esoteric doctrines, and admitted to the knowledge of its peculiar services and private ceremonies, had certain signs, marks, or tokens, called *symbola*, delivered to them, and on

---

*The first particular account of the traditional belief respecting the composition of the Apostles' Creed, is given by Ambrose, in the latter half of the 4th century; and in a sermon attributed to Augustine, who flourished a little later, the author assigns to each one of the Apostles a particular clause, or article; as to St. Peter, the article, "I believe in God the Father Almighty;" to St. John, "Maker of heaven and earth," and so on. But passing by the objection to this theory, that had the facts been as here stated, we should doubtless have had some intimation of them in the Acts of the Apostles, or in the records of the early Church, the fallacy as well as the absurdity of the statement is evident from the fact that the Article "the communion of saints," attributed to Simon Zelotes, is not found in any Creed till about 400 years after Christ; and the article of Christ's descent into Hell, attributed to St. Thomas, was neither in the early Roman, nor the Oriental Creed. It was first inserted in the Creed of the Church of Aquilia (Italy) about the year 400; and did not find its way into the Roman Creed until A. D. 600.

the declaration or presentation of these, they were admitted without hesitation into any temple, to the secret rites and worship of that god, whose symbols they had received.

Pictorial symbols, as a medium of communicating ideas, originated in the necessities of mankind, and may be traced back to the earliest period of antiquity. Their origin, nature, and use, may be best understood by considering briefly the rise and progress of written language. Let us then, in imagination, carry ourselves back to the infancy of the human race, before the use of letters was known, and when the only established mode of intercommunication among men was that of vocal language. How, in such a state of society, may we rationally suppose that one person would inform another remote from him, and with whom he could not communicate orally, of any circumstances connected with a particular object, with which he desired him to become acquainted? The first attempt would be to sketch a rude drawing of the object, and substitute that for the object itself. In this manner the idea of a man, a horse, a dog, a house, or a tree, may, as single objects, be as distinctly communicated as by alphabetic characters; while two or more houses may be made significant of a town, and two or more trees, of a wood. By the continuous copying, in successive series, of such familiar objects as the train of our ideas might call for, a kind of connected narrative of passing events might be furnished, which, though very imperfect and often quite ambiguous, might, on the whole, be generally understood. Such may be supposed to be the first attempt of men in the earliest stages of civilization, to communicate their ideas by written characters. This would be very properly termed *picture-writing*, or *object-writing*; for it would consist of delineations of the material forms or shape of objects, addressed to the eye instead of the ear, for the purpose of suggesting to the mind the idea of those objects, and certain circumstances connected with them. It is manifest, however, that the scope of this kind of imitative language would be extremely limited, and would entirely fail of delineating the internal qualities of objects, and also of expressing abstract ideas. The next step would be to remedy as far as possible this defect by associating conventionally with certain external forms and images, such properties or abstract ideas, as these forms would be likely to excite, and employ the one to express the other. Thus an eye might be made to signify *watchfulness* or *care*, if open; and *sleep*, or *forgetfulness*, if closed: an arm, *power;* an arrow, *calamity;* a chain, *bondage;* a bow, *strength*, or *victory;* a shield, *defence.* In like manner, one object possessing certain properties in a remarkable degree, might be substituted for some other object, to which one or more of the qualities or properties belonging to that object, were ascribed. Thus a fox might be delineated to represent a cunning man; a lamb, a meek or gentle one; a lion, a strong and powerful one; a tiger or leopard, a ferocious one, or a bear, a fierce and savage one. On the same principle compound ideas might be expressed by a combination of characters. Thus, if it was desired to represent a man who was both *powerful* and *ferocious*, it would be natural to make a figure compounded of the lion and the leopard; the figure of a man enclosed in a square, might denote a prisoner. For the purpose of economizing time and space, resort would next be had to abbreviation or substitution, as, for example, a part of a figure put by synedoche for the whole. Thus the idea of a man represented by the delineation of his whole figure, might now be signified by his head, or his legs alone.

What appears to be reasonable and probable in theory, is found to accord with facts among all the primitive nations of antiquity. Among the Egyptians, this kind of picture-writing, or expression of ideas by representations of visible objects and marks, was carried to the highest degree of perfection. Those historical traditions and sacred mysteries, which were regarded as of sufficient importance to be transmitted to posterity, were engraven on their pyramids, the walls of their temples, and other works of art; and hence the name Hieroglyphic, *sacred sculpture*, from two Greek words ιερος *holy* and γλυφω, to *engrave*. It was for a long time supposed that the hieroglyphic or ideographic writing of the Egyptians was a mysterious science, the secret of which was known only to the priests, and by them studiously and religiously concealed from the curiosity of the multitude. But modern discoveries have shown clearly that this writing, though called by the Greeks *sacred*—in itself veiled no mysteries, and must have been well understood by the educated class of Egyptians. The Hieroglyphics in question, though similar in form, are now ascertained to have consisted of three distinct classes, each class subserving a purpose of its own. These are denominated the

Curiologic or *figurative* Hieroglyph, the *symbolic*, or tropical, and the *phonetic*. To the *first* class, belong those in which the representation of an object either entire or abridged, conveys the idea of the object itself and nothing else. This is simple imitation, a pure picture writing and corresponds to the paintings, pictures and sculpture of the present day. This class of hieroglyphs is called, by some writers, *figurative;* not, however, in the sense in which that term is employed in rhetoric as synonymous with tropical, but as denoting that the sign employed is an imitation of the figure, shape or form of some sensible object. It corresponds analogically to words in alphabetical language taken in their primary and literal sense, and may, therefore, to preserve the analogy, be denominated the *hieroglyph proper*. Such are a circle for the sun, a crescent for the moon, an arch painted blue for the sky, the proper figure of an ibis to represent the bird itself. The *second* class is composed of those which are either the signs of objects very different in appearance from the forms of the hieroglyph, which designate them; or else denote abstract ideas which are not the objects of sense, but purely intellectual. Thus, when the figure of a lion is drawn, not for the purpose of designating that animal, but to signify strength;—of a fly, to represent *impudence, or* of a tree to denote an *obedient people*. In this class the designation is not a matter of imitation or of proper likeness, but one which merely bears some analogy to it, real or supposed, imaginative, or conventional. Hieroglyphs, of this class, therefore, correspond to words taken in a *tropical* or metaphorical sense in alphabetic language. In the *third* class, the sign or figure does not stand for the particular object which it resembles, nor for an abstract idea; but it indicates a particular *sound.* The figure delineated in the Phonetic hieroglyph, and representing a letter, was the likeness of some animal or other object, the name of which in the spoken language commenced with the sound of that letter. Thus the letter A was represented by an eagle, the initial letter of the Egyptian word signifying eagle (Ahorn) being a. Of course there would be found many objects the name of which began with the sound of A, and hence an opportunity was afforded of choosing from among the various homophonous characters, which the writer was at liberty to employ. Accordingly we find that a great number of different signs were employed at the option of the writer, to express the same letter, and this circumstance creates the principal difficulty in regard to their interpretation. The different kinds of hieroglyphics and their uses may be illustrated by their application to the name of the Egyptian god Osiris. To suggest the idea of this god by a figurative, curiologic, or proper hieroglyphic, a full picture of the god must be drawn, or at least some prominent and characteristic part, by which he would be easily recognized: just as we make a full length portrait, or merely the bust of a particular individual. To indicate the same by a symbolic or tropical hieroglyph, a picture must be drawn of the tiara and wand, the symbols of the god, with which he is always represented. To express the same by phonetic, or alphabetical hieroglyphs, a series of pictures must be drawn, of visible objects, the first sounds in whose names shall be the successive souunds in the word Osir, or, as written in the oriental manner, without the intermediate vowel, *Osr.* The first sound *O* might be represented by the picture of a reed, the Egyptian name of which is *oke;* the second, by the picture of a child, in Egyptian *si;* the third by the picture of a mouth, in Egyptian *ro.* Phonetic characters or signs, it is ascertained, form by far the most numerous class of Egyptian hieroglyphs. All Chinese writing was originally ideographic and imitative. But now, at least one half of the Chinese characters are merely phonetic or alphabetic, in the sense of syllabic. The Mexican hieroglyphs, which have come to light, were ideographic and pictorial.

We discover in Phonetic hieroglyphs the germ of alphabetical writing; and although the interval between the two is apparently very considerable, yet it does not admit of a reasonable doubt, that the latter originated in the former; that from this modified hieroglyph there arose, in process of time, a regular alphabet, constructed so as to represent and express the various sounds uttered by the human voice,—a method of communicating ideas by written characters so vastly superior to the former, as soon completely to supersede the more primitive and cumbersome method; so that in most courtries all traces of it are forgotten. The hieroglyphic origin of the ancient alphabets is evident from the names given to the letters, as well as from the resemblance which can still be perceived between their present and their original form

The names of the Hebrew letters and of those

of other Shemitic languages are *significant.* Thus *Aleph*, the name of the first letter of the Hebrew alphabet signifies an *ox*; *Beth*, the second letter, a *house*; *Gimel*, the third letter, a *camel.* These letters were at first pictures, or rude likenesses of a hut, and of the two animals, or of the heads of the two animals just specified; proceeding on the very familiar system found on the ancient Dutch tiles, and not yet entirely exploded in books for children, where an ass, a bull, and a cat, are associated with the first three letters of the Roman alphabet. The letter D, named *Daleth*, was evidently at first represented by a *door*, the name of which begins with that sound, and the picture of which would thus become the letter of that sound. The letter *vau* (ו) signifies a *hook*, particularly a *tenter-hook*, such as is driven into a wall or post, for the purpose of suspending things upon it. Now if we trace the different figures of this letter through the several Shemitic alphabets, we shall find them all derived from the same source, and all corresponding in their outlines to the original signification of the name. The letter *Heth* (ח) means in Hebrew a *fence* or *enclosure*, and is the original source of our aspirate H. In the Babylonian alphabet this letter is an exact enclosure of a triangular form; in the Phœnician, an enclosure with an opening at each end; in the old Hebrew, a close enclosure, and so on. The capital letter T in the ancient Phœnician and Hebrew alphabets precisely resembled a *cross*, (the name of the Hebrew letter Tau (ת) which resemblance is still preserved in the Roman alplabet.* That we cannot now in many instances trace the resemblance between the present letters of the ancient alphabets and the particular objects after which they were named, is owing to the various mutations to which they have been unavoidably subjected in the course of time.

It does not appear that the ancient Egyptians ever advanced beyond phonetic writing. For we know that no proper alphabet existed among them till after the advent of Christ. When the Bible was translated into their language by the

---

*The original Greek alphabet was doubtless the same as the Phœnician or Shemitic. This is evident from the following considerations: 1. The Greek letters used in the most ancient inscriptions are, as to *form*, essentially the same as the corresponding characters found in the Phœnician inscriptions and on Hebrew coins. 2 The *relative position* of nearly all the letters in the two alphabets is the same. 3. The names of the Greek letters are radically the same as those of the corresponding Shemitic letters.

The priority of the Phœnician letters is satisfactorily established by the fact that the names of most of the Phœnician letters, as stated in the text, are *significant*; but the names of the Greek letters are entirely without significance; the words *Alpha, Beta, Gamma*, &c., are merely imitations of the names of the Hebrew letters, and "simply designate certain figures." Now if we admit that the Greeks, whose language was radically distinct from the Shemitic group, borrowed the forms and names of the Phœnician letters, we see at once why those names should have no meaning in Greek. Hence in the Roman alphabet, which succeeded the Greek, the names attached to the letters are very properly dropped altogether, and the letters only retained.

early missionaries, it was done by means of an alphabet made from the Greek. The most striking difference between the two forms of writing are the following: 1. In alphabetic writing sounds are represented directly, and ideas only indirectly; but in hieroglyphical writing it is the reverse; ideas are represented directly, and sounds only indirectly. This peculiarity in the latter gives it an advantage over the former of considerable importance; viz., that when the pictures are drawn at full length, or if abbreviated, when the key of the abbreviation is known, or the tropical sense understood, it is a species of writing addressed to all nations, and may be interpreted without the knowledge of their vocal language, which is necessary to the reception of an idea from alphabetic word. Thus the Chinese written language is entirely distinct from any one of the numerous oral dialects in use in the empire, and serves the purpose of a universal tongue. This advantage, however, is far more than counterbalanced by the many disadvantages attending it. 2. When hieroglyphs represent sounds, there is an endless variety of characters for the sound; and the figures chosen to represent the sound are not arbitrary: whereas in alphabetic writing, the figures are arbitrary and conventional, and each elementary sound has its appropriate character. 3. Hieroglyphs represent full syllables; but alphabets only the elements of syllables.

From the preceding remarks it appears that, while alphabetic language may be traced back to phonetic hieroglyphs, so symbolical language had its origin in what may be called tropical or symbolical hieroglyphs. Thus we see that symbols are the representatives of other forms and other ideas than those which the material objects themselves, or their imitative figures would naturally and obviously convey, and that, consequently, they bear an analogy to metaphors and tropes in verbal language, though by no means are they identical, as some writers have supposed. When Christ calls himself "the Bright and Morning Star," it is a metaphor; but when a star is employed by the Prophet Balaam to presignify Christ, (Num. 24: 17) it is a prophetic symbol. The figure of a lion, delineated on the military standard of the Hebrew nation to signify the tribe of Judah, was a symbol: but when Christ is called "the lion of the tribe of Judah," a metaphor is employed. Symbols are always *things*; metaphors are always *words*. Symbols approach more nearly to allegories, than they do to metaphors; because the allegory, though verbal in form, like the symbol, stands for things and ideas obviously different and distinct from those expressed by it. The use of symbols and symbolical hieroglyphics for the ordinary purpose of communicating information, has been entirely superceded by alphabetic language; but, notwithstanding, many are still employed in consequence of their beauty and fitness to the ideas they are intended to convey. Thus the working tools of the operative mason are employed in speculative freemasonry, as symbols of moral truths and duties. The flag of our country is the symbol of our federative nationality. The *anchor* is a symbol of *hope*; the *cross*, of *Christianity*; the *crescent*, of *Islamism*. An ordinary finger-ring has no significance, and is worn only for ornament; but the plain wedding-ring is a symbol of perpetual affection and fidelity. The language of symbols has in every age been found particularly suited to religious purposes, as giving additional force and significance to ideas expressed in vocal language, and adapted to afford material aid in deepening religious impressions, and awakening religious emotions through the medium of sensible objects addressed to the imagination. The Hebrews, in the providence of God, were moreover brought into contact for many years with the religious rites and usages of a people, abounding in symbolical rites and ordinances. For both these reasons, we should naturally expect to find many symbols employed in the Hebrew ritual, and that not a few of them would be such as, from the accident of their position, the Israelites had become familiar with in the land of their servitude. Accordingly we find the Old Testament abounding in symbols. The worship of the Jewish Tabernacle and Temple, with the exception of the Psalmody, was entirely symbolical. Of this nature were all the sacrifices and offerings, the burning of incense, &c., &c. Even from the simple ritual of the Christian Church the language of symbols is not entirely excluded. The two sacraments ordained by Christ himself are strikingly symbolic;—the water in the one symbolizing the doctrine and necessity of regeneration or an inward and spiritual change by the operation of the Holy Spirit; the bread and wine in the other symbolizing the body and blood of Christ, and teaching the doctrine of vicarious atonement and the necessity of a vital union by faith with the Saviour of men. Symbols were also found to be an admirable vehicle of prophecy, and accordingly we find the prophetical writings, particularly of Ezekiel, Daniel, and St John abounding in symbolical hieroglyphics. Hence the study of symbolical language is eminently deserving the attention of the ministers of religion. Symbols and emblems,* like words, have a precise and determinate signification; and, like words also, are for the most part conventional, and acquire their meaning from usage. The interpreter, therefore, is not at liberty to affix any meaning he pleases to them, but only such as usage has given them. Not that symbols have or can have, uniformly, but one meaning; on the contrary, like words, they may have, and often do have, several significations as

*The nouns *symbol* and *emblem*, and the corresponding adjectives *symbolical* and *emblematical*, though not strictly synonomous, are sometimes used interchangeably. Thus the elements in the Lord's Supper, are sometimes called symbols of Christ's body and blood, and sometimes sacred emblems. The word *emblem* (in Greek ιμβλημα from ιν and βαλλιιν, *to throw in*, *to impress*) literally signifies *something inserted* or *stamped on as a mark*. It is employed most frequently in English to signify a figurative representation, which by the power of association suggests to the mind some idea expressed to the senses. Crabb represents the difference between emblem and symbol thus: "the *emblem* is that sort of *figure* of thought by which we make corporeal objects to stand for moral properties; thus the dove is represented as the *emblem* of meekness, or the beehive is made the *emblem* of industry; the *symbol* is that species of *emblem* which is converted into a constituted sign among men; thus 'the olive and laurel are the symbols of peace, and have been recognized as such among barbarous as well as enlightened nations."

employed in different relations and circumstances. At the same time these different meanings and various shades and modifications of signification all naturally flow from the radical import of the symbol. For example: The sun was among the ancients the legitimate symbol of *supreme authority*. and the stars of *subordinate authority*. Now, in strict accordance with this generic idea, the sun, in reference to the family relation, was employed to symbolize the father, the moon, the mother, and the stars, the sons; as in Joseph's Dream. But, in respect to a kingdom or empire, the sun represented the supreme power, whether vested in a male or female, or plurality of persons, and the moon is employed to represent the people or subjects of the kings. Stars sometimes symbolize not inferior magistrates, but kings. In this case, however, more than one king is spoken of, or the Ruler of the Universe is alluded to in the context as the King of kings, while the powers ordained by him are represented as stars. Now, in order to ascertain the precise meaning of a symbol in any particular instance of its occurrence, we must pursue the same course as when endeavoring to ascertain the specific meaning of a word. In the prophecies of Daniel and John, many of the prophetic symbols employed are explained; the meaning of others may be found elsewhere; and where we fail to discover it by collating other passages of Scripture, recourse may be had to profane authors.

There is one thing in relation to the employment of symbols in prophetic Scripture, which is worthy of special notice; I mean what may not improperly, perhaps, be designated their *chronology.* "In verbal description," says Carpenter, "there is no difficulty in properly adjusting the several occurrences which pass under review, and assigning to each one its respective order in the series, and its particular epoch in the general history. So also, if it be desired to trace and delineate the effects of any particular principle or transaction on different states of society, or communities of persons, a speaker or writer may do so with the greatest facility, passing from one state to the other in regular succession, and without the remotest probability of misleading his hearers or readers. Thus we have historical works extant, in which the authors have, in successive chapters, narrated the history of the community to which their writings appertained, in its social, its civil, and its political state; each of which topics has been again divided into separate branches; then has followed a review of ecclesiastical matters, synchronizing with the events embraced in the former sections of the work; which review has, perhaps, been divided into the internal and the external affairs of the Church, and each of these again into several other distinct heads of inquiry. But from such a distribution and arrangement of the several parts of the work, no inconvenience will arise, if the author but distinctly mark the limits of each, and properly adjust the whole of the general history. The reader of such a work will very naturally pass from one to the other, carrying back his mind to the common epoch, at the beginning of each of the respective divisions. It is not so, however, in symbolical or pictorial representations. If a writer employing these be desirous to place before the mind of his reader the leading occurrences of a state, throughout the entire period of its history, he will be compelled by the principles of the science, sometimes to represent distant events as existing at the *same period of time*, as in Daniel's vision of the great image and that of the four beasts; and at others, to employ a *successive* series of symbols to denote occurrences, which are strictly *synchronical*, as in the book of Revelation. And, however skilful and cautious he may be, it will be found impracticable to mark the boundaries of time, and the transition from one event to another with as much strength and clearness, as is done in verbal description or narration."*

SYMBOLICAL ACTIONS.

Intimately connected with the language of symbols is that of significant actions or signs, called symbolical actions. In the early ages of the world verbal language must have been extremely rude, narrow, and equivocal. To supply in part the deficiencies of speech or to add to the force of oral language, men were led to make use of apt and significant signs, gestures and actions; to which indeed, they were prompted by nature. Hence mutual converse was maintained by a mixed discourse of words and actions, whence came the eastern phrase of *the voice of the sign*. Ex. 4: 8. But this custom which originated in necessity, being improved into ornament, subsisted long after the necessity ceased, especially among Oriental nations, where

***Carpenter's Popular Lectures on Biblical Criticism and Interpretation.**

natural temperament inclined them to a mode of conversation which so well exercised their vivacity by motion, and so much gratified it by a perpetual representation of material images. Many of these were the natural language of creation and common to all nations; others were arbitrary and conventional. The Old Testament abounds in examples of the use of symbolical actions, or of instruction or information conveyed by arbitrary but significant signs. The New Testament also supplies some instances; but they are neither so numerous in their occurrence, nor so complicated in their circumstances, nor so uniform in their design, as are those of the Old. Thus the prophet Isaiah (ch. xx.) walked naked (i. e. divested of the mantle of sackcloth, or prophetic garment) and barefooted, to represent symbolically the captivity of the Egyptians and Ethiopians, upon whom the Hebrews placed too much reliance, instead of wholly trusting in God. So in Ezek. ch. iv. the prophet is commanded to do several things which would seem absurd, were they not symbolical; and in ch. xii. there is an explanation given of this kind of actions. The false prophet pushed with horns of iron, to denote the entire overthrow of the Syrians. Jeremiah, by God's direction, hid the linen girdle in the hole of a rock, near the Euphrates; broke a potter's vessel in sight of the people; put on bonds and yokes, and cast a book into the Euphrates—all these were symbolical acts.

Actions of this nature in the Old Testament have commonly but one object in view; viz. the adumbration of some future event, under a sensible representation of one kind or another.

Those which occur in the New Testament appear to be of a mixed character; but few as they are, some of them are vehicles of prophecy, others of purely moral instruction The act of Agabus, when he caused his own hands and feet to be bound with the girdle of St. Paul to intimate that the Apostle himself would be bound in like manner by the Jews of Jerusalem, was of the former description; to which we may add the two miracles of the draught of fishes on the Lake of Galilee, one before, and the other after the resurrection of our Lord; but both with symbolical meaning. The following are examples of the latter description: The descent of the Holy Spirit in the form of a Dove on our Saviour at his baptism was symbolical of the divine influence imparted to him without measure. When Jesus breathed on his Apostles, and said: "Receive ye the Holy Ghost," this was merely a symbolical action denoting the communication of gifts of the Holy Spirit by him, and their reception as so communicated by the apostles. When Jesus on two several occasions, placed a little child in the midst of his disciples, it was a symbolical act indicative of the manner in which divine truth should be received. When he washed his disciples' feet it was to inculcate by a most impressive symbolic act, the great duties of Christian humility and condescension. When he laid his hands upon the sick and infirm, this act was only a token or sign of the blessing to be bestowed. In like manner, when the same ceremony is performed in the ordination of ministers of the Gospel, and in the administration of confirmation to the baptized, it is nothing more nor less than a symbolic action significant of the wish and desire that suitable spiritual gifts and graces may be imparted to the individual. Symbolical actions are much more simple and obvious in their import and design than symbols, and consequently are of easier interpretation, and require no special rules.

CHAPTER XXIII.

THE NATURE AND INTERPRETATION OF TYPES.

The word Type (Gr. τυπος, from τυπτω, to *strike*) properly signifies a *mark* made by a blow or in any other manner, as a *stamp* or impress on coin produced by a die, the mark of a letter, cut in stone, &c., then 2. *form, figure, shape, pattern*, or *model*, after which anything is made. These secondary meanings all naturally spring from the primary. The word has been received into various modern languages and employed in different departments of science—the radical idea, in connexion with specific differences, being retained throughout. In *numismatics*, it has retained most of its original meaning, and signifies the impression on a coin or medal. In *philosophy*, it is used in its most general sense, to designate those forms which are conceived to exist in the mind of the Creator, according to which the character of all individual existences is determined. In *nature*, type is that form which gives the character of similarity to all the individuals of a species, and at which nature seems continually to aim. In *theology*, type signifies the *pre-or-*

dained representative relation which certain persons, events, and institutions of the Old Testament, are conceived to bear to corresponding individuals, events, and institutions in the New Testament.

The classical and biblical usage of τύπος (type) is for the most part the same. The word occurs sixteen times in the New Testament, and several times in the Septuagint; where it corresponds to the Hebrew words לְצֶם and תַּבְנִית. In its primary sense it is used twice in the New Testament, where it is employed to designate the *print* or *mark* of the nails in our Saviour's hands. John 20: 25. In the secondary sense it occurs in Acts 7: 43, 44. Heb. 8: 5. In the last two passages there is a reference to Ex 25: 40, where the Septuagint version has τύπον.

In the tropical sense of *form, manner*, the word is applied to the contents of a letter, (Acts 23: 25. 3 Macc. 3: 30,) and to a *doctrine* (Rom. 4: 17. Comp. Rom. 2: 20.) In the sense of an *example* (υποδειγμα) it occurs frequently. (1 Cor. 10: 6, 11. Phil. 1: 17. 1 Thess. 3: 9. 1 Tim. 4: 12. Titus. 2: 7. 1 Pet. 5: 3.) 3. It is applied to a person as *bearing the form and figure of another person*, i. e. as having a pre-ordained connexion one with the other, and bearing a mutual pre-determined resemblance in certain respects and circumstances. Thus in Rom. 5: 14. Adam is called a type of Christ. The same idea is conveyed by other terms in the New Testament, as by σκια, *shadow*, in Col. 2: 17. Heb. 8: 5. 10: 1. : παραβολη, *figure* in Heb. 9: 9. The correlative term, or that which corresponds to the Type, either in the way of designed similitude or antithesis, is αντιτυπος, *antitype*. See 1 Pet. 3: 21. Heb. 9: 24 Although the Theological and Scriptural significations of the word *type* coincide only in a single instance, yet this is sufficient to justify the application of the term to designate the peculiar relation subsisting between certain persons, events and institutions under the old dispensation and corresponding persons, events, and institutions, under the New, provided such a relation can be established by adequate proof. A Priori arguments against the existence of typical relations in the sense here intended, are of no force whatever. The alleged connexion, if it exists at all, is simply one of the various methods employed by the Deity to convey information in respect to future events, to establish the connexion between different dispensations of his Providence, and to display the wonderful and beautiful unity of his plan of grace in the economy of human redemption and salvation. It is simply a matter of fact, therefore, to be established on evidence drawn exclusively from the word of God; because being like prophecy, supernatural, all arguments derived from the analogy of what are called typical forms in the works of creation, though affording a presumption in its favor, are insufficient to establish such a connexion. The question then to be determined is, whether in point of fact God has employed this method of communicating divine knowledge and confirming the truth of his word to his Church —whether there is evidence of such an intimate spiritual connexion between the Old and New Testaments, that, in the history, transactions, and religion recorded in the former there are persons, events, and institutions, which have a designed foreshadowing relation to certain persons, events, and institutions in the latter. The existence of any such relation has been denied by not a few. But it is evident from various passages of the New Testament, and especially from the Epistle to the Hebrews, (see Heb. 8: 2, 5. 9: 7–9, 24, 24. 10: 1, 9. 11: 8–10, 16,) that the doctrine of Typology in the sense which has been explained, rests on a Biblical basis; and it has accordingly been held by the Church from the earliest times down to the present day. Indeed it is difficult to see how any one can clearly and thoroughly understand the revealed scheme of divine truth in its unity and completeness, and perceive the intimate connexion and beautiful harmony subsisting between the several dispensations of God, who overlooks the typical relation which is disclosed in the inspired records.

The analogy of nature warrants us in expecting that some such proceedure on the part of the Divine Being would be developed in a volume purporting to contain an inspired history of his revealed will and of his providential dealings with the human race. For the material world abounds in typical forms and special adaptations.* And this method of communicating instruction in regard to the future, for the establishment and confirmation of faith in those who may embrace the Gospel, has the advantage of imparting vividness and picturesqueness to the inspired teaching. "The truth is exhibited; not, as in systems of divinity, as a bare abstraction; not, as in the words of Scripture, by a

---

*See McCosh's Typical forms and special ends in Creation.

phrase expressive enough, but still a mere counter, bearing no resemblance to that which it represents; but by a *picture*, which the mind, as it were, sees before it. With such lively images before us, we feel as if we were walking amid living realities."

But while there is the very highest authority for real types, the absurd and ridiculous extent to which typical representations have been multiplied by the ingenuity of divines, is calculated to bring the whole subject into disrepute, and has doubtless been the cause of much of the scepticism which has prevailed in regard to it. Typology is a field in which the excursive imagination of Biblical interpreters, dogmatic theologians, and fanciful preachers, has had a pretty wide scope for exercise, and the field has in every age of the Church been industriously cultivated But the fruits produced by the toil and labor assiduously bestowed upon it, have not always been such as to afford healthful nutriment to the children of God. They have served in many instances only to stimulate a morbid appetite and create a distaste for more solid and substantial aliment. Human ingenuity has been taxed to the utmost to discover resemblances and detect typical relations in the Scriptures. All persons and facts which seemed to present some correspondence, especially in *external circumstances*, have been treated as typical. Types have been confounded with other kindred images, and analogy, real or supposed, has been the only principle on which they have been explained. Hence the importance of a proper discrimination, and of adopting some principle of typical interpretation not justly liable to the objection on the one hand of being too limited in its application, or on the other, of being too comprehensive. Much confusion on the subject of types has arisen from the loose manner in which the word *type* has been employed by theological writers, and by confounding it with other things which bear indeed some resemblance to it, but nevertheless are quite distinct.

It is important to observe that types are not *words*, but *persons* or *things*, which God intended to be prefigurative of future persons or events. There is no *typical* sense of *words*, distinct from the proper sense, as some writers have supposed. "When we explain a passage typically," says Pareau, "we only subjoin one sense to the words; the typical sense exists in the things."*

Types have not unfrequently been confounded with *allegories* and *parables*; but they are obviously dissimilar, and should be carefully distinguished. An allegory or parable is *fictitious*; a type, on the contrary, is something *real*. The one is a picture of the imagination; the other is an historical fact. Whatever it be which is designed to prefigure something future, whether a a person, thing, institution or action, the type not less than the antitype must have a real, and not a merely imaginary existence. "The essence of a type," says Holden, "consisting in its foreordained similitude to something future, requires it to be reality; otherwise it would want the first and most important kind of resemblance, viz., truth. Fiction may resemble fiction; one

*Interpretation of the Old Testament. See also Stuart's Ernesti, p. 12.

ideal personage may be like another; but there can be no substantial relationship between a nonentity and a reality. If that which is prefigured be a fact, that which prefigures it must be a fact likewise. Hence, between the type and the antitype there is this correspondence, that the reality of the one presupposes the reality of the other."† There are, it is true, some points of similarity between a type and an allegory. The interpretation of both is an interpretation of *things*, and not of words; and both are equally founded on *resemblance.* The type, moreover, corresponds to its antitype, as the *protasis* or *immediate* representation in an allegory or parable, corresponds to the apodosis, or its *ultimate* representation A material difference, however, exists in the *quality* of the things compared, as well as in the design of the comparison. When, for example, Joshua, conducting the Israelites to Canaan, is described as a type of our Saviour conducting his disciples to heaven; or, when the sacrifice of the passover is described as a type of the sacrifice of Christ on the cross; the subjects of reference have nothing similar to the subjects of an allegory, though the comparison between them is the same. And though a type, in reference to its antitype, is called a *shadow*, while the latter is called the *substance*, yet the use of these terms does not imply that the former has less of historical verity than the latter.‡

Again: The Type has been often confounded with the *symbol* or *emblem*; but they are not the same. In a type there is always some real and

†Dissertation on the Fall of Man, p. 313.

‡See Marsh's Lectures in Div. Lec. xvii, p. 89.

obvious resemblance to the person or thing typified; but this is not at all necessary in a symbol. In many instances the resemblance is entirely imaginary or of the most remote character. Hence a type is never, like a symbol, the representative of an abstract idea. Persons as well as things are typical; but persons are never symbols. Types in the theological sense, are wholly of divine origin and appointment. Symbols may be either of divine or human origin; for the most part, they belong to the latter class. Symbols indicate a known purpose, well understood from the beginning; whereas the relation of types to their antitypes is unknown, and discoverable only by a subsequent revelation. The term symbol is equally applicable to that which represents a thing past, present, or future. The paschal supper, together with all its attendant circumstances, was a symbolical representation and commemoration of a past transaction. The bread and wine in the Eucharist are symbols of the crucified body of Jesus. The images of the Cherubim over the mercy-seat, were a symbol of a present truth. The ram and he-goat in Daniel, and the white, red, black, and pale horses, in the Apocalypse, are symbols of future events.* A Type has always reference to something future, and consequently it is a kind of *prophecy*. A verbal prophecy *predicts*, whereas a type *prefigures*. The former describes in *words* what is about to take place; the latter foreshows *in its*

*Symbols, which have a prospective reference, or, in other words, prophetic symbols, like the Types under consideration, are of course exclusively biblical.

own outward similarity a future person or event. But there is nothing prefigurative in the baptismal water, or in the eucharistic bread and wine. They are merely *emblems*, not types. Thence it appears that symbols and types belong to the same *genus*, but differ in their *species*. A divine ordinance, however, may partake of the nature both of a symbol and a type; it may be at the same time commemorative and prefigurative; it may have both a retrospective and a prospective reference, and consequently exhibit the specific character of the symbol and also of the type. Such was the ordinance of the Jewish passover. The paschal lamb was both a symbol and a type. The festival of which it formed a prominent part, was intended te perpetuate the remembrance of the miraculous deliverance of the Hebrews from Egyptian bondage, and of the remarkable circumstances which attended it. Thus it primarily had a retrospective reference, and was commemorative of a past event in the history of the nation. So far it was symbolic, and was so regarded by the Hebrews. But in the divine purpose and appointment it also prefigured the propitiatory death and sacrifice of the Messiah—the true Lamb of God—by means of which the believer procures deliverance from the penalty of sin. The ritual or legal types of the Old Testament all possessed this complex character. They were symbolical in their *immediate* and *ostensible* design, as connected with an existing dispensation and religious worship. They were symbolically expressive of the great truths and principles of a spiritual religion, which were common indeed to both dispensations, but which could find only in the New, their proper development and complete realization. The New Testament declares the whole, therefore, to have been shadows (types) of the better things of the Gospel (Heb. 10: 1. 8: 5. Col. 2: 16, 17.)

Once more; The mode of conveying information by types has been frequently confounded with prophetic instruction delivered by *significant actions.* These acts, of which we have already spoken, are in common with types, *things* as distinguished from words; and they are *prophetical* in their import. Hence we commonly find them classed under the head of *prophetical types.* But notwithstanding the points of resemblance between them, the two are not identical. The significant acts in question were avowedly performed for a specific purpose, and with reference, for the most part, to some event or events near at hand. In every case they were *insulated* acts, and not interwoven into the ordinary transactions of the prophet's life. Indeed they had no relation to the prophet himself: he performed them in an assumed character, and with designed and exclusive reference to their symbolical import and prophetical relation. But *typical actions*, properly so called, arose directly out of the ordinary transactions in which the typical person was engaged. The character in which he performed them, was his own proper character, and not an assumed one. The acts themselves were performed without any consciousness of their prospective and typical relation; and the persons or events which they prefigured were remote.

It is hardly necessary to add that a type is wholly distinct from a *metaphor.* Our Saviour in the evangelical history is compared to a *door*, a *vine*, a *foundation*, a *corner-stone*; but what reasonable man would hence infer that doors, vines, foundations, and corner-stones are types of the Messiah! But when our Lord is called the *Lamb of God* which taketh away the sins of the world, the word *lamb* is indeed used in a metaporical sense, but the assertion is much more than the application of a metaphor. It intimates a designed connexion between the lamb slain in sacrifice under the Mosaic dispensation, and the great expiation to be made in the person of the Messiah. So when Christ is called *our Passover*, which is sacrificed for us, the assertion is not a mere figure of speech; but it implies that the passover bore a preordained relation to the Saviour and his mediatorial work.

From what has been said, it will be perceived that *three things* are necessary to constitute the relation of type and antitype. There must be a *resemblance* or correspondence between the two; the resemblance must have been *designed by God*, and the type must have *respect to something future.*

1. *Resemblance.*—There must be a likeness in certain respects between the person or thing prefiguring, and that which it foreshadows. Similarity must lie at the foundation of a type in all cases. This requisite is too obvious to need illustration. Indeed, writers on this subject have generally made this too exclusively the object of attention. Accordingly, when a resemblance, real or imaginary, has been discovered between two persons or events under the two dispensations, this has been deemed quite sufficient to establish a preordained connexion

between them. In this way it is easy to see how such persons as Job, Bazaleel, Aholiab, Phineas, Boaz, Absalom, Eliakim, Daniel, Antiochus Epiphanes, the unmarried brothers of him who left his widow childless, the hanged malefactors, and a thousand and one other persons and things to be met with in the Scriptures, came to be regarded as types.

When it is said that *similarity* in certain respects between the type and the antitype, is requisite to constitute that relation, this does not preclude the idea of *dissimilarity* in other respects. And when the points of dissimilarity are brought particularly to our notice, in the way of contrast, the type is called *antithetic.* We have an example of this in Rom. 5: 14.

2. The second requisite in a type is, *that it be prepared and designed by God to prefigure its antitype.* A type is not constituted such by the mere coincidence of *external* historical circumstances. There must be an *internal* union and resemblance. And this internal correspondence must be traced to the divine intention. No merely accidental or outward similitude can constitute a true type. A resemblance in very many respects may exist between two individuals, living at different periods, without there being the remotest connexion between them. Similar examples, and historical parallels are everywhere observable. One person may successfully *imitate* the actions of another. One may casually be placed in circumstances like those of another, and the conduct of the two may be very similar in a variety of respects. But this similarity alone does not establish a typical relation between them.

Guild* finds no less than forty-nine typical resemblances between Joseph and Christ, and seventeen between Jacob and Christ, not scrupling to swell the number by occasionally taking in acts of sin, as well as circumstances of the most trifling nature. Yet this does not prove that either Joseph or Jacob was really a type of our Saviour. If mere similitude were sufficient to constitute the relation of type and antitype, then would Capt. Fluellen's celebrated theory of a typical connexion between Alexander the Great and King Harry of Monmouth, be strictly true, being based on the following indubitable facts. 1st. That the birth-place of both commenced with an M. 2d. That both were great fighters; and 3d. That there was a river in Monmouth and also a river in Macedon, the name of which, however, the honest gentleman had forgotten. The connexion between a type and its antitype must have been originally preconcerted and preordained by God himself. And it is this original design and preordination, which constitutes the peculiar characteristic of a prefigurative type, and distinguishes it essentially from all mere examples of natural phenominal resemblances and other typical forms. Where this does not exist, the relation between two persons or things, however similar they may be, is not the relation of type and antitype.† But Cocceius,

*Moses Unveiled.

† "To secure its purpose," says Dr. Dick, "the type must be instituted by God, who alone can establish the relation; and it is by no means sufficient that, between two distinct persons or events, there should be an accidental resemblance. The essence of a type consists not in its similarity to another ob-

on the contrary, a distinguished Hebrew scholar and learned expositor of Scripture in the 17th century, advanced the opinion that *every* event recorded in the Old Testament, which in any way resembled something to be found in the New, was to be regarded as *typical.*‡ Upon this broad foundation a multitude of writers soon commenced the erection of an edifice spacious enough to accommodate as many types as the ingenuity of man chose to create. So that, for more than a century and a half, the principle was universally admitted that *where the analogy*

---

ject, but in its being divinely appointed to be a representative of it." Theol. vol. 1. p. 144. "The great point to be established is, that the likeness was designed in the original institution. It is the *previous purpose* and *intention,* which constitute the whole relation of type and antitype." McClelland's Manual, p. 94. See also Marsh's Lec., pt. 2, Lec. 6. Chevallier's Hulsean Lectures, p. 6.

‡John Cocceius (Koch) was born in Bremen in 1603, and died in Leyden in 1660. He successively held the Professorship of Biblical Philology in his native city, Bremen, and in Franeker; and that of Theology in Leyden. He belonged to the Reformed Church, and was among the first to vindicate successfully the right of theology to an exegesis free and independent of dogmatics, in opposition to the scholastic divines of the age. The views of Cocceius in regard to the typology of Scripture, were embraced by his two eminent pupils, Hermann Witsius and Campegius Vitringa. To the same school of interpreters belonged the English writers Mather, Keach, Worden, J. Taylor, and Guild, nearly all of whom lived towards the latter part of the 17th century. These have since been followed by McEwen, Ridgley, Brown of Heddington, Laurentius, and a host of others.

is evident and manifest between things under the law and things under the gospel, the former are to be regarded (on the ground simply of that analogy) *as types of the latter.* The excessive and absurd multiplication of types resulting from the adoption of this principle, tended at length to bring typical interpretations into disrepute, and either led to the rejection of prophetical types altogether, as a mere human invention, or disposed sober men to regard the subject of typology as hopelessly involved in conjecture and uncertainty. We have said that the *divine intention* enters fundamentally into the relation of type and antitype. But *consciousness* of such a relation in the mind of the sacred writer is not necessary. He need not know or feel that there is an established correspondence between the person or thing foreshadowing and that which is prefigured. Nor is it needful that a typical person should be aware of the fact that he was designed to be such, or that he was manifested as bearing that relation. In like manner it is unnecessary that a typical institution should be known to be such by those among whom it was established.

3. The last requisite in a type is, *that it must have respect to something future.* The Old Testament types shadowed forth good things to come. "Types were not appointed to represent *present* but *future* realities. They were a temporary mode of instruction, pointing to another and clearer way of educating humanity in the highest truth." In consequence of possessing this prophetic character, types may be employed to *prove*, as well as to *illustrate* the gospel. Examples, analogies, and resemblances, not announc-

ed as typical, are illustrative only. They explain truth rather than prove it. The ulterior and prophetic reference, however, was not the only purpose for which a religious institution was anciently appointed. It might, and generally did, subserve other purposes, subordinate perhaps, to this, but nevertheless in themselves highly important and beneficial. And that subordinate, but immediate purpose, was, probably, the only one which at the time was clearly and distinctly understood by those who observed the rite. Many, if not most, of the Mosaic ordinances, in point of fact, served a twofold office and purpose. While they pointed significantly to the better dispensation to come, as their ultimate reference, they symbolized to the Hebrews *present duties* and *responsibilities*, and inculcated moral virtues and religious obligations of vital importance.

The vital question now presents itself: how are we to determine, whether an acknowledged resemblance between two persons or things in in the Old Testament is typical of something connected with Christ or his Church recorded in the New? Is there any principle which will guide us with sufficient accuracy for all practical purposes in deciding whether there exists a special relation between the two, designed or ordained by God?

The previous design or preordained connexion constitutes, as we have seen, the typical relation. Now this must be shown by competent testimony. It will not answer, in a matter of this kind, to be guided by fancy and mere conjecture. What testimony then is sufficient to establish the relation in question? A proper and sufficient answer to this question, we think, is this: *No person, event, or institution should be regarded as typical, but what may be shown to be such from the Scripture itself.* Here is a plain and simple law, which furnishes a sure and safe criterion, by which all *fanciful resemblances*, dignified with the name of *typical relations*, are excluded. The reason of the rule must commend itself to the sober judgment of every man: viz. that no one is competent to make known to us the divine intention, except God himself, or some person inspired and authorized by him. This law does not demand that there should be an express and formal declaration or explicit assertion *totis verbis* to that effect. It is enough that *the allusion be of such a nature, and the connexion in which it is found be such as to afford a reasonable presumption in favor of this opinion.* And where there is room for doubt, that doubt may fairly be resolved on the affirmative side. The following quotations show conclusively that this principle accords *substantially* with the views of some of the ablest English and American divines in the present century who have given their attention to the subject.

Bishop Marsh:—"The only possible source of information on this subject is Scripture itself. The only *possible* means of knowing that two distant, though similar, historical facts were so connected in the general scheme of divine Providence that the one was *designed* to prefigure the other, is the authority of that work in which the scheme of divine Providence is unfolded. Destitute of *that* authority, we may confound a resemblance, subsequently observed, with a resemblance *preordained*. We may mistake a comparison, founded on a mere *accidental* parity of circumstances, for a comparison founded on a *necessary* and *inherent connection.* There is no other rule, therefore, by which we can distinguish a *real* from a *pretended* type, than that of Scripture itself. There are no other possible *means,* by which we can *know,* that a previous design and a preordained connection *existed.**

Bishop Van Mildert:—"It is essential to a type, in the Scriptural acceptation of the term, that there should be competent evidence of the divine *intention* in the correspondence between it and the antitype,—a matter not to be left to the imagination of the expositor to discover, but resting on some solid proof from Scripture itself."†

Ernesti:—"Those who look to the counsel or intention, as they call it, of the Holy Spirit, act irrationally, and open the road to the unlimited introduction of types. The intention of the Holy Spirit can be made known to us only by his own showing."‡

Prof. Stuart:—"If it be asked how far we are to consider the Old Testament as typical, I should answer, without any hesitation, just so much of it is to be regarded as typical as the New Testament affirms to be so, and *no more.* The fact that any thing or event under the Old Testament dispensation was designed to prefigure something under the New, can be known to us only by revelation, and, of course,

*Lectures pt. 2. Lec. 6.
†Bampton Lectures, p. 239.
‡Terrott's Ernesti, Vol. 1. p. 25.

all that is not designated by divine authority as typical, can never be made so, by any authority less than that which guided the writers of the New Testament."§

Prof. Stowe:—"In regard to types and allegories, we know of none, excepting those which are explained as such in the Bible itself. All the rest are merely conjectural, and, though often ingenious, are worse than idle, leading the mind away from the truth, perverting it by false principles of interpretation, and making it the mere sport of every idle fancy.†

Dr. T. H. Horne:—"Unless we have the authority of the sacred writers themselves for it, we cannot conclude, with certainty, that this or that person or thing, which is mentioned in the Old Testament, is a type of Christ, on account of the resemblance which we perceive between them."‡

Chevallier:—"The connection of typical events with those which they foreshow, can be determined by authority only. For unless the Scripture has declared that the connection exists, we can never ascertain that any resemblance, however accurate, is any thing more than a fanciful adaptation, and we may go on to multiply imaginary instances without end." Again: "The error of those who suffer their imagination to suppose the existence of types where they are not, should warn us that no action must be selected as typical of another, unless it be distinctly declared or plainly intimated in some part of Scripture to possess that character."§

§Stuart's Ernesti, p. 13.
†Introduction to the Study of the Bible, p. 35.
‡Introd. vol. 2. p. 530. 7th ed.
§Hulsean Lectures, pp. 34, 54.

Christian Observer (London):—The truth of the whole matter (viz. of types) unquestionably lies in a short compass. The interpretations of this nature, which are adopted by Scripture itself are infallible; but when they stand alone upon the authority of human invention and imagination, or, what is sometimes absurdly introduced as the analogy of faith, they are simply fallible, and often very simple indeed. No man of common sense will pretend, on such points, to any superior inspiration or judicial authority over another. Here the right of private judgment must take its most legitimate stand. The Scriptures, no doubt, are suited to every turn of mind and taste. The very large place which the imagination occupies in the mind of man cannot have been unknown to him who framed the Scriptures *for* man. Hence we may justly admire that ineffable wisdom which has given forth enough for the dullest and most sterile understanding of the wayfaring man, to guide him; and has superadded an abundance of most instructive and impressive analogics for every higher grade of intellect or imagination, not even refusing food to the most soaring and aerial of all minds, by the construction of narratives, occurrences and doctrines, which, with almost a miraculous closeness of application, may be made to fit into one another, and into the *analogy of faith*. It is, however, we repeat it, where these applications are warranted and made to our hands, by the words of inspiration itself, that we deem them either positively certain or absolutely wise and safe.||

||Christ. Obs. vol. 27, p. 236.

McClelland:—"This (the previous *purpose* and *intention*) must be proved, and there is only one way of doing it. Show me from Scripture the existence of such a connection. Whatever persons or things in the Old Testament are asserted by Christ or his Apostles to have been designed prefigurations of persons or things in the New, I accept. But if you only presume the fact from a real or fancied analogy, you are drawing on your imagination, and assuming the dangerous liberty of speaking for God."¶

Ellicott:—"We should not positively assert the existence of typical relations between persons, places, or things, unless it appears either directly or by reasonable inference that such relations are recognized in Scripture."

In the application of this principle, we find in the Old Testament two classes of types. 1. *Ritual Types*, and 2. *Historical Types*,—embracing 1. historical *persons*, and 2. historical *events*.

But it has been the singular fortune of the principle in question to be opposed on opposite grounds. Some object to it as being too narrow and restrictive; while others object to it on the ground that it is too broad and comprehensive. To the former class of writers belong Fairbairn and Dr. Davidson; to the latter Dr. W. L. Alexander and Mr. Lord. 1. Fairbairn expresses strong disapprobation of the Cocceian system, based on analogy; but he at the same time declares his dissent from the principle which we have laid down, based on authority, and in his elaborate work on the subject of typology has sought to lay open a *via media* between the two. But we

¶Manual of Bib. Int. p. 94.

do not think he has been entirely successful. We have failed to discover in his instructive but diffuse treatise any clearly intelligible, well defined and substantial basis, on which the mind can rest with satisfaction. He regards the types which would fairly come under the Rule here prescribed as simply "*examples*, taken from a vast storehouse, where many more may be found." While he contends in the main for Scripture authority in some sense to distinguish what is typical from what is not, he often converts *his own theological ideas into the warrant.* "Thus," says Davidson, "we are told that the cherubim were set up for representations to the eye of faith of earth's living creature-hood, and more especially of its rational and immortal, though fallen head, with reference to the better hopes and destiny in prospect. From the very first they gave promise of a restored condition to the fallen; and by the use afterwards made of them, the light became clearer and more distinct," &c., &c.* All this is groundless and far-fetched. The tree of life was also a type of immortal life and paradisaical delights yet to be enjoyed by the people of God in Christ.† Enoch is undoubtedly to be viewed as a type of Christ‡ Noah was the type of him who was to come, in whom the righteousness of God should be perfected.§ Abraham was the type at once of the subjective and the objective design of the covenant, or in other words, of the kind of persons who were to be the subjects and channels of blessing, and of the kind of inheritance with

*Fairbairn's Typology, 2d ed. vol 1, p. 240, 241. †P. 214 ‡P. 218. §P. 295.

which they were to be blessed.|| Pharaoh's destruction was typical of Antichrist.¶ The tabernacle was 'a type of Christ, as God manifest in the flesh, and reconciling flesh to God.'** Such things as these in the region of a biblical typology clearly indicates that a certain school of divines create types in abundance by the aid of their peculiar theology. Thinking that they magnify Christ and his dispensation in this manner, they virtually convert Judaism into Christianity, instead of keeping them in their proper relations. They mistake the essential, concrete thing which constitutes a type."†† Dr. Davidson objects to our principle chiefly on the following grounds: "It is admitted," he says, "that types partake of the nature of prophecy. Now in order to connect the thing or person described in prophecy as future with its counterpart, we do not require the exposition of the Scripture writers themselves. A prophecy *is not said in Scripture* in most cases, to be fulfilled in a person or event, even where we have reason to believe that it is so. No one dreams of demanding the express testimony of an inspired writer for demonstrating the meaning of what is fulfilled. What was predicted is not identified with its counterpart when the latter takes place. Why then should a different rule be applied to types? Why should their spiritual sense be every where pointed out by the Scripture writers themselves? Are we not warranted in assuming that there are predictions in the Old Testament which were at least partially fulfilled

||P. 306. ¶Vol. 2d, p. 56. **P. 236.
††Davidson's Horne's Intro vol, 2. p 444.

in circumstances and persons belonging to the New, without its being expressly said that they *were* so fulfilled? In like manner, may it not be inferred that some types are not indicated in the New Testament which must nevertheless have been really such? The prophetic Scriptures have their character. We cannot always fix their meaning or determine their scope. There is no key to the interpretation of prophecy in the New Testament. Neither is there, in many instances, an express declaration that a passage is prophetical in its nature; so that we may sometimes mistake history for prophecy, and *vice versa*. Types should be regarded in the same manner."* Much of this objection lies against the principle as stated by Bishop Marsh and Prof. Stuart, viz that an express declaration by Christ or his apostles to that effect is necessary to establish the typical relation. But its force in this particular, we think, is obviated by the more comprehensive character of the principle as expressed above. The case drawn by Dr. D. from prophecy, does not seem to be altogether parallel. Prophecies in general may be ascertained to be such from the nature of the subject, the form of expression, or the context, and from these sources we may satisfactorily determine their proper meaning and fulfilment, irrespective of any declaration or intimation to that effect in the New Testament. But it is impossible in this way to ascertain what is typical and what not, in the Old Testament. Types are indeed a species of prophecy, but they are *concealed* prophecies, which only their comple-

*Davidson's Horne, vol. 2, p. 439.

tion can indicate or explain. There may undoubtedly be typical persons and things in the Old Testament which are not alluded to as such in the New; but we have no means of ascertaining what they are. Indeed we should not have known of the existence of typical persons and institutions in the Old Testament at all, had we not been so advised in the New.

2. But there is another class of interpreters who object to the principle in question as admitting of too wide an application, and who would greatly curtail the typical matter of Scripture. Thus Dr. W. L. Alexander* defines types to be "symbolical institutes expressly appointed by God, to prefigure to those among whom they were set up certain great transactions in connection with that plan of redemption, which, in the fulness of time, was to be unfolded to mankind." The same view has been adopted and defended at length by Mr. Lord.† According to this writer types must possess the following distinctive marks: They must have been specially constituted such by God: they must have been known to be so constituted and contemplated as such by those who had to do with them; and they must have been continued till the coming of Christ; when they were abrogated or superceded by something analogous in the Christian dispensation. By the definition of Alexander and the distinctive marks of Lord, historical types in the Old Testament are en-

*Connection and Harmonies of the Old and New Testament. 1841.

†See Lord's Ecclesiastical and Literary Journal, No. 15.

tirely excluded, and by the latter especially; nothing is admitted as belonging to this character but what appertained to "the tabernacle worship, or to the propitiation and homage of God;" this, in his judgment, embraces the entire sphere of the typical. All the distinctive and essential marks of a type which Lord lays down, are, in the sense intended by the writer, incapable of Scriptural proof. "The strictly religious symbols of the Old Testament worship were not specifically constituted types, or formally set up in that character any more than such transactions as the deliverance of the Hebrews from Egypt, or the preservation of Noah in the deluge, which he denies to have been typical. In the manner of their appointment, viewed by itself, there is no more to indicate a reference to the Messianic future in the one than in the other. Neither were they for certain known to be types, and used as such by the Old Testament worshippers. They unquestionably were not in the time of our Lord; and how far they may have been so at any previous period, is a matter only of doubtful speculation. Nor, finally, was it by any means an invariable and indispensable characteristic, that they should have continued in use till they were superceded by something analogous in the Christian dispensation."‡ In point of fact, many of them did continue in use until the redemptive work of Christ was finished on the cross; as, for example, the sacrifices and other ritual observances of the Temple worship; and the commemorative ordinance of the Passover. But most of

‡Fairbairn's Typology, vol. 1, p. 51.

the historical types, whether persons or events, were of such a nature as not to admit of being repeated even by a symbolical or commemorative rite.

Types have been variously divided and classified by different writers. They speak of natural, moral, historical, legal, prophetical, and other types But for most of these classes there is no foundation whatever. The classification proposed by Chevallier is probably the best which has been made. It is the following:—1. Those which are supported by accomplished prophecy, delivered previously to the appearance of the antitype; as Moses, (Deut. 18: 15), Joshua, the High Priest. Zech. 3: 8. 2. Those supported by accomplished prophecy, delivered in the person of the antitype; as the brazen serpent, (Num. 21: 5, 9. Comp. John 3: 14); the manna eaten by the Israelites in the Desert, (John 6: 32, 49); the paschal sacrifice, (1 Cor. 5: 7, 8. Comp. Lu. 22: 14–16); the miraculous preservation of Jonah in the belly of the great fish, (John 11: 32. Matt. 12: 40). 3. Those which in Scripture are expressly declared, or clearly assumed to be typical, after the prefigured events had taken place; as the numerous types contained in the Levitical priesthood and sacrifices, (the Epistle to the Hebrews *passim*) also Adam, Melchisedec, Joshua, the son of Nun, David, Solomon, Elijah as a type of John Baptist, etc.

In the interpretation of types the following rules should be observed:

I. *The analogy between type and antitype should not be urged beyond the points to which revelation has extended it.* This rule is founded on the principle that the relation between type and antitype is, and must be, *general*; and consequently it was never designed that the comparison should be extended to every particular circumstance. In every case, especially of typical persons, there are many things in the type which *have* and *could have* no place in the antitype, because the persons and things related are respectively earthly and spiritual, imperfect and perfect. And for the same reason, some things are peculiar to the antitype, and could have no counterpart in the type. It is not, therefore, throughout the entire compass of their history, but only to certain specific acts, or to certainly divinely appointed offices or relations, that we care to look for what is properly typical. In some instances we may discover *other points of resemblance* also, which it may be interesting and instructive to consider; but these being, as far as we know, *accidental*, do not enter into the typical relation. Thus Jonah was a type of Christ only in reference to his being three days in the belly of the great fish, and coming forth at the end of that period alive and unharmed. His disposition, conduct, and character, have no concern with the typical relation he bore in that part of his history to which we have adverted. To regard the sinful acts of typical persons as prefigurative of Christ, as has sometimes been done, is little short of blasphemy. Indeed, it is never in their personal or private characters that individuals are types of the Messiah. If they were official persons, then the typical relation belongs not to their private, but their *official* character. Thus Moses typified Christ as a prophet, lawgiver, leader of the children of Israel, and head of the ancient dispensation. Interpreters of the Cocceian school, however, not satisfied with this general and official relation between Moses and Christ, have enumerated various particular actions of his life as typical. He married an Ethiopian, a stranger, and a black woman; so Christ espoused the Gentiles, who were strangers to God, and by reason of sin, as black as hell could make them. He sweetened the bitter waters of Marah by a tree cast into it; so Christ sweetens all our afflictions by means of his cross. He led Israel through the Red Sea; so Christ leads his Church through a sea of tribulation. As Moses was transfigured on Mt. Sinai and seemed so glorious that the children of Israel could not behold his face; so Christ was also transfigured on Mount Tabor so that his disciples were amazed and knew not what to say.*

The *Prophets*, as a class, prefigured Christ the great teacher; so likewise the *priests* and *kings* of the Old Testament. But we are not warranted from this to regard the particular acts of individuals belonging to either of these classes as typical of Christ. It was only in their public and official position, and not in their private capacity that they were thus related to the Son of God. The Levitical priesthood and the ritual sacrifices of the Mosaic economy prefigured Christ our great High Priest, and the sacrifice of himself offered for sin on Calvary. Yet there were many things in that priesthood which have no counterpart in the antitype. The High Priest was to offer sacrifices for his *own* sins (Heb. 5: 3) as well as those of others, which cannot apply to Christ (Heb. 7: 27). The Aaronic

*Keach on the Metaphors, p. 960, ed. 1779.

priesthood, moreover, was weak and unprofitable—attributes which certainly did not belong to the Redeemer. The Tabernacle, with its furniture and religious services, as a whole, is affirmed in the epistles to the Hebrews and the Colossians to have been of a typical nature; but it was never intended that the relation of type and antitype should be extended to every minute particular. The following examples, however, will show to what lengths the comparison has been carried by writers of the Cocceian school. The ark of the Covenant, (says Witsius), being partly of wood and partly of gold, aptly represents the two natures of Christ.* The table of shewbread was a type of Christ, because it was covered over with gold, and had a crown about it, denoting the purity of Christ's humanity with the glory of his deity and the majesty of his kingdom; because it had food set upon it, of which none were to eat except the priest, signifying that spiritual nourishment which is in Christ, which none receive or partake of but believers only, or the royal priesthood of the faithful. The bread was always to be upon the table, which signifies that in Christ there is food continually for our souls. There was much bread, twelve loaves, which signifies that in Christ there is food or nourishment enough for all who realize their need of him; or it shows how plentifully God feeds his elect; his poor shall not want bread, his table is always spread, always richly and abundantly furnished.†

The burnt-offering of fowls was a type of

*On the Covenants, vol. 2, p. 208.
†Keach, p. 969.

Christ, because they were turtle doves or pigeons, signifying his meekness and innocency. The neck of the fowl was to be pinched with the nail, that the blood might flow out; but not that the head should be plucked off from the body. All this signified how Christ should die and shed his blood; yet, thereby his deity, as the head or principal part, should not be divided from his humanity; nor yet by his death should he who is our head be taken from his Church, but should rise again, and be with them by his Spirit forever. The blood thereof was strained or pressed out at the side of the altar, before it was plucked and laid upon the altar to be burned; signifying thereby the straining or pressing out of Christ's blood, in his grievous agony in the garden, before he was taken and stripped to be crucified: and so on *ad nauseam.*‡ Now there is no way of avoiding this palpable error, and egregious trifling with the word of God, but by strictly confining our expositions of types to those express points in respect to which the Scripture itself authorizes us to consider them as typical; or which immediately flow from the nature of the particular relation or character, which we are taught to regard as constituting the analogy between the type and antitype.

II. *No doctrine should be regarded as fundamental which is founded solely on typical analogy.* The great and essential truths of the word of God, are taught in plain and unequivocal language. They are not concealed under the veil of types and shadows, or left to be deduced from obscure

‡See Keach's metaphors—quoted in Davidson's Horne, p. 443.

and figurative passages. The typical manifestations of the divine counsels will be found in perfect harmony with these truths. They serve to illustrate and confirm the great doctrines of salvation; but they do not reveal them for the first time, nor exclusively. They strengthen our belief in the truth and reality of what is made known elsewhere and in other and clearer forms. Our belief, for instance, in the doctrine of atonement, may be greatly strengthened by contemplating the fact that it was not only revealed to our fathers by the clear intimations of verbal prophecy, but prefigured in the numerous sacrifices which were offered from the time of Adam to the death of Christ. At the same time, it is highly improbable that Jehovah would conceal, under the veil of figure, parable, and type. truths necessary to salvation, and nowhere disclosed in plain and literal terms. No person, therefore, can be expected to receive, as a necessary article of faith, any doctrine, founded exclusively or primarily on the types and shadows of the patriarchal and Mosaic dispensations.

THE END.

ERRATA.

The reader is requested to correct with his pen the following errata. Other typographical errors of minor importance will be easily detected, and need not be noticed here:—

Page 65, line 14 from bottom—for "not able" read "not be able."

Page 66, line 8 from top—for "Coccaous" read "Coccius."

Page 190, line 7 from top—for "1341" read "1841."

Page 137, line 11 from bottom—for "with tropes" read "in tropes."

Page 166, line 16 from top—for "arising from" read "suggested by."

Page 175, line 5 from bottom—for "rationally" read "soberly."

Page 211, line 5 from top—for "profess" read possess."

Page 224, line 9 from top—for "expressive" read "express."

Page 229, line 9 from bottom—for "they rest" read "it rests."

Page 253, line 8 from top—for "its answer" read "it answers."

Page 271, line 17 from top—for "excite" read "suggest."

Page 288, line 6 from top—for "is" read "are."

www.ingramcontent.com/pod-product-compliance
Lightning Source LLC
LaVergne TN
LVHW020222110826
845151LV00003B/790

* 9 7 8 1 4 2 5 5 3 2 7 2 7 *